When Your Aging Parent Needs Care

Candy Arrington
Kim Atchley

HARVEST HOUSE PUBLISHERS

EUGENE, OREGON

Published in association with Hartline Literary Agency, LLC, of 123 Queenston Drive, Pittsburgh, PA 15235.

Cover by Garborg Design Works, Savage, Minnesota

Cover photo © Image Source Photography / Veer

WHEN YOUR AGING PARENT NEEDS CARE
Copyright © 2009 by Candy Arrington and Kim Atchley
Published by Harvest House Publishers
Eugene, Oregon 97402
www.harvesthousepublishers.com

Library of Congress Cataloging-in-Publication Data
Arrington, Candy.
When your aging parent needs care / Candy Arrington and Kim Atchley.
    p. cm.
Includes bibliographical references.
ISBN 978-0-7369-2526-6 (pbk.)
1. Adult children of aging parents—Religious life. 2. Aging parents—Care—Religious aspects—Christianity. 3. Caregivers—Religious life. I. Atchley, Kim, 1968- II. Title.
BV4910.9.A77 2009
248.8'619897—dc22

2008049415

Printed in the United States of America

09 10 11 12 13 14 15 16 / VP-SK / 10 9 8 7 6 5 4 3 2 1

To Mama

Thank you for taking such good care of us all these years. Now it's our turn to take care of you. Daddy, I still miss you but know you are building the best mansions in heaven.

I love you both.

Candy

The lines are fallen unto me in pleasant places;
yea, I have a goodly heritage.
(PSALM 16:6 KJV)

■ ■ ■

To Mom and Dad

I love you both dearly for opening your hearts to me in so many precious ways; for allowing me to share the journey when the road felt treacherous beneath our feet; and for allowing me to experience your spiritual strength and wisdom in times of physical weakness and uncertainty. Thank you for the lessons of the heart no book or school could match.

We miss you both, but still feel your love from Heaven every day. Thank you for the butterflies.

Kim

Contents

Y ou do so much for me and I know I'm a burden," Edith said to Shirley and me. Tears filled her eyes as she added, "I know I get cranky, and I'm sorry if I get impatient."

She talked for perhaps a full minute and tears came to our eyes. She was Shirley's sister—older by thirteen years—and had been the mother figure for her until our marriage. Now it was our turn to care for her.

That was one of the best days we had in caring for Edith.

"I'm not going to take that rat poison!" she cried out a few days later. For several minutes Edith ranted about the medication her doctor prescribed.

That was one of the worst days we had in caring for Edith.

Most days were a combination of ups and downs. No matter how hard we tried to do everything for her, we went to bed with unfinished items on our to-do list. Either it was something we hadn't been able to do for Edith or a task we didn't have time to finish for ourselves.

Sometimes we resorted to a form of tough love by clearly stating boundaries; sometimes we held each other and prayed because we felt we had failed. During most of the seven-and-a-half years we felt pulled, pushed, or shoved in several directions. Or as Candy Arrington and Kim Atchley say it, "Caregivers often feel that even if they've gotten things under control in one aspect of life, other things suffer and still need attention."

We cared for Edith in our home for many reasons. Although there was a brother, we felt it was the right thing for us to invite her into our home. We stayed with the sometimes joyful task of repaying her love given during Shirley's childhood. We stayed with the sometimes thankless task because it was the right thing to do. After Edith died, we grieved, but we were at peace. We had given as much as we knew how.

We didn't have access to a book such as *When Your Aging Parent Needs Care: Practical Help for This Season of Life*. Most of the books we read were either personal experiences or technical books written by experts such as lawyers or doctors. We functioned as nurses, parents, confidants, and children, and the roles shifted from day to day.

By contrast, *When Your Aging Parent Needs Care* does what we rightly expect of good how-to books. The authors share their own histories and illustrate various caregiving problems by citing others' experiences. After each example, they explain the principles involved and offer practical advice for coping. They start at the beginning stages of caregiving and follow it through until the death of the loved one.

This book also does something few others do: Candy Arrington and Kim Atchley provide an especially helpful chapter on making the transition from the death of a parent toward rebuilding a life. Too many books stop before they reach that point. Another plus is chapter 23 that explains the forms you, as a caregiver, will need, and they clarify the purpose of those documents.

So now you have become a caregiver. Some days you may see yourself like the performer on a tightrope. Balance becomes the goal you strive for each day. On the best days, you'll experience some of that, but it's not an easy lifestyle. If you can accept this phase of your life as an opportunity to serve your aging parent as well as a time for your own spiritual growth, this book can enhance your life in the midst of the daily chaos.

If you follow suggestions by the authors, many of these practical tips can offer you balance as a long-time caregiver. As you take on this task, you need to focus on your loved one, but you don't want to neglect your own needs. You may not be able to reach true balance, but you'll be closer to that by using this book.

CECIL MURPHEY
coauthor of *90 Minutes in Heaven* and
When Someone You Love Has Cancer

Acknowledgments

With special thanks from Candy:

- To Jim for encouraging my writing pursuits, providing for our family, and being a voice of reason when I try to look too far ahead. I love you.
- To Neely and Jay for being the kind of young adults who make a mama proud and for loving the Lord your God with all your hearts, souls, minds, and strength. You are both gifts from God.
- To Kim—I've learned so much from you about this balancing act called caregiving. Thank you for your friendship and for collaborating with me in this endeavor. A cord of three strands is not easily broken.
- To "Chinkie"—We're on this path together and I promise to hold up your arms when you can't anymore.
- To Dalene Parker for manuscript review and critique in the midst of caregiving.
- To Rod Morris for seeing the potential in this book and offering us a contract.
- To Cec Murphey for being a role model and an encourager to me.
- And to those who took care of Mama while I finished this book.

With deepest thanks from Kim:

- To my loving husband Ryan, whose encouragement has been beyond measure and who thankfully kept the cars happy and the family running.
- To Alison, Emily, and Guy Henry, who keep me smiling in the tough times with their amazing insights, hugs, tickle fights, and giggles.

- To Joan and Phil, the best in-laws in the world, who've always been there for all of us.

- To Candy—without whom this precious baby would never have been born.

- To Tamela Hancock Murray, the most uplifting agent anyone could hope for and whose vision has helped ours to grow.

- To the many medical professionals who shared in interviews and helped us navigate difficult terrain as a family.

- And to all the amazing people who opened tender hearts to us all by sharing their stories.

Introduction

While it may be argued that every generation is squeezed between others, ours more than any other is the "Sandwich Generation." Many of us have delayed marriage and parenthood. Our parents are living longer because of prevention and cures. And thus we take on the dual role of parenting our children and caring for our parents.

Candy and Kim met for coffee one day to discuss writing and quickly discovered they were each writing a book on the same topic—caring for aging parents. *We're competitors,* they thought, but then realized they were looking at the topic from different yet complementary perspectives. That's when they decided to collaborate, creating one voice from their wide range of experiences. To further broaden perspectives, they've included other caregiver stories.

Candy and her husband, Jim, have two adult children. Candy's mother is a widow, cancer survivor, and an octogenarian. Her mother-in-law, in her nineties, is a widow who lives alone. Both Jim and Candy are only children and thus have sole responsibility for their mothers. The caregiving roles have increased in recent years with health challenges. Candy's father died in 1991, five months after a cancer diagnosis. Jim's father died suddenly in 1984 from a brainstem hemorrhage.

Kim and her husband, Ryan, have three children—college age, middle school, and elementary school age. Kim cared for both of her parents. Her 81-year-old father died in 2006, following a four-year battle with cancer. Her mother moved in with the Atchleys in early 2007 and died in November 2008 as a result of complications following surgery for her second bout with cancer.

Caregiving is a difficult and challenging job. This book is not an effort to convince you it is an easy task. We understand the mental and physical exhaustion caregiving entails and recognize the emotional intricacies involved in role reversal. We've experienced the guilt and frustrations and coped with parental stubbornness, forgetfulness, accusations, fears, and childishness. We understand what it's like to be crying inside as you miss your son's last musical performance at school while you sit with your parent in the emergency room.

Most of the time, we don't talk about caregiving. We tack it on to our already over-full schedule and swallow the myriad feelings that threaten to bubble to the surface. We acknowledge lost identity in the complexity of balancing multiple roles.

Although it's easy to get mired in the difficulties of caregiving, joys also exist during this phase of life. With an open mind and heart, you'll receive blessings far beyond any you asked for or dreamed of along with the assurance of God's loving, guiding hand.

In writing this book, we validate your feelings and link arms with you on this journey. While the scenarios presented in this book will not be identical to yours, you'll find similarities. You'll discover nuggets of encouragement to help find a solid footing on the shifting sands of caregiving, new perspectives for discovering treasure within your family bonds, and refreshment as you dip a toe into the truths of living water.

Above all, we acknowledge God as the creator and sustainer of life and offer support in the task of obeying the fifth commandment to the best of our ability.

> "Honor your father and your mother, so that you may live long in the land the LORD your God is giving you" (Exodus 20:12).

May Jehovah Jireh bless you richly for honoring your parents and this commandment.

Grace and peace,
Candy and Kim

Chapter 1

Welcome to the High Wire
Balancing Your Life with Caregiving

Alise popped the succulent appetizer into her mouth, surveyed the faces of her friends, and joined in their laughter. The warmth of friendship and an all-too-infrequent sense of relaxation flooded her senses. But the feeling proved fleeting when she realized her cell phone was ringing.

While the chatter around her continued, Alise heard the voice of her college-age daughter.

"Mom, our flight's been cancelled. We'll be in Chicago overnight."

"Did the airline get you a hotel?"

"Yes, but they've given Tom and me a room together."

"What? They can't do that!"

"Really, it'll be okay, Mom. Besides, I'm afraid to stay in a room by myself in this airport hotel. We'll see you tomorrow morning at 11:00. You *can* pick us up, right?"

"Yes, I'll be there."

Alise pushed the red button on her phone, realizing she now needed to find a substitute teacher for her Sunday school class and come up with the best way to tell her husband their only daughter was about to spend the night in a hotel room with her fiancé.

Sometime during her phone conversation, the server had brought the entrées. Alise carved her steak, took a bite, and tried to refocus on the conversation.

Across the table, Sarah continued the saga of her mother's week-long hospital stay following her fall. In addition to a urinary tract infection, Sarah's mother was hallucinating. Sarah had missed a whole week of work and was now searching for a full-time sitter for her mother.

As Alise voiced her understanding of Sarah's situation, her cell phone jangled again.

"Mrs. Brooks? This is Susan at Falling Leaves Manor. You're number one on the emergency list for Mrs. Bobo. I'm calling to let you know she slid out of her wheelchair."

"Even with the safety belt alarm?"

"Unfortunately, yes. Her back is scraped and we're concerned about her hip. She seems slightly disoriented so we're transporting her to the ER. Can you meet us there?"

"Yes, of course."

After fishing in her purse for enough money to cover her meal, Alise gave a fleeting glance at her hardly touched plate, accepted the consolation of her friends as she gave hugs around the table, and headed for the parking lot. Tears threatened to escape her brimming eyes, but she swallowed the emotion and resisted the urge to crawl into her car and drive as far away as possible.

■■■

They call us the Sandwich Generation. We are pressed, sometimes not too gently, between caring for our parents and living our own lives at the same time. A large number of us are still raising children. Some are helping to care for grandchildren. We come in all ages, shapes, sizes, and life situations. We're becoming an increasing majority among today's population, shouldering additional responsibilities and silently struggling with the ramifications. This stage in life is one that surpasses age barriers in the same way that parents, at any age, can share the joys and challenges of parenthood.

But others rarely want us to haul out a photo account detailing our search for supplies for incontinence or the struggles of medication management. We're all just trying to get through each day and survive the seemingly endless challenges.

And it may not be until you're stuck between the platforms of your own life and that of your parents that you realize you're not only on a tightrope, but teetering with no pole for balance.

Here's your pole. It's our gift to you.

We're navigating the same tightrope you are. The only difference is we've had just a little more experience and have learned how to use the balance pole. Don't look down or be afraid. You're not alone, and we know that can make all the difference.

In this book, you'll read our stories and those of others. We'll share what we've learned and help you realize that your frustrations, fears, and seeming failures are normal. When tightrope-walking caregivers share their experiences, they form a unique bond. They can pass each other, even at a distance, smile, nod, frown, or just shrug shoulders and speak volumes of support without even saying a word. It's a special sisterhood. Though care isn't given just by women, we're still filling in the gaps of care with skills that gender predisposition and society have trained us to accept.

Baby boomers are hitting retirement age and finding themselves caught between caring for their aging parents and spreading the wings their parents taught them to use. Boomers have defined decades with an "I can do anything, anywhere" attitude. Now, when many of them are looking to show the world just how active and productive they can be, caring for their parents stops them in mid-flight.

But caring for aging family members encompasses others:

- A college student balances beginning her adult life with work and studies, while also filling in a generational gap to care for her grandparents.

- Sixty-two-year-old John is in a unique situation as caregiver for his brother and sister-in-law. While he has his own health issues and is a grandparent, John takes care of a childless brother nearly twenty years older than he. Although a capable adult, he often has to work through the "little brother" mentality still held by his older brother, while trying to offer support and care.

- Singles are finding new ways to adjust their full lives to the needs of aging parents whether they are living nearby or across a continent.

Who belongs to this sister- and brotherhood of caregivers? Nearly everyone has a caregiving story to share. Perhaps a sibling has taken the lead role in giving care to a parent, or other relatives or friends step in when you just can't be the one to do it. Regardless of how active a role you take, you'll doubtless find yourself feeling like an unwilling participant at some point.

You may be the one sitting by watching it all happen, or you may be aiding the primary caregiver. But you'll be there in one way or another. Finding the right support for your situation is essential. And there is no method that works for everyone. Family dynamics, situations, and personalities, as well as sibling and parental relationships, all factor in.

"You just go through this and feel yourself moving along even if you don't know exactly where you're going. You have to do it step by step or day by day. You can't look at the long haul or try to predict the future," Paula says.

"It's like I'm learning to drive a car with a manual transmission with no directions for learning how and when to shift," says Terri.

Though this book is not a manual, there are tips that may make your situation less stressful. In the chapters that follow, look at the situations you may encounter as you take on caregiving responsibilities. There will be laughter, heartache, and cheers along the way. But most of all, you will find encouragement to look ahead and to place one foot in front of the other, knowing others understand and care.

As you read through this book, you'll find many of the following features in most of the chapters:

- **Sensitivity Alerts:** Issues that may be sensitive for those receiving care.

- **Reality Checks:** Issues that may not make sense but are part of the reality of your situation.

- **Through the Looking Glass:** First-person narratives from elders receiving care.

- **Viewpoints:** Narratives and aids to remind you that you're not alone.

- **Living Water:** Scriptural nourishment for maintaining a healthy perspective on caregiving (Candy is the author of all the Living Water segments).

- **MOPs** (Medical Office Procedures): Rules specific to doctor's offices.

- **Forms:** Forms you might find helpful (see chapter 23).

Viewpoint:

Life Changes—wife and mother of two

"My mother was picking my children up from school for me, helping me with them in the afternoons and even cooking dinner. She could do it all. Though she was beginning to have some health challenges, nothing prepared me for finding my mother lying on the floor after I got a call from my aunt that she couldn't be reached by phone. I arrived in Mama's driveway at the same time as E.M.S. In an instant, Mama's life changed, and so did mine," Terri says.

Terri's mother had had a stroke while cooking breakfast. By the time Terri arrived, smoke was billowing out the door from still-cooking eggs. After a three-week hospital stay, Terri's mother came home. For months, her mother spent part of each day in her own home and part with Terri and her family. Terri managed two sets of finances, daily life for the family, and work. Eventually, they sold both homes and bought a larger one. They lived full lives between the medical crises they faced.

As a paralegal, Terri was able to work out a flexible schedule with her boss. She keeps her cell phone on, answering calls from her mother when she's at work and answering calls from the office when she's taking her mother to appointments.

Though her brother is supportive, he lives three hours away.

When Terri tried to be away for a weekend, the worry she faced took away from the reprieve. And, in fact, she got the dreaded call. Her mother had fallen and broken a bone in her wrist. Racing home, Terri jumped back into her new role.

"It's like a child carrying a security blanket, and I'm that blanket. I always knew I'd take on this role, if needed. I saw my mother unselfishly care for her in-laws and how she made that work. I love her and wouldn't have this any other way, but that doesn't mean it isn't hard," she said.

Terri has had to tell her mother that her days behind the wheel of a car and using a skillet are over.

"It's hard to talk to my mother that way, but also hard for her to accept it," Terri says, admitting the role is not comfortable and guilt often creeps in.

Living Water

> I will instruct you and teach you in the way you should go;
>> I will counsel you and watch over you.
>>> (Psalm 32:8)

> For I am the LORD, your God,
>> who takes hold of your right hand
> and says to you, Do not fear;
>> I will help you.
>>> (Isaiah 41:13)

When you take those first tentative steps into caregiving, the tightrope sways and threatens to flip you upside down. The parents you previously went to for comfort, support, and wisdom are now leaning heavily on you, sometimes expecting more of you than you feel you can provide.

Thankfully, you don't have to navigate caregiving in your own strength. God provides a wealth of wisdom and resources to those who ask. He promises to take hold of our right hand, steady us, educate us, counsel us, and calm our fears, one day or perhaps even one minute at a time. While it's great to be organized and capable, we are at our best when we're leaning completely on God, trusting that He is our stability in this otherwise shaky endeavor. In realizing and accepting the mortality of our earthly fathers and mothers, we enter into a new and deeper relationship with our heavenly Father.

Take a moment right now to ask God to be your Abba, your Daddy, and provide balance, support, guidance, and peace in the days ahead.

Additional Information

Online resources:

AARP is a wonderful resource for issues affecting the over-50 age group. The AARP *Bulletin Today* is their regular publication that covers a multitude of related topics to help you understand senior living issues: http://bulletin.aarp.org.

Another helpful online resource, www.helpguide.org, has a separate section on seniors and aging.

Books:

Caring for Your Parents: The Complete Family Guide (AARP), Hugh Delehanty and Elinor Ginzler (New York: Sterling Publishing Company, 2008).

Chapter 2

Assessing Your Juggling Act
Relationships and Caregiving Dynamics

S teven tiptoed into his mom's room. Even as an eight-year-old, he knew the importance of maintaining quiet in the household for as long as possible. He gently shook his mother's shoulder until she woke.

"Mom, Grandma's chasing chickens again," he whispered.

It wasn't the first time Jan's mother had "chased chickens" in the middle of the night. Grandma had lived on a farm her entire life. Now, she often got up in the middle of the night, scrambling through the family's living room to catch chickens only she could see. On this night, however, she did it without her nightgown.

Jan, a single mom, didn't have enough money to pay for assisted living or other supervised care for her 64-year-old mother, a long-suffering Alzheimer's patient. The trio lived by their own resourcefulness on a farm far from town. Jan's mother's mind was gone long before young Steven was old enough to remember anything other than a nude chicken-chasing grandma.

■ ■ ■

Jan is in the center of a wobbly tightrope walk. How long can she and her young son continue to balance life with a semblance of normalcy given their circumstances?

Balance for the caregiver and the care recipient is the hardest issue of all and one that often creates feelings of guilt and inadequacy. In Jan's case, her son's friends were scared away by her mother, leaving her feeling she wasn't providing a normal childhood for her son. She also felt inadequate to meet her mother's needs, yet was bound by limited financial resources. Like a plate-spinning sideshow performer, Jan felt pressure to keep all facets of her complicated life moving.

"You can never provide the care you really want because you can't be there all the time and do everything. Don't look back with regrets. Each time, you make the best decisions you can. When you do all you can to provide the best care and comfort, trust that it will be all right, so you can move forward on the calling God has for you in the other areas of your life," says Paula, who once walked a tightrope caring for her in-laws, a seriously ill husband, and their own family.

Caregivers often feel that even if they've gotten things under control in one aspect of life, other things suffer and still need attention. They're standing on a platform while someone else is swinging precariously above a net waiting to be caught. There's just no time to take comfort in even the small footing. They feel they must continually jump in, be active, and get another job done. If the momentum stops, can it ever be found again?

While caregivers provide strength and support for others, they need to look for support for themselves. Some caregivers are the counselor for so many others they forget they need to sound off to someone occasionally too. There is benefit in talking to a spouse, friend, or coworker. Having a way to vent frustrations and gain new insights is only part of the picture for finding balance.

When a caregiver chooses to stop scheduling social activities, it's like cutting off blood supply to a vital organ. Caregivers need to make plans with their own families and friends, and it's essential that those plans not include the person, or people, for whom they provide care.

However, it doesn't make sense to plan large social gatherings or a long vacation when a parent is fighting for life on a hospital bed or if a doctor is suggesting major surgery. Balance and practicality are important. Keeping some time sacred for life to continue in a semi-normal state allows an opportunity to breathe life into the tired caregivers.

Even if a caregiver is very close to her parents, including them in everything is a recipe for trouble. First, it provides no mental break for the caregiver. Second, it can make any planned event awkward for all.

A party for fifteen four-year-olds is probably not a good time to include an aging parent. Tolerance for noise and confusion is reduced during the aging process so bringing a parent to a kids' party isn't ideal. A smaller family-only celebration at home or in a restaurant, in addition to the children's party, allows grandparents to be involved and reduces stress for all.

In turn, your aging parent may occasionally want dinner out without his caregiver. Combining nights out can be a solution. A caregiver can provide chauffeur service, then go out to a different restaurant.

Boundaries

Tasks that take you ten minutes to complete take Dad half a day. It may be something simple like sorting through the mail or folding a load of laundry. It may even irritate you when Mom doesn't want you to just zip through the task. Don't do it. As long as a task won't hurt her, and she is physically capable of handling it, take the time issue out of it and let her do it. You have plenty of other things to do. She, however, does not. Completing simple daily living tasks helps maintain independence.

Social Boundaries for the Caregiver

As you become more and more involved in your parents' affairs, you'll make contacts with their friends. Those friends may begin asking you about their health issues. Why not tell a caring friend everything? Because your parents still deserve to make decisions about who knows the nitty-gritty details of their care. That Garden Club may be the last social group your mother has where she feels that she's looked up to for her abilities. Knowing that every other person in the group knows she has to wear adult continence pants at night will only take away her self-esteem.

Take a few minutes to consider each person to whom you're passing information. Would Dad really want Aunt Sally to know he has a catheter?

It's usually the closest family members or very close friends with medical backgrounds who will be able to support you by listening when you've had a rough day caregiving. But maintaining dignity is an issue. If you are providing updates on your parent via e-mail, perhaps you need two lists—one for those who receive all the details, another for those receiving general updates.

Having compassion is not just about doing what makes you comfortable if you were in your parent's physical condition. You need to consider mental and emotional issues for your parents as well as for yourself.

The Parents You Love, or Not

Balance depends greatly on understanding the nature of parent-child dynamics. Some relationships are as close as Siamese twins; others are polar opposites. At times the very foundations of the relationships involved in caregiving are shaken. When parents blame us for things we have no control over, it's difficult to bridle anger and remain loving. At times someone other than an adult child is more successful making suggestions. The key to managing emotions is to accept the nature of relationships—they change, sometimes daily or weekly.

Empathy is a powerful tool. Unfortunately, reciprocal empathy doesn't always happen. Consider the following scenarios:

> Elizabeth watched as her daughter, Fran, unloaded bags of groceries. *I could do this,* Elizabeth thought, but didn't say anything because she appreciated the help.
>
> Fran's cell phone rang.
>
> "Mom, I need to get this, but I'll be back in a minute to finish." Fran stepped out of the tiny kitchen.

From the kitchen, Elizabeth heard every word including her daughter's tone of exasperation. "Hi Shelley…yeah, I've got a minute, but I'm at Mama's…I *might* be able to, but I have to finish here and it may take a while…No, she's fine, but she's been a little difficult, if you know what I mean…Okay, I should be able to get out of here in an hour. I'll meet you then."

I thought we had a nice morning together, but from now on, I'll find another way to get to the store, even though Fran is willing, Elizabeth thought.

■■■

Jamie stopped by her mother's house to deliver stamps. Dishes were stacked in the sink and the kitchen counter was littered with crumbs. Several weeks' worth of newspapers and mail covered the kitchen table.

"Mama, has your back been bothering you?"

"Well, yes, how did you know?"

"Things are a little cluttered. Would you like for me to straighten up?"

"I'll do it later. Why don't you come in the den and sit with me."

Jamie ignored her mother's reply and began sorting mail. Then she turned her efforts to the counters and sink. Rounding the corner to the laundry room, Jamie almost stepped in a plate. Several dishes were directly in the path to the washing machine.

"Mom, why are these plates on the floor?"

Jamie's mother hobbled into the room. "Oh, those are from my dinners. I let Poodles have a taste when I'm finished with them."

Hearing her name, Poodles came into the laundry room wagging from head to tail and began licking one of the plates.

"Mama, I don't think you should leave these out here. You could stumble over them, and besides, they attract bugs."

"Oh, Poodles," Jamie's mother said, directing her answer to the dog. "Our Jamie just doesn't know how we do things around here, does she? She comes in and takes over, storming around and messing up how we do things. She means well though, we know that don't we, girl?"

Jamie was shocked and hurt that her mother directed her reply to the dog. *I'm unappreciated. I've got plenty to do other than listen to Mother talk to the dog,* Jamie thought.

In both cases, whether intentional or not, feelings were hurt. Thoughtlessness can come from a caregiver or a parent. Many times these situations are rooted in a general frustration, either from a lack of balance in the caregiver's life or from embarrassment or a grasp for independence on the part of the person receiving care.

Often neither party knows how to address the situation when hurt feelings are involved. It is hard enough to get down to business and talk about finances and end-of-life decisions, but when an ego has been bruised, several things are likely to come next. The injured party may rebel by getting angry and arguing about unrelated issues or adopting a clipped, irritated tone to express frustration. Or the party may withdraw and refuse to talk.

Communication is vital, but it's equally important *how* you talk. It's very easy for caregivers to talk down to the person they're caring for without even realizing it.

When Dad starts behaving like your four-year-old, it's easy to start treating him like a child. Yet the same approach you'd use with a child may work to accomplish the task at hand. When you catch yourself telling your mother not to turn on the stove because it will hurt her, you may suddenly realize you're treating her like a toddler. The role reversals cause an emotional twist that can tear your heart out if you don't work toward balance. That's when you pretend this child in an adult's body isn't the person who changed your diapers and helped you survive your first broken heart. Although challenging, try to maintain compassion and awareness.

Everyone has issues. Some adult children detest their parents. Some are "guilted" into caregiving and resent the role. Others have even looked forward to the day when they can take care of aging parents. Ultimately, caregiving is a very individual journey.

For caregivers who feel they're not even wanted in the role they've assumed (or have been pushed into), this is an ideal time to face unresolved issues. Sometimes emotional aspects need attention more urgently than physical situations, and that attention must occur before healing or peace can come. It takes a willing, although sometimes bruised, heart.

When opportunities for healing are ignored by parent or child, the sudden death of a parent can bring fresh wounds. Caregivers may find scars have formed along their journey, but scars are better than gaping wounds and provide stronger footing for the future.

Caregiving Beyond Blood Ties

Deaths of family members or fractured relationships frequently leave people with no one to care for them when they reach the point of needing help. A study of grown children of divorce conducted by Elizabeth Marquardt, a vice president of the Institute for American Values, and sociology professor Norval Glenn at the University of Texas at Austin found that strained relationships still exist in families of divorce once children reach adulthood. Many adult children of divorce struggle with whether they should, and how they should, care for estranged fathers who are ill and often living alone. The relationship between stepparents and stepchildren is even more precarious, with no clear definition of expectations.[1]

But sometimes, special people step forward to fill a caregiving gap. They may be neighbors, friends, former coworkers, or church volunteers.

A Caregiving Friend

Allie has been caring for her friend Virginia for more than a decade. Although Allie stood by her when Virginia's husband died 14 years ago, the two bonded years before. Allie is young enough to be Virginia's daughter, and Virginia tells everyone she is. Although no blood binds them, they share mutual love and concern.

Virginia's son, stepchildren, and adult grandchildren live states away. No family lives close enough to take on the primary caregiving role. Virginia's care is a labor of love for Allie. But accepting this role hasn't been easy. Virginia was hospitalized seven times in one year alone.

Allie has navigated the choppy waters of finding specialized medical care and, at times, juggling the services of more than a dozen different doctors. She also found around-the-clock caregivers, which allowed Virginia to stay in her home. And Allie keeps Virginia's family informed on the ever-changing landscape of her health and care.

Allie's husband manages Virginia's finances. They don't need or expect anything financially from Virginia and go to extremes to make sure Virginia's resources are protected.

"What we're so thankful for is that Nana (Virginia) can live the life she's always lived. She's stayed in the home and community she loves and has the lifestyle she's been accustomed to for so many years. It's what makes her happy. None of us has been in a position to provide that for her, though we wish we could. We're thankful beyond words that God brought Allie to us and Nana," says Virginia's granddaughter.

▪▪ Through the Looking Glass ▪▪

In the mirror: Lucy, a 74-year-old living with her husband in a house that holds fond memories.

> "This is a critical time in our lives. We both feel good and have no major illnesses, but in the back of our minds, we wonder if we'll remain independent for ten or fifteen more years.
>
> "Our major concern is the possibility of having to sell our

beautiful lake home at some point. The house belonged to my parents and was the only permanent location our family had as we moved from parsonage to parsonage. Since my husband was a pastor, we moved many times while the children were growing up.

"We vacationed in this home and came here for holidays and special occasions. Our three sons lived here while they worked summer jobs. It is a special, sacred place to us.

"We'd like this house to be an inheritance for our children when we're gone. Yet, if our health fails quickly, none of them live nearby to be our caregivers. Then we'd be forced to sell the house and use that money to enter a retirement village. But we hate the thought of our family grieving the loss of this place.

"These thoughts can become burdens, but we know we have to trust our Lord to lead us in making wise decisions."

Viewpoint:

Out of the Mouths of Babes—A lesson for Kim from her daughter

"When I'm grown up, I'll have to deal with you like you deal with Grammi and Papa," our seven-year-old said.

Although her frankness shocked me, I realized she was responding with a child's acute sense of nailing a situation. Her perspective gave me a glimpse at the future and provided a reality check for me.

It had been a particularly full and frustrating week. Though I always tried to remain positive about all we were juggling, the strain must have shown. I didn't view our situation as "dealing with" my parents, as if they were a deck of cards I had to shuffle because it was my turn or duty. So, I had a talk with that wise seven-year-old about the gift of caring for others.

Kids, however, have varying degrees of involvement in the caregiving journey, and it's important to take note. Seeds are being planted in their minds for the future. Helping those seeds grow positive roots is important.

When caregiving is part of their small world, it does something to children's developing sense of themselves and the world at large. It helps them see that the world does not revolve around them.

Communication is important to put things in perspective. You may be so exhausted that thinking of the effect the strain you're under is having on your children is something that gets put aside. Or perhaps that has become your primary worry. Again, communication makes the difference. But don't wait too long. Those oh-so-observant children often have a few nuggets to share with you that lighten your load.

For Steven, whose chicken-chasing grandmother frightened away his friends, he learned empathy for others and a sense of his own ability to deal with hard situations. His experience took away some of the fear of things he may face one day. It was tough, but they made it, chickens and all.

Necessity teaches us all lessons. I used to be the mom who had to have everything in order before anyone came to our home to visit. Now, if friends come over, I've discovered that they usually feel comfortable if the house isn't immaculate—it's more like their own homes. That works for me, even though I still have high standards. The kids are learning important lessons, even if this isn't the way I'd planned to teach these lessons.

Not long after going through a series of medical crises, we decided to have friends from church over to our house. One of my friends called me and asked me if I was nuts.

"No, I'm just trying to live my life," I answered.

My life I share with my husband and children still includes others. Could I have used the time to just sit around and rest? Yes. Did I need to peck away at a couple of months' worth of cleaning and chores I'd gotten behind on? Yes and no. Having people over gave me incentive to get in gear and get the work done. I felt great when they came. Tired but great. When they left, the house was in order and I was energized for whatever came next.

Had an emergency with my parents arisen, we would have cancelled the gathering. Everyone knew our situation and would understand.

Living Water

> Respect your father and mother—God, your God, commands it! You'll have a long life; the land that God is giving you will treat you well (Deuteronomy 5:16 MSG).
>
> Love is always supportive, loyal, hopeful, and trusting (1 Corinthians 13:7 CEV).

God commands us to honor our parents and includes the promise that we'll enjoy long life if we do. But there may be days when treating our parents with respect is so challenging we're willing to forfeit this provision! When parents are stubborn, whiny, or uncooperative, we have to draw from the well of grace to remain patient and loving.

Honoring parents is most difficult when the baggage of unresolved hurts and misunderstandings weighs us down. Often, a disrespectful phrase flies out of our mouths before we even realize it, springing from a wound deep within that we don't even know is there. But rehashing some long-ago injustice, perceived or otherwise, may not be prudent.

Instead, write a letter to God. Be sure to include the injustice, your feelings, then and now, and as much information as you want. It may take you several days to complete. Then make a decision to forgive your parents. You don't even have to mention this to them. This is a transaction between you and God, a time when you choose to let go of bitterness and resentment. Pray, asking God to help you forgive your parents and to forgive you for harboring hostility all these years.

First Peter 4:8 reminds us that love covers a multitude of wrongs. Choose to forgive and love your parents as God forgives and loves you.

Additional Information

Online resource:

Caring Connections offers a wide variety of resources to help care-givers assess their situation and needs: http://www.caringinfo.org/CaringForSomeone.

Books:

How to Care for Aging Parents, Virginia Morris (New York: Workman Publishing, 2004).

Chapter 3

Understanding and Caring for the Primary Caregiver

Caregiving Roles

Kendra turned off her headlights, eased up the driveway, and into the carport. She gathered her purse and briefcase, got out of the car, and resisted the urge to flip on the carport light.

Fumbling with keys, coat, purse, and briefcase, she finally located the keyhole. She walked carefully into the dark kitchen, deposited her burdens on the counter, and groped her way toward the hall. The next thing Kendra knew, she was sprawled on the floor beside the dog crate, and Sassy was barking at an earsplitting decibel.

Within minutes, the phone rang. Kendra stood and hobbled to it. A sigh escaped her lips when she saw the caller ID.

"Hello."

"Kendra, you're home! Are you all right? I think someone is trying to break into your house. Maybe I should call the police."

"Mother, I'm fine, really. Please, don't call the police…again."

"But it's dark at your house and I heard noises. Are you sure you're okay?"

"Yes, I just got home."

"Well, for heaven's sake, why don't you turn on some lights? I'm standing at my bedroom window and your house is pitch dark!"

"I like it that way," Kendra mumbled.

"What? Kendra, you've got to speak up. I don't know how you keep that job of yours when you don't speak clearly. I raised you to enunciate your words. All this mumbling is a result of these cellular telephones—people whip those contraptions out in public places and even in church, mind you…"

"Mom, I need to go. I haven't had supper yet."

"Well, come on over. It won't take me but a minute to warm up my mobile meals leftovers."

"Thanks, but I'm really tired."

"Well, you work too hard. Why won't you let me feed you? I'm just trying to help. Besides, I need you to do a few things for me."

"Mom, it's late, and I was over there for four hours yesterday afternoon. Surely whatever you need can wait until morning."

"But if you don't help me, who will? I'm just stranded here since I can't drive anymore. I'm depending on you. Besides you leave early and I don't want to have to get up that soon. I need my rest, you know."

"Okay, Mom. I'll be over there as soon as I change clothes."

"Don't take too long. My program comes on in thirty minutes."

Kendra clunked the handset back on the base without even saying goodbye. *What kind of life is this?* she thought. *I'm staying at work later and later and sneaking in my own house to try to gain a little privacy, but it never works. I feel like a slave.*

The Role of Primary Caregiver

Like many of us, Kendra feels overwhelmed by her role as primary caregiver. Whether an only child or one who has landed in the lead care position because of proximity, personality, birth order, or sibling default, the primary caregiver takes the lead in caring for aging parents. No matter the size, dynamics, or geography of the family involved, one person emerges wearing the top hat.

Like the ringmaster in the circus, the primary caregiver oversees everything that happens. Often, there are more acts than one can comfortably keep an eye on, but most primaries never admit this. They stoically press on because it's harder to take an honest look at the physical and emotional intricacies of caregiving and to admit help might be required than it is just to do everything.

Primary caregivers do what everyone else is expecting—they take control. There's a reason that one family member rises to the top. Others around the primary caregiver already know that person is going to be okay because he or she possesses the skills and strength to manage the job. This person is likely the most organized, assertive, or even controlling family member, and is a natural for the job.

Primaries really don't talk much about all they are juggling. Even if many family members live nearby, this person usually stands alone and ends up doing all the extra errands and checking on Mom and Dad once a day or more. But if you are the sibling, spouse, friend, or coworker of a primary caregiver, listen up. Your support is vital, even if not asked for. While the primary caregiver may claim *things are going just fine, thank you,* notice the haggard look and pasted-on smile. The primary caregiver may be only one thin strand away from a breaking rope.

Caring for the Primary Caregiver

Here are some suggestions you can implement to help a caregiver circumvent burn out:

Start a support network. This group may consist of coworkers, friends from a local church, a caregivers' support group, or a counselor. More than likely, it will end up being a combination of several. It is vitally important to communicate feelings, fears, and frustrations to someone or in the pages of a journal.

Become a listener. Primary caregivers deal with a number of situations that fuel frustration and resentment. Often, siblings or others call the primary repeatedly to ask how a parent is doing when they could just as easily call the parents or drive the two blocks to visit. Having a friend who is willing to listen while the primary caregiver vents, whether by phone or even through e-mail, helps defuse frustration. Contact from someone beyond the everyday stresses of caregiving allows the primary caregiver to remember that the world is larger than the tasks at hand, and other people are out there. It may not be necessary to offer advice. In fact, ask first if input is wanted. Acknowledge what the primary caregiver is saying and validate feelings. Rather than addressing each item in a three-page e-mail, pare it down to a simple, "Wow, it's been rough over there today, and you've reached your limit, haven't you? I'm praying for you."

Actively shift control. Since primary caregivers have to juggle so many things at once, look for opportunities to relieve them of at least a portion of that burden once in a while. Nurture the person who is putting everyone's needs ahead of her own. The easiest way to do this is by shifting her focus.

When offering long-distance support, your initial thought may be to send a card to the person who is receiving care. Instead, or in addition, send a card to the caregiver. Include a gift certificate to a coffee shop or bookstore. It may go unused for months, but the thought will be appreciated. Or send her children some form of entertainment—a puzzle they can work together, or balloons or bubbles they can amuse themselves with for a while. Find a local caterer and have some casseroles sent over. You've relieved one decision—what to cook for dinner when she finally gets home.

For those supporting locally, when the primary caregiver balks about taking a break, push the protests out of the way. Send her to the movies while you do the laundry. Offer a shoulder to cry on, a receptive ear, and reminders that reason, communication, humor, and taking breaks will lighten the load.

Embrace reason. The primary caregiver needs to listen to an internal voice of reason and other trusted friends or family. Remind the primary caregiver that it's okay to feel brokenhearted, even in the midst of decisions made with reason.

> "I remember the exact moment I had to sign a DNR (do not resuscitate) order on my father. My heart said I was killing him, but my head knew it was what he wanted, and the right thing to do. But I still remember exactly where I was standing in the doorway, and even the way the bush outside looked when I did it."—Paula

Although the primary caregiver may already know what's involved in a DNR document, and all the common sense behind it, when signing a DNR for your own parent, emotions often overshadow reason.

Learn and share. Primary caregivers who have investigated the full prognosis of their loved one may need to share fears about the uncertainty of what lies ahead. Although doctors have no guarantees, they can give an idea of what others have experienced in similar situations and provide suggestions for what kinds of support care may be needed, now or later. Be available to listen, console, or cheer a primary caregiver who realizes the prognosis isn't matching reality.

Keep in touch. A number of primary caregivers manage full- or part-time work through flexible hours and the modern miracle of the laptop and cell phone. However, once home, a primary caregiver often wants to turn off the computer and phone and feel disconnected. But communication with a supportive cheerleader may be just what is needed to help the caregiver refocus.

Support-network members can create an e-mail or phone update chain so a primary caregiver doesn't arrive home to six messages from people wondering how Mom made it through the latest test. Caring-Bridge, a nonprofit organization, provides "free, personalized websites that support and connect loved ones during critical illness, treatment, and recovery" (caringbridge.org). Here family and friends can check in and get updates. You can offer to create and help update such a site for your friend.

Find the humor. Whether it's sharing a laugh with the whole family about the new potty chair or the everlasting mountain of laundry, find a way to laugh. It's not laughing at the person you're caring for; it's about finding humor along the way. Help a primary caregiver see these chances for laughter. Supporters do not have to be stand-up comedians to help bring stress relief through laughter.

Provide a break. At some point, the primary caregiver *must* escape, even if only to run out for an ice cream cone or a quick cup of coffee. Supporters can volunteer or hire help for routine chores, or call in extended family members to pitch in. Others feel helpful, and the primary caregiver regains strength and perspective. But be realistic about what is actually feasible. If a primary caregiver's sibling offers to come 700 miles to offer relief, this may be more stressful for the primary caregiver because of preparations involved in housing the relative and explaining everything necessary for the caregiving situation. The hassle may prove more stressful than the help.

> ■ ■ ■
>
> **For spouses:** Over the years, husbands and wives hurt or disappoint each other with words or deeds or by failing to respond in times of need. Now, during these caregiving days, is when you can really bless your spouse by stepping up to support emotionally and actively. Little acts of kindness, like unloading the dishwasher, running a load of laundry, paying the bills, or volunteering to check on your spouse's aging parent so he or she doesn't have to that day, demonstrate your love and support for your spouse during these difficult days. Be observant; then volunteer. Your spouse will love you for it!
>
> ■ ■ ■

Calling in Reinforcements

As Regan prepared for a business trip, she lined up extended family members and neighbors to grocery shop and pick up medication for her father. Before leaving town, she stocked her father's pantry, deposited checks, and mailed bill payments.

As she kissed him goodbye, Regan reminded him that her plane arrived around midnight on the night of her return and she'd need at least a day to right her own household before returning to "the routine." She placed the pad beside his chair that contained the phone numbers of her backups and dashed to the airport.

Around 4:00 p.m. on the day after Regan's return, her father called.

"I'm out of my blood pressure medicine," he said without preface.

"I thought Uncle John was picking up meds for you while I was gone."

"He couldn't do it. The doctor sent him for tests."

"Why didn't you call Mr. Jones? He's right down the street and he'd be happy to help."

"I didn't want to bother him. Besides, I knew you'd be back today in time to get it. It can't wait until tomorrow. I'll die without it."

Scenarios such as this one are what make most caregivers long to hop on the next plane to a Caribbean destination. Even with careful organization, plans sometimes go awry. But resist the urge to try to do everything yourself because something might not work out if you delegate. There really is merit in having help. Someone else can care for your parent. While it may not be in a manner your parent is accustomed to, someone else is capable of doing the job. There comes a point when, even if your parent protests, it's time to call in reinforcements.

Viewpoint:

Keeping Perspective—Candy, an only child

Sometimes caregiving can feel like a life sentence. When I'm in the middle of an especially demanding and intense period, I remind myself that this chapter of my life won't last forever. While making a trip across town to pick up the insurance card before going to the pharmacy, I realize the day will come when I'll wish I could see my parent one more time.

I've found it helps to keep a variety of CDs in the car. The music can be either soothing or lively, if I need energizing. I also listen to Scripture tapes as I travel. Other times, I turn off all noise and pray aloud as I drive.

Although I often feel stress, I try not to view caregiving as merely a list of chores to complete and check off the list. This time with my parent may be shorter than I anticipate, so I try to find some level of joy in each encounter. Journaling the triumphs and joys, as well as the frustrations, helps. Spending more time looking for the positives rather than dwelling on the negatives in my current life situation allows me to keep perspective.

Living Water

> Plans fail for lack of counsel,
>> but with many advisors they succeed.
>>> (Proverbs 15:22)

Many times we labor under the burden of feeling it's all up to us to make things happen. As a caregiver, you may believe no one else can provide the level or the manner of care you are currently giving your loved one. There's just one problem with that train of thought. It's faulty. It's also a little arrogant. When you take this much responsibility and control, you are crossing God out of the equation.

Although he was in a different situation, Moses tried to handle every legal dispute that arose during the time the children of Israel were wandering in the wilderness. The Bible says Moses stood, and the people crowded around him from morning until evening in an effort to have their cases heard and judged.

Jethro, Moses' father-in-law, was the voice of reason. He came to Moses and said, "Why do you alone sit as judge, while all these people stand around you from morning till evening? What you are doing is not good. You and these people who come to you will only wear yourselves out. The work is too heavy for you; you cannot handle it alone" (see Exodus 18:13-18).

It took the wisdom of a man who was outside Moses' regular group of advisors to see that Moses was ruining his health, and alienating his family, by trying to handle this huge task on his own. His father-in-law advised Moses to select capable people and delegate authority to them so he wouldn't have full responsibility for the job.

View your caregiving role the same way. Look around you and select people who are capable and trustworthy to help you. In taking this step, don't view yourself as lazy or incapable. You are very competent, but you need to employ wisdom in handling the demands of the job. God will bless you for relinquishing some of the control, and you will be stronger and more refreshed by accepting help.

Additional Information

Online resources:

The www.webmd.com and www.revolutionhealth.com are excellent sites for looking up any issue a primary caregiver is dealing with, particularly stress.

Books:

The Caregiver's Survival Handbook: How to Care for Your Aging Parent without Losing Yourself, Alexis Abramson with Mary Anne Dunkin (New York: Berkley Publishing Group, 2004).

Chapter 4

Long-Distance Caregiving
Managing Across the Miles

Long-distance caregiving presents a different and more complicated set of challenges. The ability to drop by and check on parents daily, or even several times a week, is an impossibility. Daily care must come through agencies, other family members, friends, neighbors, or hired caregivers, and sometimes, entrusting your parent's care to others is fraught with problems.

Following are several long-distance caregiving scenarios. While each situation is different, there are the commonalities of need, concern, and balancing normal responsibilities with travel.

Millie's Story
"When Mom fell and broke her hip, she went to a rehabilitation facility at a nursing home, and then into the nursing home. My sisters and I were appalled by the conditions in the facility and the lack of care she received. She became very depressed, so we made the decision to care for her at home until she was well enough to go into assisted living.

"My two sisters and I began alternating caregiving stints. It was very difficult for all of us. I was traveling back and forth between South Carolina and Michigan. Although my sisters live in Michigan, each was several hours away from Mom's town. One sister was working full time and she took the weekends, beginning Thursday afternoons. I was concerned about her because she worked all week, had little rest on the weekends, and went back to work on Mondays, arriving late after dropping my mother off for a blood transfusion. My mother has a blood disease that requires her to have blood transfusions twice a week. The process takes about six hours.

"We made the caregiving switch on Mom's transfusion days. I went to Michigan every two weeks and stayed about ten days. While there, I was able to work it out to go to some water aerobics classes on the days Mom was getting blood. Other times, I'd leave the house briefly for a brisk walk around the block, even in the freezing weather. That helped me keep my sanity.

"Also, my aunt was able to come and stay with Mom so I could go to the grocery store or do other errands. That was a tremendous help. My sisters and I alternated caring for Mom for almost a year. Although I knew this is what we needed to do, I dreaded the approach of my time to be there. Not because I didn't want to see my mother, but because of the travel and the feeling of being unsettled.

"Eventually, she was well enough to go into assisted living. We found a wonderful privately owned facility that meets her needs, both physically and socially. The staff is very attentive, and they really do care about her.

"I find that I have a lot of resentment toward my mother's church, because she was always so involved, serving on committees and attending faithfully. Her church is very important to her, yet no one has been willing to volunteer to pick her up for services or Bible study, and she misses that interaction with people. I don't think anyone in a leadership position at the church has even visited her. I am bitter about that."

■ ■ ■

Millie and her sisters were able to formulate a long-distance care plan for their mother that worked. While the schedule was challenging, their sacrifices enabled their mother to recover sufficiently to enter an assisted living facility.

This story also brings to light a situation that frequently occurs.

Often churches do not have a system in place for providing either transportation or visitation for their senior members. But senior adults feel a great loss when they are cut off from the fellowship of a body of believers.

Perhaps you can serve as an advocate for your parent in this area, encouraging her church to make continued connection with senior adult members a priority.

Flora's Story

"When I was a child, my mom always took me swimming at a crowded New York City public pool. While I played at the shallow end of the pool, she'd watch from a nearby bench. One day, a large man knocked me into the deep water. Unable to swim, I panicked, flailing and struggling to keep my head above the water. In a flash, I saw my mother dive into the water, and she pulled me to safety.

"Many years have passed since that day, and my mother is now struggling in another kind of deep water—that of infirmity and old age. Although I have since moved to Florida and she remains in our native New York, our roles have reversed and it is I who rush to her aid.

"After she fractured her hip six months ago, I have traveled up and down the east coast three times. I am now preparing for a fourth trip. This involves dropping everything I am doing in my home and my writing career. And it all stays dropped until I return home and am able to pick it back up.

"Because my husband is retired, he is able to accompany me. This is helpful for me because my health is not the best. His presence is also helpful for my mom because while I clean her apartment and do her laundry, my hubby puts his 'fix-it man' talents to use and repairs things.

"We also do my mom's shopping, stocking her cabinets with items that require little or no preparation and that use as few dishes as possible. These include frozen dinners, microwaveable soups, powdered milk, packs of crackers with peanut butter, and vacuum-packed containers of orange juice.

"My motivation is best summed up by the title of a compilation *My*

Turn to Care by Marlene Bagnull. When I was drowning, my mom came to my rescue. I am now coming to hers."

■ ■ ■

Flora's story highlights the importance of maintaining an attitude of gratitude in the caregiving process. Sometimes it's easy to adopt a martyr-like mentality, but here are some ways to cultivate gratitude.

Praise. We live in a society where people often demand their rights and sue if they feel victimized. This attitude focuses more on self than on God. Praise helps shift our focus off ourselves and onto God. Start each morning by reading one of the Psalms. Think about God's attributes and His great love for us (Psalm 18:46).

Joy. Do you ever find yourself just going through the motions of daily existence without experiencing joy? God's desire is for us to live victorious lives here on earth. Take a moment to recognize and rejoice in God's great gift of salvation, freely given (Isaiah 25:9).

Freedom. We are so blessed, yet we often feel sorry for ourselves regarding some aspect of our lives that isn't going exactly as we'd like. We enjoy the freedoms of living in America, but also experience liberty from the penalty of sin because of Christ's sacrifice on our behalf (John 8:36).

Anticipation. Each year, farmers live in anticipation of a bumper crop. They watch the sky for signs of rain, pray for just the right temperatures, and hope the current year's yield will be the best ever. We have the hope and promise of eternal life through faith in Jesus Christ. Let us live a life of gratitude in anticipation of our heavenly home (Hebrews 6:19-20).

Inell's Story

"Although Pop was 93, he made the decision to have heart valve repair and bypass surgery thinking it would extend his life a little longer. Unfortunately, it really didn't turn out that way. He was in the hospital or restorative care almost three months following his surgery.

"My father's doctor wrote to tell me I was needed in caring for my father, and I was able to take accumulated sick days as family medical leave, thus safeguarding my benefits and saving my vacation days. Several of my coworkers offered to donate their vacation days for my use, also.

"My sister-in-law and I spent all day, every day, either at the hospital or restorative care. When Daddy finally came home, he needed 24/7 help in addition to the two of us, so we hired a service. He died about two weeks after coming home.

"Now, my husband's mother is in an assisted living facility for those with Alzheimer's. Prior to that, I was helping to care for her in her home.

"When I think of what some families go through, I know I was blessed with my situation. But caregiving is emotionally and physically draining. There are some battles I fought that I probably shouldn't have. Looking back, I'm glad I worked years ago in admissions at a nursing home. I believe the Lord allowed that experience to give me insights into the caregiving process."

■ ■ ■

While long-distance caregiving takes many forms, it is especially stressful because it alters schedules for an indefinite period of time. Sometimes companies allow employees to come up with a creative plan for adjusting work schedules to accommodate caregiving needs. Be sure to investigate all the options.

Kara's Story

"When my father's health reached the point where he could no longer care for himself, I lived 1000 miles away and was a single mom struggling to make ends meet. My brother, who lived 15 minutes from Dad and had grown children, could have helped, but he did nothing.

"I traveled from Orlando to Pennsylvania as often as I could, but the guilt was overwhelming. When I was with Dad, I felt guilty about not being with my daughter. When I was home with her, I felt guilty not being with my father. It was an excruciating time for us physically, mentally, and emotionally. It helped Dad when hospice came in, but I still felt helpless. I read a book published by hospice about how both the patient and their loved ones experience anger. Reading the book helped, but I still feel angry about various aspects of the caregiving process.

"Dad never lost awareness of what was happening. That was both a blessing and a curse. Up until the moment he died in my arms, Dad recognized me and realized I was there for him. I knew how ready he was to die because he suffered the trauma of bedsores and other pain that even medication didn't ease.

"There were other issues, like 'friendly' neighbors who came by and stole Dad's pain pills, and a hired caregiver who took presents from under his Christmas tree. I couldn't be there to follow up the way I wanted to.

"When I came home after my father's death, I discovered I'd lost my job, even though I'd been told repeatedly that everything was taken care of. My manager at work never turned in the 30-day leave I requested. From this experience, I learned to get everything in writing, hard copy, not just by e-mail.

"I've also had trouble handling Dad's estate, even though it's very small. It would have helped if I'd been involved in the estate planning, but I wasn't. Dad was from the old school and thought everything would be done right, but the lawyer he trusted proved untrustworthy.

"I never thought I'd be in a position to need help from the American Bar Association, but the stack of estate papers is a constant reminder of all that still needs to be done. I long for closure so I can salvage happy memories, even the bittersweet ones we had together at the end."

■ ■ ■

Kara's story is a reminder that our aging parents are targets for unscrupulous individuals, particularly when there isn't a family member on-site. Guarding your parent from fraudulent offers, untrustworthy professionals, and thieves presents one of the greatest challenges to caregiving long distance. But there are some things you can do to deter this type of activity. Arrive unannounced to get a better view of day-to-day care. Make it clear to caregivers that they are not to leave neighbors, their own friends or relatives, or others alone with your parent, or allow them access to other parts of the house. Remove as many valuables as possible from the home. Do the best you can.

Ginger's Story

"The hardest part of being several states away from Dad is having him call and say, 'I hurt.' Although I've made three trips in three months to be with him, I feel so helpless when he calls and says he's in pain.

"My father had a stroke last year, and while he was still in the hospital, I realized how important it is for our parents to have an advocate. There are issues not just with medical care, but with communication.

"We had an incident where an RN gave my father an injection of insulin while I was trying to explain to her that he is a borderline diabetic and not on insulin. She bluntly told me there is no such thing as a borderline diabetic and ignored my protests. I was so frustrated that I felt physically ill after she just popped him with an injection without checking his blood sugar again to confirm he actually needed insulin. It had been five hours since he'd had a blood sugar check.

Contact information

"We live in Florida. My daughter lives in South Carolina. My son, though in Florida, is 120 miles away. It helps that our neighbor has all our important contact numbers.

"When my husband and I had an accident, we were both air lifted to the hospital. Our neighbor made sure the paramedic knew my husband had diabetes and notified our family about what had happened. My sister was at the hospital before we were. Having a neighbor who will do this brings all of us peace of mind."—Betty, 75

"I wrote a letter to the hospital about the incident, but my father asked me not to mail it until he had completed the hospital rehabilitation program. In the letter, I made sure I complimented another RN, who was especially helpful and courteous, instead of just complaining about the incident with the injection.

"Eventually, I received a reply. The supervisor had called the nurse into her office and asked her to read my letter. The nurse was upset to realize how her abruptness and actions had affected my father and me, and she is now taking a class to increase her communication skills.

"Now that my father is home, he has a friend who helps him. The stroke affected his left side and his vision, so he needs help all the time. I'm just thankful the friend is willing and available to help."

Ginger's experience highlights the critical element of both acting as an advocate for your parent and communicating with medical staff. Although communication issues will be addressed in subsequent chapters, it's important to note Ginger's approach in reporting the incident. She used the "sandwich method," complimenting one of the nurses before bringing up a complaint about another nurse, and then ended the letter with words of appreciation.

Often in our frustration or anger, we go into a situation with guns blazing. It is helpful to gain a little distance between the incident and your encounter with medical or administrative personnel, unless the incident is so critical that your parent's welfare is immediately at stake.

Many hospitals now have patient advocates who can assist in communicating with hospital employees or administrators. Most patient advocates are genuinely interested in hearing the patient's perspective on situations and willing to help. Unfortunately, others sometimes appear to be more of an advocate for the hospital than for patients. But definitely look into patient advocate programs.

Tips for Long-Distance Caregiving

- Talk to your parent's friends, neighbors, and relatives who might be willing to help on a rotating basis with various needs.

- Set up a monthly schedule. Request permission of all those involved to list their contact information so they can find a substitute rather than calling you at the last minute if they cannot be available.

- Create a notebook to leave at your parent's home that includes your contact information, emergency phone numbers, doctors' office phone numbers, a list of prescriptions your parent is taking, and a calendar that highlights all appointments.

- Investigate services that provide in-home care.

- Check to see if a mobile meals program is available in your parent's town. Not only will this provide your parent with one hot meal a day, but it will also ensure your parent is checked on during the day.

- Schedule your trips to coincide with important medical visits. While a friend or neighbor can take your parent for something like routine lab work, you need to be present to ask questions and act as an advocate for your parent during appointments with doctors. Many times, aging parents either do not answer the doctor's questions honestly or do not understand or remember instructions or reasons why tests are ordered and additional medication prescribed.

Living Water

> Look straight ahead,
>> and fix your eyes on what lies before you.
> Mark out a straight path for your feet;
>> stay on the safe path.
> Don't get sidetracked.
>> (Proverbs 4:25-27a NLT)

Perhaps today you are dealing with all the guilt, frustration, and fear that surround long-distance caregiving. Concern for your parent niggles at the back of your mind during work, conversations, attempted relaxation, and in the wee hours of the morning. A ringing phone jangles nerves as you wonder if this is a call informing you of your parent's illness, injury, or death. How do you cope? There is a tendency to ignore the inevitable—the prospect of greater in-home care or a move to a facility. But Proverbs encourages us to take an honest look at what lies ahead and make a plan.

It's easy to get sidetracked because life interrupts and there is always something that seems more urgent. But start making a list of steps you need to take before your parent requires the next stage of care. This may mean locating important papers, scoping out assisted living facilities, or having your name added to your parent's bank account. Pray for wisdom, prepare, and trust that God walks this path with you.

Additional Information

Online resources:

www.longdistancecaregiving.com offers specific information for geography-challenged caregivers.

Books:

Parenting Mom and Dad: A Guide for the Grown-Up Children of Aging Parents, Michael T. Levy, M.D. (Upper Saddle River, NJ: Prentice Hall Press, 1991).

Chapter 5

A Survival Manual

How to Set Up a Primary Caregiver's Notebook

The filling out of copious forms is synonymous with a visit to a new doctor's office. If you're new to caregiving, the forms are daunting because they require answers to the same questions about numerous conditions. In many cases, after filling out forms, a physician's assistant or nurse asks the same questions again, sometimes while holding information-laden forms in hand. A patient or caregiver often feels the urge to shout, "Read the form!"

There's a reason for the paperwork and question-and-answer session. People forget. It's as simple as that. Although every bit of a medical history is not pertinent to every doctor's office visit, it is all important. But a doctor and his or her staff cannot know that without having all the information at hand.

In today's lawsuit-happy society, paper trails sometimes offer security, even if the trail is a computer file. Doctors, staff, and patients alike find that the latest in digital charts have their good and bad points, but the bottom line is the need for accurate information.

Keeping track of one illness—its tests, treatment, and medication issues—is one thing. Having the knowledge of a lifetime medical history is totally different. Often a caregiver is in the fourth doctor's office in a week, struggling to catch up with a new diagnosis to manage and realizing the need for help in keeping up with vast amounts of information. Ideally, a caregiver will have a notebook to organize everything.

Enter one large, three-ring binder—THE NOTEBOOK. It's a

lifeline and a safety net. Ideally, aging parents will take a proactive approach and start their own notebooks, but that rarely happens.

The Primary Caregiver's Notebook

In setting up a notebook, divide it into sections that make sense to you. Here's a recommendation of topics:

- General information
- Insurance
- Medications, with room for drug information sheets
- Medical history with separate lists of surgeries, tests, and hospitalizations
- Medical contacts

General Information

For each person you care for, have their full name as it appears on official documents, date of birth, home address, and phone numbers accurately recorded. It's best to memorize the Social Security number rather than recording it in the notebook because someone other than a family member may take your parent to the doctor and this number needs to remain secure. Record the insurance company and policy information, as well as the telephone numbers. It is helpful to keep records of previous addresses and phone numbers, too, especially if you need to reference doctors and records created in other towns. Keep this information in the front of your notebook for quick reference.

Word of Caution. The notebook contains important information, so don't leave this book lying around and accessible to sitters, those cleaning your parent's house, or a casual waiting-room thief.

Insurance

Copy insurance cards front and back and keep multiple copies in your notebook. Take insurance cards with you to each appointment. You may want to get an extra copy of your parent's insurance card and keep it in your wallet. It helps if you've numbered the cards or copied them in the order in which insurance filing occurs.

Reality Check: Having copies of insurance cards circumvents those times when Dad is fumbling through everything in his wallet to find his cards and growing frustrated because they've disappeared. After all, if you're juggling your own family and work responsibilities, there's a good chance you'll be running late for this appointment. Some office systems require the cards be scanned each and every visit regardless of how ridiculous it is to you, so have them available.

Sensitivity Alert: Dad still wants to carry his cards in his wallet because this makes him feel he still has some control. Remember the first time you slipped your new driver's license in the windowed compartment in your wallet? That feeling doesn't go away. Just carrying that wallet with the evidence of a full life tucked inside makes a difference to your parent whether that license is still used or not. Honor your parent's feelings by allowing him to carry his cards, even if you're organized, have copies, and don't need his.

Medications

A list of current medications and dosages is essential for your notebook. Make sure to include prescription and nonprescription medications, including that herbal supplement Mom ordered out of a catalog. At each appointment, a nurse should review medications with you. Keep a current medication list on your computer. Update it regularly and keep copies in the notebook. It's also handy to keep a list of any drug allergies right on the medications list. The Universal Medication Form (see chapter 23) is also available.

Even if you use the Universal Medication Form, keep a master list in the notebook in a format and style that works for you. Where possible, note on your master list the date a medication was started, which doctor prescribed it, and the condition the medication is treating. If you are the one calling in refills, mark on your personal calendar when you need to either mail or call these in so you receive them before running out. Over time, you may feel you've mastered the art of coordinating prescriptions so you have to call the refills in only once every three months, or at worst, once a month. But it rarely works that way. Some medications can be three-month, refillable prescriptions. Others are more strictly regulated. Then, of course, present illness meds are filled locally as issues arise. Being organized helps save emergency calls to doctors' offices to try to get samples to see you through until the prescription arrives.

Keep a section of your notebook for the Drug Information sheets that come with filled prescriptions. They have important information, particularly about drug interactions and possible side effects that will be important to access if you get that late night call that all of a sudden Mom's urine has turned orange. These sheets can also help if a medication reaction develops over time. Mom may have been taking medication X for years, but it caused a reaction only when medication Y was added.

In the medication section of your notebook, include reference information for local and mail-order pharmacies you use. A quick reference sheet for pharmacy contact can help when asking doctors to call in prescriptions or if you need to check the status of refill requests. Having fax numbers helps, too, as often doctors fax the pharmacies. And remember the personal touch. It's always good to get to know the pharmacist at the drive-through window by first name.

Reality Check 1: If you're calling in a prescription refill, you're likely to have the bottle in hand so you can reference the Rx or refill number printed on the bottle. While holding the bottle, write the order confirmation number right on the bottle along with the date you called in the request. Don't throw away a prescription bottle until its replacement has arrived. Try to use up the oldest prescription first.

Reality Check 2: It is most helpful to be aware of the information *not* listed on the paper prescription written by your doctor. Though many doctors' offices now digitally shoot a prescription from the office directly to the pharmacy, paper prescriptions are still used. Gener-ally, the patient's name is written on the script, along with perti-nent medication and physician information, but additional infor-mation required by the pharmacy may not be. If you're having the prescription filled locally, it helps to write the patient's name, date of birth, address, and home phone number on the back of the pre-scription. You may also want to note "insurance is on file." This helps even if you've used the same pharmacy for decades.

> ■■■
>
> ### MOPs
> **(Medical Office Procedures)**
>
> Some medical offices post signs that patients are expected to bring all their medications with them to all appointments. Ask ahead of time if bringing an up-to-date list serves as an acceptable substi-tute. Some will say yes, others no, but why go through the trouble of brown-bagging the entire contents of the medicine cabinet if you don't have to?
>
> ■■■

You may want to consider cre-ating and printing some labels for your notebook with this informa-tion so you'll have one ready when you need to drop off a prescription. Mail-order pharmacies usually require a patient order form that includes that information. Also, keep in your notebook addressed, stamped envelopes for the mail-order pharmacy. That way, when you've just gotten a new long-term pre-scription, you can pop it in the envelope and drop it in the mailbox before you've ever gotten out of the car. One thing crossed off your to-do list equals increased peace of mind.

Medical History

Compile a medical history for each person in your care. Include sur-geries, and if possible, the year of the surgery, the surgeon's name and contact information, along with notes about the conditions leading to the surgery. For example, if Dad had pancreatitis of unidentified causes three times before Dr. M took out his gall bladder, this information would be helpful if he's suddenly having unexplained abdominal pain. Obviously, all this information may not be available, but do the best you can. And it's okay to enlist help from those you are caring for in compiling medical history. It allows them to feel a part of the process and removes some of your burden. It's fine to go back and check their work, but here's a great opportunity to reinforce that you are treating your role as that of a team member, not a dictator.

Reality Check: While it may be irritating to answer the same questions over and over again, reviewing the history often reveals information overlooked the first time and provides doctors with a missing piece of the medical puzzle they're trying to fit together.

It helps if caregivers let patients answer for themselves, but be prepared to offer additional information if it's left out. This gives the doctor an idea of how that patient views his own medical history. Talking to the patient also allows the doctor to see the patient's personality (see chapter 8, "Effective Communication"), which can have a great impact on how the doctor discusses treatment. If the patient is a know-it-all armchair physician, the doctor may use technical terms rather than layman's terms.

Medical Contacts

Keep a list of current doctors' names, addresses, and phone numbers as well as fax numbers and names of nurses you deal with regularly. Here also make notes about the staff's personalities to treasure or avoid, and logistical notes that will help you know the easiest side of the building to park on when you're pinched for time and perhaps don't want to wait for elevators. Why bother? Well, if the primary caregiver has a crisis, someone else will be using these notes to step in. Make them good, and it will ease your mind if you're sick and your brother, neighbor, or friend has to take Mom for her chemo that day.

Keep a separate list of contact information for former physicians and, if possible, list when they were care providers, even if it's an approximate guess. *Tip:* You can call the offices, talk to the records department, and just ask for the dates of service. Most will give you that information without making you jump through hoops. You may have to provide the patient's Social Security number and date of birth.

Reality Check: When Bill's parents moved from their home in Ohio to Illinois so he could help care for them, he had all the records he knew about sent to the new doctors. Two years after they moved, his father went in for neurological testing. Bill and his mother vaguely remembered that he'd had a neurological work-up "a while back." Had anyone sent those records? No. Did anyone remember where the CT scan was performed? No. Bill tracked it down, but just having that doctor's office listed would have been easier than searching through an old phone book and guessing which office it was. He was just lucky it was a small town and his mother had kept the old phone book.

▪▪ Through the Looking Glass ▪▪
Who's in control?

In the mirror: A 69-year-old widow living with her daughter and family

> "I was 59 when I lost most of my vision quite unexpectedly. In the last ten years, I've had many times when I had to give up control unwillingly, by medical necessity. It's still hard. It makes me angry and frustrated.

> "I was an active volunteer, but after nine eye surgeries over the course of a year, I was limited in what I could do. But I managed to stay active, thanks to my husband's willingness and ability to drive. However, when he became sick, that all changed again.

> "We moved and adjusted to living in a retirement community. I was as active within that community as I could be, serving on various committees and developing friendships. Though transportation was offered it was often hard to schedule, and

we lost the opportunity to just go where we wanted to when we wanted to.

"During the time my husband was sick and since his death, I've had to rely on my daughter to make appointments for me. I could do that myself, but since I need her to take me to them, it's been better for her to do the scheduling around her many other obligations. She comes with me to appointments and sits in the exam rooms with me, and she did that with her father too. I've appreciated her concern and efforts, especially with all the medical issues we've faced (at one point, both my husband and I were receiving treatments for cancer). It helps to have two sets of ears, and in my case, an extra set of eyes.

"But I must confess, on occasion I have resented her efforts because it has taken away my independence in areas that I still believe I could handle. It's easier all around the way we handle things together, but that doesn't mean it isn't hard to give up control. I try to keep track of my appointments and medications, but again, she has to help because of my eyesight. Mentally, I can take care of these things, but when it's time to call in refills, I can't see all the tiny numbers on the bottles, and even with a magnifier, managing all that and the automated phone refill directions is so frustrating!

"When my husband died, I relied on her help for handling the estate. I felt guilty for that and wanted to hire an accountant, but she didn't want me to have the expense, so we did it together. She's handled things beautifully.

"Even though we've worked through so much together and have become much closer than we'd ever imagined we would be, it's still hard to rely on anyone, let alone my child, for so many things.

"I take medication for anxiety, but I work hard to focus on the things that I can do. Now that I live with my daughter and her family, I can help with household chores, and it makes me feel good to do them. I do that quite well. It relieves some burden for them, and I feel better about myself when I do. I know at first it made my daughter feel she wasn't taking care of me, but we talked about it, and she finally understands that letting me do these things is taking care of me by letting me feel good about what I can still do."

Viewpoint:

"Bag It"—Medication management

Many patients enter doctors' offices toting brown grocery bags filled with medicine bottles. Sometimes, they don't even know all the bag contains or why certain bottles were in their medicine cabinet. They've just dumped it all in because they were told to bring all medications. It's a daunting task for nurses to inventory the bag and attempt to create an accurate picture of what it represents for the patient's health. But it's better than not knowing all a patient is taking.

"The key to medication management is accuracy and thoroughness," says Elaine Olson, RN, with more than 25 years experience working in medical offices. Here are her answers to some frequently asked questions.

Q: *Why ask patients to bring all medications?*

A: A lot of offices have that posted and there is a reason. Many patients think they don't need to bring in, or tell us about, medicines another doctor prescribed. We need to know everything they're taking, even vitamins, herbal remedies, and aspirin. We also need to know things that aren't taken every day.

Q: *But what if they take something like aspirin only when needed? A patient might think what they take for a headache doesn't matter if they're having a hysterectomy or their gall bladder removed.*

A: Again, it's about being informed. If we know they take a medication on occasion for headaches, it might remind them they've been having headaches lately when we ask them if they've needed it. That can be a key to the whole picture. Then, of course, if they're having surgery and they take aspirin, that can cause blood thinning, which a surgeon really needs to know.

Q: *Why not just ask for a list?*

A: That's easier, of course, but sometimes even that isn't accurate. Some patients or caregivers aren't as conscientious about these things, and we really need to be sure. A handwritten list is just fine, too, but we want to make sure nothing is left off the list and that it's updated.

Q: *How do you handle the brown bags?*

A: I thank the patient or the caregiver for remembering that they were asked to do that. Then I try to show them why we ask them to bring all medicines and give them a Universal Medication Form. I tell them they can start using it, and if there's time, I show them how.

Q: *What is the Universal Medication Form?*

A: It's a form that's becoming more common. It's very simple to use and hopefully will become standard for all doctors' offices rather than having different types of forms in each one. It makes it easier on the staff and the patients. The nice thing is once you have one filled out correctly, you can make copies of it.

Q: *Why would you need copies if you give it to the doctor or nurse?*

A: There are two reasons. First, once you have one done, you can take it with you to each office and eventually all of your doctors have the same information. That makes taking care of you easier. Then you can keep copies in your wallet, which is really helpful if there is any kind of emergency.

Living Water

> Therefore, since I myself have carefully investigated every-
> thing from the beginning, it seemed good also to me to write

an orderly account for you, most excellent Theophilus (Luke 1:3).

Commit to the LORD whatever you do,
   and your plans will succeed.
      (Proverbs 16:3)

Dr. Luke knew the importance of organization and structure in conveying information. His training as a physician helped him analyze the data once he'd collected it and place the facts in a framework that was informative and made sense. Luke didn't rely on hearsay as the basis for what he recorded. He took the time to carefully research and note all that had transpired, going back to the beginning. He interviewed eyewitnesses, checked dates and details, and had the goal of presenting the most accurate account possible. Once Luke gathered and organized all the information, he shared it with others.

Like Dr. Luke, by carefully researching, organizing, and recording information, we can be prepared for questions and situations that arise regarding the care of our parents. Taking the time to gather and record information in an orderly fashion takes some of the stress out of the caregiving role. But don't leave God out of your planning. The success of our plans and preparations depends on our committing whatever we do to Him.

Additional Information

Online resources:

www.caregiverslibrary.org—The national caregivers' library offers information on a multitude of topics to help you create a useful notebook and backup plan to give yourself the support you need as a caregiver. See checklists and review other key issues.

Chapter 6

The Essential Back-Up Plan
Formulating a Plan for a Caregiver in Crisis

Jim sat in his doctor's office, his wife by his side. The physician came in with file in hand and no definable expression on his face.

"Well, Jim, Susan, this isn't the news we wanted."

With hands tightly linked, Jim and Susan heard the diagnosis of bladder cancer, listened to the list of treatment options, and then asked to hear them again.

"I recommend at least two courses of chemotherapy before surgery. That way we hope the tumor will shrink before we go in to remove it," the urologist said.

"Where is all this done?"

"Well, we do the chemo here at the Cancer Center, then you'll need to decide where to go for the surgery. You can go to the main hospital in Mason or you can go to the University Medical Center in Madison. Between now and then, you'll have to meet with the oncologist here, then later with whichever surgeon you choose."

"But what about David?" Jim said to Susan. Though he'd just received news that his own health and life were in jeopardy, Jim's thoughts went straight to his brother, whom he'd cared for over the last five years.

"Jim, this is about you. We'll figure out how to take care of David later."

"But I'm all he has," Jim said.

■ ■ ■

A team mind-set, established early on in a caregiving relationship, can help when a caregiver has a medical crisis of his or her own. For the primary caregiver, realizing that a team is in place can make handling personal crises easier. The unexpected happens, so if you are the primary caregiver, set up your team even if you don't need all the players right now.

Primaries are the head coach, managing most of the game plan for getting through day by day. But the person, or people, being cared for are still the team owners. It's their life, resources, and best interests that need to be met, even if they've lost or relinquished their ability to manage. But when the head coach is down, who is the assistant coach?

First, don't keep secrets. Tell the person you care for that you have a crisis of your own. Hiding information about your own struggle only increases tension and can lead to short tempers, fights, and miscommunication. Listen to suggestions from those you care for about whom they want to help them. It may be a distant relative you've lost touch with but with whom they talk regularly. It may be a long-time friend you wouldn't consider asking for help, but with whom your parent has a closer relationship.

Details for creating backup plans come from living arrangements. Does the parent you care for live with you, independently, or in a retirement or assisted-living community?

In Jim's case, his brother lived in his own house about six miles from Jim and Susan. David had few neighbors and lived about 20 minutes from doctors and the local hospital. Jim fixed David's breakfast every morning, left sandwiches with him for his lunch, and brought dinner in the evenings. Jim and Susan shared the upkeep of the house, but had considered hiring, though had yet to select, a housekeeper to relieve their cleaning and cooking duties. Locating someone to help David while managing Jim's medical care and planning wasn't easy.

Formulating a Plan for a Caregiver in Crisis
Step One: Honesty
Be realistic about where you are. Find out your own prognosis

and plan for the worst. If you can get all the caregiving bases covered, that's ideal. Here's where you step back and say, "Okay team, play ball." It's better to be a bench coach than still at bat when you've got your own crisis. You may not have horrible side effects from chemo, but you might. With a backup caregiver, you won't need to worry about getting Mom to her therapy on the days when you thought you'd be up to it but aren't.

Step Two: Resources

Find out who is in the best geographical position to provide support and what kind and amount of help they're willing to give. If possible, discuss this with the person you're caring for as well as those who will be your support. A good start is to use your notebook. Look under the main headings you have created and see if one person or more than one could cover keeping up with those areas of care.

Be willing to hire help, as needed, to fill in the gaps. If you are hesitant to look for hired help, either for financial or other considerations, look into which public agencies can provide assistance. Most people don't become familiar with home healthcare companies, city or county transportation, or hospice until they need the services, and they often wish they'd accessed them earlier. Resources are available, and if you take the time to learn about them before you need them, you'll save time and energy when you need them the most.

Respite care is often offered at retirement communities. No, these aren't "nursing homes." That term gives caregivers and their loved ones cold chills. Even if you'd never think of allowing your parent to live in a retirement community (see chapter 14), you might still be able to utilize some of those services on a short-term basis. If handled in the right way, it can be like a vacation for the person receiving care and give the primary caregiver time to handle his own surgery and recovery.

Having your NOTEBOOK (see chapter 5) organized will help. This book can be passed on to siblings, friends, or trusted neighbors should the primary caregiver become sick or need to be out of town.

Step Three: Finances

Money management can be a major issue in caregiving and should not be left up to short-term hired help. It's just not safe, even if you've hired from an agency. If you are paying all your parents' bills, this is the time to see if a sibling can step in. No sibling? Consider a spouse or close friend. For short-term needs, consider paying some bills a month or two ahead, and leave a hidden envelope of cash for the neighbor bringing groceries in. Setting up automatic payments of certain bills can also ease burdens. It might be good to talk to your bank service representatives about what is happening and ask for help. If nothing else, they can flag the account to warn of excessive withdrawals or any unusual activity.

Step Four: Information

Once a plan is in place for who will take care of what, it's time to inform all the players of their duties and who is covering all the other bases. Caregiving issues overlap, often intricately. When cousin Suzie volunteers to take Mom to physical therapy, but the therapist says it's time for an appointment with the doctor, Suzie needs to know who gets that information. Is she supposed to set up the appointment? And who will see to it that Mom gets to it? It helps to distribute a list of caregivers, their duties, and contact information to all involved. If Suzie has an emergency and can't get Mom to therapy, then she knows she can call one of your mom's Sunday school class members who brings her a meal once a week.

If you've always been the one to take Dad to his appointments, and suddenly your neighbor is doing that, it would help the doctor's office to know what's going on, and what information can and cannot be given to the neighbor. This is when friendly relationships with the staff at the doctors' offices, banks, and other service organizations are beneficial.

Letting Go

An important thing for caregivers to remember is that life will move on without them. Primaries often get so wrapped up in their role that they have difficulty letting go or feeling they can. This is when caring for the caregiver becomes multifaceted. Those who love the caregiver can offer new perspectives. Caregivers, let go a bit. It's hard, but worth it. If you take care of yourself, there will be a healthier you to offer again later. But risking your own health to provide for another will only cause more trouble later. Realize that having backup doesn't mean you or your importance to your loved one can be replaced.

The Jealousy/Guilt Factor

Often, when caregivers do let go and allow others to help, they experience an odd mixture of jealousy and guilt. Mom might rave about the meal your sister made and continue to sing her praises long after she's gone. But you've been cooking for Mom every week for a year with rarely a thank-you. It's perfectly understandable to resent this and feel jealous of the praise offered to someone who hasn't worked nearly as hard as you have to provide love and care. The key is stepping out of your own emotional soup long enough to look at perspectives.

■ ■ ■

**MOPs
(Medical Office Procedures)**

Remember those Health Insurance Portability and Accountability Act (HIPAA) forms you have to fill out each year? One of them lists the names of the people authorized to receive information about care. If a person not on that list calls for test results, major frustration lies ahead. If you're the one on the list and know the staff in the office well, you can call or send a letter before the appointment explaining the situation and delineating how information can be conveyed and to whom. You may have to update the HIPAA forms.

■ ■ ■

Any change in routine, especially for an elderly parent, promotes continual chatter. In the life of many of our elders needing care, there just isn't much to talk about. Anything new becomes a novelty worth several discussions. Your mother has a new topic to focus on. It makes her feel loved and cared for to think and talk about the things someone else has done for her. That doesn't mean you, as caregiver, are any less important. Understanding your parent's perspective helps to regain focus rather than succumbing to hurt emotions.

However, it's easy for resentments to build within a caregiver's heart. Caregivers generally incorporate the extra duties into their lives so well that most tasks become automatic. It isn't until they stop, or are forced to stop, that they realize how hard they've been working and how little thanks they've received. Caregiving can be a lonely journey. Sharing the journey with those who can appreciate what you're juggling and who aren't directly involved in it will help keep perspectives balanced. Your friends will offer pats on the back for all you're doing even if the person you're doing it for forgets.

Viewpoint:

Cancer x 2—Donna's story

"At age 57, Mama received a breast cancer diagnosis, two years after Dad died with lung cancer. He lived three months following the diagnosis, and Mama took care of him the whole time he was sick.

"While he didn't suffer, it was totally different with Mama. The doctor did an x-ray in his office because she'd been having more than her usual back pain. A needle biopsy revealed breast cancer cells. The cancer was also on the chest wall. Ironically, following the biopsy, she received a report from her annual mammogram telling her everything was clear.

"She went from her home, into the hospital, to restorative care, and then came to stay with us so we could help her through the chemo. We thought this was a temporary arrangement so we had home health coming in to help her learn to do things on her own. In the back of our minds, we wondered if it would work, but we wanted to support her independence because we knew it was important to her.

"Sometimes it was hard though, and I had feelings of resentment. I'd rearranged my hours at work, but still she was the one who was there when the kids came home with news and our baby had some of his 'firsts.' At times, I felt like she was stepping into my role even though deep down I knew that wasn't true.

"The doctors tried four different types of chemotherapy, all of which she couldn't tolerate. She grew sicker with each attempt. Five months after her diagnosis, she was under hospice care.

"The oncologist wanted all the daughters in the family to have mammograms because of Mama's diagnosis. My sisters' reports came back fine, but mine didn't. I received a breast cancer diagnosis just days after I turned 30.

"My relationship with Mama got really rocky then because I couldn't talk to her like I always had. It was hard to talk to someone you knew was dying from what you had. I couldn't go to her for comfort because she couldn't offer any. We could talk about anything else, but not that.

"I remember when I was having such a hard time, she looked at me one day and said she was sorry.

"I said, 'Sorry for what?'

"'I'm sorry that you're getting all of the attention. It upsets me that people used to come here to see me and care about how I was doing. Now they're just coming for you.'

"I felt as if I'd been stabbed in the heart! I loaded up the kids, went to Wal-Mart and just sat in the parking lot and cried. Somehow, she always made me the bad person, even while caregiving and dealing with my own illness.

"The only way I managed through that time was with a morning ritual. After everyone had gone to school and Andy had gone to work, I'd get two-year-old Zach settled and I'd go and sit on the side of my bed and just cry.

"I'd tell myself, 'If God wanted you now, He'd take you. This isn't a death sentence. He's getting you prepared. You have three beautiful children and they need you.' I'd give myself my pep talk, then get up. That was the only way I got through.

"All the while my aunts and cousins were coming in to help with Mama. Although it was a help, at times it made us feel like we were losing control of our own home. It put a lot of stress on my husband too. It's hard to have someone else doing your laundry and rearranging your cabinets.

"In December, I had the first of four surgeries I'd have within the next year. Mama went to live with her sister while I had surgery. I remember being so scared that it would be my last Christmas with my kids. I had 52 staples across my chest, but I rode with them on the four-wheelers they'd gotten for Christmas because I wanted them to have that memory. Mama stayed with her sister so we could have that Christmas together, just the five us.

"My aunt couldn't manage doing all that Mama needed. We wanted Mama to come back, but I couldn't handle it either.

"By February, we'd sold our house and Mama's and moved down the street from my sister, Penny. We knew Mama would want to come home with us if she could, but the end seemed near when she had to go back to the hospital. She rallied, but I still wasn't able to take care of her. I needed to heal and knew more surgeries were coming. It was very hard for me to explain to Mama that I couldn't go through my surgeries and take care of her. I had to be like the tough parent she had always been. My sisters weren't in a position to take her. Deanna lived in Florida and Penny was running her own business while raising her three kids. So we made a really hard decision and put her in the closest hospice house, which then was more than an hour away.

"Mama didn't cuss, but she told me and Penny to go to hell. She said things to me that she later didn't remember saying. It may have been the medicine she was on then, but it was so hard to hear.

"Sometimes she would apologize, but an apology doesn't take away the hurt. I look back on it now and I wonder how I got through it. I thought that if I just died, the rest of my family would have to take care of Mom. I could be out of it and hand the burden off to Andy and the kids. But then I'd think rationally and realize I wouldn't want to put my kids through that. You think all these wild things, but ultimately, if I hadn't had a belief in God, I wouldn't have made it through.

"Mama was at the hospice house March through June. In July, she went back to her sister's house because, at that point, they were only treating the pain and she was much more manageable.

"I had my final surgery in December.

"It was still Mama's wish to live with us, so she moved back in January. We had help from hospice, plus the family. I was still trying to work. My aunt and cousins helped in the mornings, and the aide came when they had to leave. Andy would do whatever was needed when I had to work nights. Mama's personal care was intense. Andy did things for her most husbands couldn't handle. He could call Penny, and she'd come to help him when I was gone because it took more than one person to take care of her. God and family are what made the end of Mama's life manageable. Deanna offered emotional support even though she lived far away and Penny from nearby. We all pulled together for our mama's sake and for each other."

Living Water

> People who don't take care of their relatives, and especially their own families, have given up their faith. They are worse than someone who doesn't have faith in the Lord (1 Timothy 5:8 CEV).

Paul's words to Timothy are straight to the point and may cause some to bristle. But perhaps we all need the reminder that just because a job is difficult or hard to think about, that doesn't mean it can be ignored.

I've discovered over the years that half the frustration of doing something unpleasant or challenging comes from my resistance and procrastination. Once I stop delaying, take a look at what's required, and move forward with a plan, anxiety and stress diminish.

On the other hand, finding someone to help you when you are physically not your best or simply need a rest is not the same as not providing for your loved one.

Ecclesiastes 4:10 reminds us that with a friend (or backup caregiver) available, if we fall down or get sick or need help, that person is there to provide a necessary life rope. And verse 12 provides that wonderful imagery of the strength of a cord made up of three strands—you, your backup network, and God—all intertwined and working together to provide the necessary support for your aging loved one.

> If one falls down,
>   his friend can help him up.
> But pity the man who falls
>   and has no one to help him up!
> Though one may be overpowered,
>   two can defend themselves.
> A cord of three strands is not quickly broken.
>   (Ecclesiastes 4:10,12)

Additional Information

Online resources:

Respite care is a family preservation and support service intended to reduce family stress. Planned and crisis respite can occur in out-of-home and in-home settings depending on the needs of the family and available resources. The ARCH National Respite Network helps caregivers locate respite services in their community (http://chtop.org/ARCH.html).

Books:

Hiring Home Caregivers: The Family Guide to In-Home Eldercare, D. Helen Susik, M.A. (Atascadero, CA: Impact Publishers, 1995).

Chapter 7

Interacting with Practitioners
Developing Effective Perspectives

One of the keys to successfully interacting with practitioners is accepting that personalities are different. Primary caregivers experience them all—first hand. And they'll most likely experience them all the way home from a doctor's appointment when all Mom can talk about is the doctor's poor bedside manner. But riding the wave of personalities doesn't end there. When Mom calls Aunt Sue to tell her all about the ordeal of the day, you'll hear it again while you're doing her laundry.

If you accompany your parent to every appointment, you'll have a perspective on the reality of the day rather than just her emotional reaction. Sometimes, saying that a doctor "wasn't nice" is simply her way of dealing with a diagnosis she didn't want to hear.

Chapter 8 gives a more in-depth picture of the different types of personalities you'll encounter, as well as a perspective on your own personality. Just accepting them for what they are makes managing the day-to-day interactions easier.

Getting What You Need from Practitioners

Here are a few tips to help you get what you want and need from practitioners.

Appointments. When scheduling appointments, be clear about how many issues you need to discuss. This helps schedulers know how much time to allot with the doctor. Also, if you're really pressed for time, see if you can get the first appointment of the day. But make sure your parent can be ready in time for an early appointment. Many sleep later, need extra time to get going in the morning, and don't function well if their normal routine is rushed. If you schedule an early appointment but arrive to find your parent still in her bathrobe, your stress level, and hers, will skyrocket.

If you're going for a follow-up visit with a specialist after having tests done, call ahead to make sure the report from the lab or the radiologist has arrived. Often, a nurse will flag that page before you even get there.

You can also call ahead to ask if the doctor is on time or way behind for the day. If the situation isn't urgent, you may want to reschedule before you ever leave the house if you're looking at a wait of several hours.

Some doctors—particularly gynecologists, who are often on call for deliveries, or specialists who are on call for emergency surgeries—experience delays that can throw an office schedule into turmoil. It's a good idea to make notes about these dynamics when you are getting information about the practice.

Go prepared. Take a book, knitting or cross-stitch, or pick up a new magazine on the way to the office. Waiting happens. Getting angry about it is not likely to change it. It's okay to go to the receptionist and make sure you're all checked in, but beyond that, making a big issue is likely just to cause you aggravation.

Medications. Have your medications list updated when you walk in the office. Be ready to explain any change from the last visit. That helps one specialist know what the others are doing and why.

Questions. Save everyone time and frustration by having your parent start a list of questions a few days ahead of the appointment. When you arrive for the appointment, let the nurse know you have questions and give her the list. She'll pass it on to the doctor before he even gets in the room, and everyone will be on the same page.

Concerns. In some caregiving situations, the primary will need to clue the doctor in on issues the patient may not want to discuss. Caregivers can send or fax notes to the doctor's office or slip a note to the nurse before the doctor comes in. Doctors understand that caregivers are there to help and provide vital additional information.

Physicians

While doctors and nurses know much more about medicine than you do, you're likely to know much more about their patient than they ever will. Some people are intimidated by physicians because it is a highly respected career, or an element of fear and a what-I-don't-tell-can't-hurt-me mind-set exists. Some older patients expect their doctor to know everything without having to be told. Today's caregivers know that's just not how it happens. Remember, your loved one is the patient and is paying for services offered by the doctor. In essence, doctors are your employees. Sometimes just accepting that part of the relationship helps break some self-imposed barriers people bring with them to appointments.

Doctors can work only with the information they receive. They mix that information with their medical knowledge to make well-educated choices for treatment. But there is a reason it is called "practicing" medicine. If one medication for a problem doesn't work, they try another. Medical care is an intricate process. Mix in personality issues and emotions and the complexity of maintaining a successful doctor-patient connection intensifies.

Lucy didn't like Dr. J because he seemed pompous. Later, that perception changed, but only after she had taken her father to Dr. J for three years. Lucy finally figured out that the pompous attitude was merely Dr. J's way of expressing confidence in his ability to care for his patients. For some patients that was comforting, but it struck Lucy the wrong way. Eventually, she looked beyond that and saw how hard Dr. J was working to save her father's life. The doctor even showed emotion and seemed more human and caring in his responses when treatments didn't achieve the desired result. The doctor's caring side was there all along. He just didn't show it in a way Lucy recognized. When Lucy's father died, Dr. J wrote a personal note of condolence, and Lucy was deeply touched.

The point here is that you may not get that warm friendly feeling you'd like to have at each appointment. Remember that doctors are caregivers too and are doing the best they can. You are dealing with one patient; they deal with dozens in a single day. Will there be bumps along the way in relationships with doctors and care staff? Of course. Are they human? Most definitely.

Each physician approaches the job differently. Leaving personality issues at the door will help you not compare or focus on physicians' "bedside manner," when their medical expertise is what you need.

General Physicians. A "family doctor" is generally the first line of attack for a medical problem. They look at the whole picture of care and know when to refer to a specialist. They can treat most issues and need to be informed of what's going on with specialists. Often specialists send a summary note to the family doctor to give him details about the piece of the puzzle they are dealing with. Not all general physicians can admit patients to the hospital. If this is the case, the general physician often has connections to an internist nearby who can handle hospital admissions quickly. Those who can admit to the hospital often turn in-hospital care over to hospital staff doctors (hospitalists). Check this out before it becomes an issue.

Gerontologist. A physician who specializes in the medical problems and care of the aged.

Internist. The internist works with adults only and can have more insight into care issues affecting adults. Though considered more of a specialist than a general physician, an internist can handle anything from a sinus infection to a hospitalization.

Specialists. Medicine today encourages specialization. That means that the list of physicians a caregiver encounters is usually long.

Specialists may make caregivers feel brushed aside if they bring up medical issues that aren't in the realm of that doctor's specialty. There are two main reasons for not being offended by this, which is often the first response of a caregiver or patient.

First, doctors may be limited in what they are allowed to treat based on insurance guidelines. Doctor A might be willing to do a cholesterol study or provide the flu shot you asked about while in her office, but if she knows that insurance will give her staff (and eventually you) a hard time about paying, it is really saving you some hardship to suggest you get that done elsewhere.

Another reason not to be offended is that doctors in specialty practices have spent years fine-tuning their skills on a focused area of care. They know all the basics of medicine, but they've focused on the many nuances of care pertaining to their specialty. It's better for that oncologist to know everything he possibly can about all the treatments for cancer, even if it means he has neither the time nor expertise to advise you on why your leg is hurting. Yes, the specialist needs to know this, because it could be a side effect of medication or other treatment; however, he may feel that another doctor, with a different specialty, would give you a better answer or treatment option.

You're likely to have a long list of players on your care team with the initials M.D. behind their names. As members of the team you're managing, they each have something important to offer. The game plan, including the defensive and offensive strategies for winning, requires the whole team. Despite the number of appointments that fill a calendar, it really does work in the best interests of the patient. No one physician could be an expert on everything no matter how much you or they would like it to be so. As head coach, you're the one bringing all they have to offer together. You get one office to fax test results to the others and ask doctors to update each other so that everyone is working together. That's your job as primary caregiver.

Still, some doctors just do not do their jobs. Once you put personality issues aside, if you still believe that the needs of the person you are caring for are not being met, then by all means find someone else. Sometimes it's a personality issue that just can't be overcome. Other times, you realize the job is not getting done. It's okay to trust your instincts and the knowledge you've gained in your caregiver role.

The next step is to find another doctor. If you need a new specialist, you can approach a doctor on your care team that you trust and ask for a referral. You may or may not want to give details about the reasons for changing physicians. That will depend on the relationship you've built.

Nurses

You'll find all kinds, but the vast majority are absolute angels.

Dr. Snow, on a first appointment with his patient, Marianne, confided that he considered his nurse "the boss" and expert in his office. Many doctors do not have the wisdom to realize just how true this is, let alone verbalize it. In many instances, a caregiver is not very concerned whether or not the doctor calls back. It's the voice of the nurse she's waiting to hear.

As with the doctors, nurses also specialize, and within those specialties are a wide range of attitudes and personalities.

In one office, a lab nurse drawing blood was asked about another procedure. Though she said it very nicely, the message came through loud and clear that the question was not within her realm of knowledge and she wasn't going to help find the answer. There's a difference between being told "I don't know," and "I don't know, but Julie down the hall may be able to answer your question, and you can see her after we're done."

Bedside manner isn't an issue just for doctors, but for all medical staff, even office workers. It's about offering care and courtesy the way you'd like to have it extended to you. The golden rule works, but it isn't always applied.

Some staff members are just rude, and it is up to the caregiver to decide how, or if, to address the situation. If the nurse is shouting at your mother that she needs to use the personal wipes so she can get a clean urine specimen, and your mother is embarrassed, something should be done. Some nurses cajole or talk-down to elderly or infirm patients. Your first line of defense for these circumstances is a good offense. Model the communication style you wish them to have with your parent.

You can ask the nurse to please lower her voice when addressing intimate issues, and give a little smile when you do to let her know it's not her you're addressing but your mother's modesty. Nurses work with these situations daily so the modesty factor can be lost after a while. It's fine to remind them you need them to be sensitive to your parent's needs. Successful interactions with practitioners center on the choices you make.

Some caregivers and patients resort to passive-aggressive techniques, such as stubbornness, sullenness, procrastination, or intentional ineffi-ciency, to deal with their dissatisfaction. But passive-aggressive behavior rarely works because most people don't catch the nuances of passive-aggressive speech and behavior.

Emily's mother never liked the way the receptionist at the doctor's office talked to her. So she delayed calling when she needed to sched-ule an appointment. She also discouraged Emily from calling, but never explained why. Finally, Emily realized her mother was avoid-ing the receptionist because she had been brusque with her mother in the past. But Emily reminded her mother that an appointment was needed and that avoidance would never convey the message to the receptionist that her phone skills are lacking.

Office Staff

Stickler Office Worker. These are the kind that no matter how many times they see you, they're by-the-book all the way. Honor them. If it means carrying your healthcare power of attorney (HPOA or Health-care Proxy) with you to every appointment, just accept that. The HPOA should be in your notebook anyway. Don't go in complaining that their office procedures are ridiculous and so-and-so does it better. Rant in the car, to your husband, or to the mirror. Don't do it in the elevator as you might be ranting beside the office manager you've never met. No need to make enemies. And remember, they're just trying to do, and keep, their jobs. One day, this office worker may be just the one to call when you want to make sure a report gets faxed to another office quickly.

Slack Office Worker. These are the hardest to deal with. Primary caregivers spot these quickly. They're the ones who take way too long to schedule a follow-up appointment because they can't find the right screen on their computer or constantly mention a "new system." Put their names down as people to avoid, if possible. If you're next in line to check out after an appointment and discover it's their line, find a distraction until another scheduling staff member is free. The alternative is to call later to confirm that the appointment was actually entered into the computer.

Reality Check: Should it be necessary to have to follow up? No, of course not. But accepting that you simply must take this path to ensure the appointment is scheduled makes the inconvenience easier to swallow. Should you complain? Yes and no. You are within your rights to mention that a certain person told you the wrong appointment time, yet again. If this is a doctor you'll be seeing a lot, it might get the point across to just say, "I was told to come at 9:00, not 10:00." There are times when that can help and times when it can hurt. Only you can make that decision.

The old adage that you attract more flies with honey really is true. Saying anything to office staff, even if it is criticism, with a smile on your face and a comment about how you know they're working hard, softens your complaint and makes them more receptive to what you have to say.

The Gem. Here's the one you won't need to put on any list, but you should. You'll remember her face because she made your life easier, even if for a fleeting moment. She'll do it more than once, and you'll catch yourself trying to sneak a peek at her name tag. You sneak because she remembers you from the last time you were in, and you're embarrassed because you can't remember her name. She knows you because your face screams PRIMARY CAREGIVER. When she sees that, she automatically wants to help. If you're scheduling one treatment, she'll try to help you by scheduling several around your calendar, and she smiles when you take that big breath of relief. She's a rare gem. Bask in her glow.

■■ Through the Looking Glass ■■

Doctor appointment via teleconference

In the Mirror: At 62, Ann Jones has experienced her own acute renal failure. Her husband of three years, Phillip, 66, has had chronic issues with anxiety. Doctors are now monitoring him closely for symptoms of Alzheimer's disease.

"With my own health issues, I've found that what makes the difference for me is a doctor who listens. I can't stand feeling like a doctor is rushing me through. When that happens, I feel that my body and healthcare are of no value. Thankfully I have found doctors who are encouraging. But with my husband, the situation is very different.

"When we married, I knew that Phillip used VA (Veterans Affairs) benefits for his healthcare, but I had no idea what that would entail. With the VA we've found that he's treated pretty much like a number. At a point when his anxiety was increasing, we had to go through a central number to reach a doctor. We never had our calls returned, and each time we'd call again, we were told the doctor was getting our messages.

"After three days we found out the doctor was no longer practicing! With this news, I was desperate. Then we were told we'd either have to see a practitioner or use TeleMed. Practitioners are fine, but with Phillip's complex history, we wanted the specialist. With TeleMed, you don't actually see the doctor in person. You sit in a room and look at a television screen. You see the doctor and the doctor sees you. The thought of using a system like that was terrifying to us. But we felt it was our only choice.

"Thankfully, the system doctor is excellent. I've had to deal with doctors in person that had much less bedside manner and who had no interest in what I had to offer as a wife. It really is important for both of us to have a feeling of worth in the process, whether we're in the caregiving role or seeking care for ourselves.

"As we age, the problems we deal with feel so complicated. A doctor (and caregiver) who is encouraging and involves you in the process helps you maintain your self-worth. It's the kind of encouragement you give a small child. I don't see that as belittling. I see it as being sensitive. Listen to me. Talk directly to me and explain what I need to know in terms I can understand."

Viewpoint:

The Waiting Game—Kim and her mother

My mother was always a clock-watcher. She'd get highly agitated when waiting in an office. Because of the nature of our relationship, I'd tease her gently about it when she'd start huffing and looking at her watch every few minutes once her appointment time had passed.

Once, when her behavior was really bothering me, I gently threatened to take her watch away, and actually held out my hand for it. She got the point. Through many years and many trips to doctors' offices, I also learned not to get to offices too early and to bring new magazines with us. Other times, we'd simply position ourselves near enough to the television where she could listen to a show.

My personal perspective on doctor's office waits is very different from my mother's. I never mind waiting for my own appointments, especially for Dr. Hicklin. His manner is such that I know when he walks into the room, he's left everything else at the door and is focused on my needs. He speaks warmly and takes time to really listen. He'll discuss what's going on and different ways to approach a medical problem. He listens when I give my opinion and knows I wouldn't be there unless necessary. He makes me feel that we're working together and that he values me as a person. I know he'd never run out of the room because the time the appointment scheduler allotted him is up.

But I also know to expect to wait at his office. So, I bring my knitting or a book I really want to read. I don't look at the clock. I don't plan much else for the day because I know I might have to wait.

If a doctor is giving the kind of care I expect to the patient in the next room, and it happens to take longer than expected, that's okay. He's going to give me the time and care I need too. I'd rather it take longer to do the job right than to stay on any impersonal schedule.

At one appointment, when I had to wait nearly two hours, I could see the strain on Dr. Hicklin's face when he came in the exam room. He apologized for the wait. I smiled and told him my perspective.

"I am so relieved to hear that," he said. "Do you know that the number one stress in my day is the wait my patients often have? It really bothers me very much, but my hands are tied. Sometimes folks come in and I think they're here for one thing, and then they have four or five other issues they want to discuss. I can't just tell them their time is up and we've handled their one issue for the day. So, if it takes more time, I give it to them. My patients are people, and I really do care about them."

Living Water

> Finally, all of you, live in harmony with one another; be sympathetic, love as brothers, be compassionate and humble. Do not repay evil with evil or insult with insult, but with blessing, because to this you were called so that you may inherit a blessing (1 Peter 3:8-9).

Most of the time, it's the little things that trip us up, annoy us, and cause us to say and do things we later wish we could take back. Sometimes, we can jump one major hurdle after another with grace, and then trip over the perceived slight of a receptionist or the overloud voice of a technician. But like it or not, our witness is ever before us, and that flare of temper or unkind word will be mentally catalogued by those in the waiting room and behind the desk.

James 3:10 reminds us that both blessings and curses are uttered from the same mouth, even though it shouldn't be that way. Remember that your actions and reactions provide the most accurate picture of your spiritual maturity, and many are watching to see if they match up to the name "Christian."

Right now, stop and ask God to help you think before responding, live in harmony with those around you, practice compassion, bless rather than curse, and above all, love with the love of Christ.

Additional Information

Online resources:

www.netofcare.org—a site where caregivers will find links explaining the healthcare system along with specifics for getting the most out of communications with providers.

Chapter 8

Effective Communication

*Breaking Communication Barriers
and Understanding Personality Types*

One dictionary definition of *communication* is "a transmitting; a giving or exchanging of information, etc."[2] Sounds simple enough, doesn't it? But communicating with parents and other family members may prove a huge caregiving hurdle because lots of factors have the potential to inhibit communication.

The ability to communicate effectively is central to good relationships. Therefore, let's have a look at the role emotions, personality types, history, and a whole host of other factors play in communication.

Emotion Commotion

Emotions are the biggest challenge to effective communication. Often, deep feelings about certain subjects surface during simple conversations. Suddenly, anger, pain, or tears emerge.

As people age, they begin to display more emotion. A previously stoic father now frequently cries over seemingly nothing. Or a prim and proper mother occasionally peppers her conversations with profanity. These more emotional responses may be the result of medications, declining mental faculties, or simply feeling age exempts them from behaving in a certain manner. Whatever the reason, emotions can make communication difficult.

Issues that have always been hot-button subjects are probably going to be even more so now. Therefore, give thought to circumventing expected reactions—yours and theirs. In some cases, the best way to communicate may be to pass the job to someone else. If a sibling historically has had more success communicating with your parents, and is willing to broach the subject, pass the baton. Don't feel guilty if you need to do this. Everyone has a role to play in the process of effective communication.

Identifying Personality Types

What do you envision when you hear someone described as having a great personality? Most often, we think of personality as the way a person acts around others, whether they are friendly and outgoing or quiet and reserved. But personality types go much deeper than outward expression and affect the way we act, react, and interact with those around us. How we communicate with our parents, siblings, extended family members, and others is determined by our personality type.

Melancholy

John firmly believes that organization is the key to happiness. He keeps meticulously organized file folders on every aspect of his life, including his wife, children, and mother. Although he's efficient, he's not the warmest person around. While family members know he loves them, they rarely see displays of affection, and most humor is lost on John. He often spends time alone in his study at home and doesn't appreciate being interrupted. When things don't go as he planned, John often thinks there is a conspiracy against him. Inefficiency and mismanagement annoy him, and he sometimes complains to his wife that people don't treat him fairly.

John attempts to keep his interaction with his aging mother on a strict schedule. He goes to work an hour early three mornings a week so he can leave work at precisely 2:00 p.m. every Thursday and make the 30-minute drive to his mother's home. Attached to the memo pad on his dash is a list of errands, which he requires his mother to submit to him the day before. When he arrives at her house, he expects her to be ready and waiting to begin their rounds.

This week, as John pulls into the driveway, he notices a week's worth of newspapers dot the walk leading to his mother's front door. Styrofoam cat food plates litter the yard, and mail spills from her bulging mailbox. Muttering to himself, John exits the car and picks his way through the debris. He inserts his key into the lock and pushes the door open. It halts at a two-inch swing, hindered by the chain latch.

"Mother, I'm here!" John yells.

After several more unanswered announcements, John trudges back to his car, jerks the door open, reaches for his cell phone, and dials his mother's house. He can hear ringing coming from inside. On the sixth ring, the answering machine picks up.

"*Mother*, I am in your drive and we're running late. I'm waiting," John shouts to the answering machine. Glancing at his watch, he counts the minutes. Exactly seven minutes and twenty-nine seconds later his mother releases the chain and opens the door. With dismay, John sees that she is dressed in her bedroom slippers and robe.

He tries to control his anger as he walks to the door. "Mother, this is our day to run errands and you're not ready."

"Oh, is it? I thought we were going on Thursday."

"This *is* Thursday."

"Well, I'm not ready. I'll have to dress."

Twenty minutes later, John's mother emerges from the bathroom. During that time, John has vacuumed the den, dumped the trash, loaded the dishwasher, and restarted the soured clothes in the washer. After a five-minute search for his mother's cane, he helps her walk to the car and buckles her in. By now, they are thirty minutes later leaving than he anticipated, and he'll be stuck in traffic going home.

"John, I need to go to the bank and cash a check first."

"The bank? That's not on our list."

"But I have to have some money."

"I have your debit card. We'll use that."

"No, I need real money."

"The debit card deducts money from your checking account. Remember? We've been over all this before."

"I just don't understand how that works and I'm already trying to pay off one credit card."

"This is a debit card, not credit."

"I just think I need some cash."

"Fine, we'll get cash back when we check out at the grocery store. We don't have time to go by the bank."

"I just wish you'd let me have some money." A steady sniffing begins. Then, a sob escapes her lips.

"Mother, please tell me you aren't crying! What is there to cry about?"

"I just wish I could drive."

"You haven't driven for three years. Why are you bringing this up now?"

"I just want to do things the way I'm accustomed to doing them, and you won't let me."

John swerves into a nearby parking lot and throws the car into park. He clenches the steering wheel and stares out the window. His mother's sobs punctuate the silence. John realizes he should try to comfort her, but he's angry. Her tardiness has messed up his whole schedule, and now her emotional outburst requires him to either comfort her and do things her way or follow his original plan and feel guilty later for doing so.

In the end, her tears wear him down, and he takes her by the bank on the way to their other stops. But John is frustrated by the change in routine and annoyed with his mother for spilling her emotions on him. In his mind, the day is ruined.

■■■

The melancholy personality is rigid, organized, and private. Melancholies expect perfection of themselves and everyone around them. They rarely share thoughts or feelings and don't quite know how to handle it when someone else does. Melancholies often hold grudges for actual or perceived offenses, but they would never tell the offender because that person should just know.

The melancholy member of a family is the one who wants to set up a meeting and follow a pre-approved outline when discussing issues. If your parent is a melancholy, you may be used to his "Eeyore-ian" view of life and realize that much of your communication with him requires encouraging reassurances.

The positive side of the melancholy personality in communicating is his accuracy in details and precision in recording and keeping facts and figures.

Sanguine

Sandra, Silvia, and Stan sat around the table at a local coffee shop. Stan had driven from a town two hours away to be at this meeting to discuss selling their mother's house and placing her in an assisted-living facility following her stroke.

Stan drummed his fingers on the table. "So where do you suppose our charming sister Stella is?"

"I left a message on her voice mail yesterday reminding her again that we were meeting today," Sandra said.

"I sent her an e-mail last night," Silvia said.

"Did either of you get a response?" Stan asked.

"Well, no," Silvia and Sandra said in unison.

Forty-five minutes and two cups of coffee later, the three decided to go ahead with their discussion. As they exited the coffee shop an hour later, a familiar red sports car squealed up to the curb and stopped in the handicapped parking space.

"Hi, siblings all. Ooh, I'm so glad to see you. You're not leaving are you?" said Stella as she leaped from the car. "I can't believe you didn't wait for me!"

"Stella, our meeting was at 4:00. We decided you weren't coming," Stan said.

"I wanted to be here, I really did, but I finally got an appointment with that new manicurist I've been trying to get in with for six weeks, and I simply had to take it. You do forgive me, don't you? I knew you'd understand. You're just the best!"

In a word, the sanguine personality is loud. Often a flashy dresser, this person is usually trying to be the center of attention. Sanguines love to talk and love a party. They have lots of friends, but always have room for a few more. Although sanguines are fun to be around, it's hard to catch them giving serious attention to much of anything. While they like to communicate, they want to do all the talking, and frequently they are their favorite topic.

Although they may be one of the first to volunteer to help, they feel no remorse about failing to follow through, especially if something better, or more fun, comes along.

If one of your parents has a sanguine personality, you're going to find it difficult to corral him or her long enough to communicate seriously on any subject, especially end-of-life issues. If your sibling has a sanguine personality, don't be surprised if she doesn't return your phone messages or e-mails that request a meeting to discuss urgent issues. If a sanguine does agree to come, she may not show up. But despite her lack of follow-through, the sanguine lifts spirits and eases communication tensions with her presence.

Choleric

"Charles, this is Connie. You need to take mother to the doctor tomorrow at 10:00."

"I can't. I have a meeting with an out-of-town client."

"Well, reschedule it. I have a deadline that won't wait."

"Connie, my meeting won't wait either."

"It will have to. I've taken mother to the last four appointments and it's your turn. Deal with it."

"Connie...Connie?" Charles' attempted reply was met with a dial tone.

The choleric person takes charge. She knows the best way to do things and doesn't mind telling you that your way is no way at all. Other personality types often feel cholerics boss or shout orders. Cholerics are no-nonsense folks who have little time for chatting. Their communication style is an abrupt delivery of information, and they really aren't open to hearing alternatives from others.

Cholerics often speak while gesturing or pointing a finger for emphasis. They expect rapid action from their edicts and are easily annoyed by those who want to take time to discuss all the options. The choleric personality is in control and focused on getting jobs done. They make rapid decisions and bulldoze their way through the consequences. Often, other members of the family step aside with the approach of this steamroller personality.

If your father has a choleric personality, you probably dread trying to discuss anything with him other than surface, inconsequential trivia. A choleric sibling may either totally take over caregiving issues regarding your parents or be too busy to be bothered with them.

The strength of the choleric is the ability to tackle even the most difficult communication barrier or task and see it through to completion.

Phlegmatic

Phyllis arrived at her father's house late Sunday afternoon to find her father and brother, Patrick, lounging on the sofa watching a basketball game. Dirty dishes were stacked in the sink and on the counter. The trash can was overflowing, and several days' worth of newspapers littered the living room. On the kitchen table, amid cereal and snack food boxes, was a blank tax organizer.

After kissing her father, Phyllis motioned Patrick into the kitchen.

"I thought you were going to be here this weekend to help Dad organize his tax information. He has an appointment with the CPA tomorrow."

"We're getting to it," Patrick said. "We just wanted to visit and relax a little first."

"Pat, you've been here since Friday afternoon and you haven't done a thing except eat, visit, and relax, apparently! Your mission was to help Dad with his taxes."

"Don't get so bent out of shape. I'll make sure we finish it before I leave."

"It's already 5:30 and you have a three-hour drive home. When, exactly, were you planning to begin?"

"Is it that late already? Oh, well."

■ ■ ■

The fourth personality type is somewhat more elusive because, although it has distinct traits, it also exhibits flashes of the other personalities. The phlegmatic is the person who has to be coaxed off the couch and away from the TV when you're attempting to have a family meeting. Phlegmatics are relaxed, nonconfrontational, laid-back people who speak softly and rarely have opinions about much of anything. They are the ones who say, "Whatever you decide is fine with me." The choleric personality may be alternately annoyed or pleased by the phlegmatic, feeling the need to light a fire under him to get action or happy that someone agrees with them without argument.

If a parent is a phlegmatic, communication may not be much of a problem. If your sibling has this personality type, you may grow frustrated by his lack of input or failure to see needs and take action.

The strength of the phlegmatic comes in his ability to bring a sense of calmness to communication deadlocks or quietly broach subjects with parents when others spark conflict.

Communicating with Other Personality Types

Gender really has nothing to do with personality types. People often have strong traits of two of the personality types, and the person you have the most difficulty communicating with may share your personality type or be your opposite.

For example, if you and a parent are both cholerics, you usually butt heads over issues and end up shouting at each other. If you are a melancholy, you may grow exasperated with your phlegmatic mother, who puts off making decisions and has little regard for schedules.

The melancholy personality needs to learn to lighten up. Melancholies are serious and often see humor as unnecessary and flighty. But communication will go much better if melancholies practice smiling and making a few light-hearted comments occasionally. The word *practice* is essential here. It won't come naturally.

Another thing melancholies actually can do is talk! Since melancholies are thinkers rather than communicators, they are usually sitting in a corner internally correcting the grammar of the person speaking rather than paying attention to the content of the conversation and interacting. By looking for the good in what is being said rather than criticizing, the melancholy allows others to feel more comfortable discussing things with him.

The sanguine personality can aid communication by talking less and listening more. And remember, listening involves more than not talking. Focus is required. Look the other person in the eye and pay attention rather than practicing in your mind what you're going to say next. When sanguines speak, they should make an effort to lower their voices. Unless your parent is deaf, there is no need to shout. Realize that communication requires give and take.

While others may hesitate to speak around melancholies for fear of being critiqued or criticized, with cholerics, folks want to avoid being yelled at, cut short, or made to feel stupid. As a choleric, you have the bad habit of talking over others and not allowing them to finish a sentence.

Cholerics have a hard time with those who process thoughts as they speak. But practice patience by letting speakers finish what they are saying. Even if you can anticipate where they are going with the thought, pay attention and show interest in what is being said.

This may prove challenging for those with a choleric personality, especially when a parent is retelling something for the umpteenth time. But realize that your abruptness in communication often shuts down other personality types from saying anything else. Accept that others have opinions and the right to express them. Learn to ask what others think. Be sensitive to expressions in your communication style that may be offensive and hurtful. Give the gift of your time and attention.

The personality makeup of the family your parents grew up in also has an impact on conflict and communication within your family. Your parents may mirror one of their parents' personalities or function in direct opposition to it.

For example, if your father's mother was a choleric-melancholy who demanded the house always be neat and orderly and her children make stellar grades, today your father may be messy around the house and unfocused or rebellious when pushed into doing anything. Conversely, if your father grew up with a strong choleric father, he may model that pattern and impose rigid, no-nonsense rules on family.

By understanding the personality types, you can begin to see what causes communication barriers and make adjustments in how you respond to and approach situations. Realize you are in control of only your own adjustments. You can't change the personality or perceptions of others.

The important thing to remember is no one personality type is best. God made all the personalities, and aren't we thankful He did? Otherwise, we'd be boring cookie-cutter copies of each other without that special spark that makes each of us interesting and unique.[3]

Tips for Breaking Communication Barriers

Work on relationships before crisis comes. Often, lack of communication within families happens when everyone is waiting for someone else to make the first move. When unresolved conflict is present, communication suffers because family members can't discuss much of anything without hauling out old baggage that has nothing to do with current circumstances. Fostering communication may involve saying you are sorry for something you don't think is your fault or asking forgiveness for something you don't remember doing. Realize that you must take the first step toward reconciliation and better communication because others likely aren't going to. Work to break down barriers by editing your responses. While you can't change others, you can alter your reactions, thus ending old patterns and opening the flow of communication.

Be prepared. When broaching a difficult subject with parents, do your homework. Research, gather, and digest information so you have answers for inevitable questions. You never know when the opportunity to discuss issues will suddenly present itself. If you aren't prepared, the moment is lost.

Stay focused. If a topic needs to be discussed, try to avoid getting sidetracked by other subjects or issues. Sometimes parents avoid communicating about difficult subjects by redirecting conversation to other needs or projects. But sometimes you just have to force the issue.

Talbot traveled to his mother's home in another town, at her request, to discuss the location of her important papers. Over the course of several visits, each time his mother spent the entire weekend pointing out projects she wanted done around the house and requesting he do them immediately. By Sunday afternoon, when Talbot tried to direct her attention to the reason for the visits, she proclaimed exhaustion and told him he would have to come another time. Eventually, Talbot appeared at her door, unannounced, and told her he was there for only two hours. With reluctance, his mother led him to the file cabinet that contained her estate information and they spent two hours talking.

Determine a strategy for discussion. In some cases, it works best to call a family meeting and have all present for the discussion. At other times, the best plan is to look for a logical opening to interject the topic and seize the moment. If your parent talks about a friend's sudden death, you might be able to slip in a comment like, "I wonder if she had a will?" That could lead to discussion of where your parent's will is located, or if she has one. If she doesn't, make an appointment with an attorney as soon as possible and take your parent to the appointment.

Listen. As noted in the personalities portion of this chapter, some people have a harder time listening than others. If this person is you, cultivate the art of listening. This involves not just hearing words, but reading the underlying fears and frustrations beyond what is being said. Once you gain this skill, communication goes much better.

Recognize fears. You may chalk up your parents' unwillingness to communicate to stubbornness, while the underlying emotion is, in fact, fear. As our parents age, they become childlike in their need for stability, routine, and security. Any discussion of something that may jeopardize those needs may be viewed by your parent as a conversation not to have. End-of-life discussions or conversations that lead to big decisions may be something your parent works hard to avoid because these talks have the potential to flip the lid on a Pandora's box of fears.

Realize thought processes are different. Many of our parents grew up during the Great Depression and have a higher level of anxiety about financial issues. They don't make a distinction between debit and credit cards, and many are accustomed to paying cash for everything. You may especially encounter reluctance or stubbornness in communicating about finances. At times, you may even be accused of commandeering your parents' funds. Try not to take this personally. But if you are handling any of your parents' funds, do so with integrity and careful notation so your management is beyond reproach.

Grow up. Your biggest barrier to communication may be you! Take your "little boy" or "little girl" head out of the sand and take a big bite of reality. There are things you need to know, and that requires communication. Even if you aren't on the front line of caregiving, it's your responsibility as an adult child to know and face these issues. You may choose not to deal with them or to assign the duty to another family member, but there are important issues that are or will be part of your reality. It's time for you to be the grown up.

Plant seeds. As long as you're not in a crisis situation, it's okay not to deal with everything in one sitting or even get to the point right away. Dealing with one issue at a time might make it easier for you and others. But make sure you don't wait too long because you might not get the answers in time. Look at the issues and assign priority.

One strategy for broaching a subject is to find an article that brings up an issue you believe needs discussion. Read the article in your parents' presence, then initiate conversation. An alternative is to mail a copy to them and ask their opinion later.

Don't force it. If you sense your parent isn't ready to discuss a subject, don't push it. Realize that you may have to mention something several times before your parent is willing to talk about it. Be patient and gauge the willingness and receptiveness of your parent to communication on the topic. Timing is important, so determine when your parent is most alert and open. You should never force a serious discussion late at night or when you or your parents are hungry, tired, or in a hurry.

Stay cool. It's easy to lose your temper when discussing emotionally charged issues. Save your anger for a rant to your spouse or a close friend. Expressing anger will invariably shut down further communication on the topic because your parent will likely remember your outburst and want to avoid your anger in the future.

▪▪ Through the Looking Glass ▪▪

Communication from an aging parent's perspective

In the mirror: An 87-year-old widow and mother to one daughter

> "My husband's been gone now for 31 years, so I've handled all my affairs by myself for all this time. Now, though, I wish my daughter would communicate with me more about issues, particularly financial ones. I don't want her to have any surprises or difficulties when I'm gone.

> "My daughter has my power of attorney and is listed on my accounts. I've asked her to take over paying some of the bills so she knows where things stand, but she won't hear of it.

> "She says, 'Mom, you've been handling it well on your own for so long, and since you can still do it, you should.'

"I think she feels that if I stop taking care of these things I'll slow down and become less alert, and that doing these things makes me feel independent. But I don't see handling these things as an independence issue. I just think it would be easier for her later.

"When it comes to paying my rent, or paying the utilities, taxes, and other expenses for my home in another state, she has no idea where I stand or what is in my accounts. She knows the basic types of bills that get paid because she deals with that for herself, but she doesn't want to know about mine.

"If I ever had a time that I ran short, I know she would jump in and help. It's never come to that, but I know she could and would willingly do that if it ever became necessary.

"My daughter knows I have a living will and a will, and everything I have is hers. Right now the only issue I have is declaring an alternate beneficiary. I'm not sure I should list her husband because what if something happens to them both?

"My daughter knows where I want to be buried even though it isn't where I live now. And which church I want for the funeral. But these aren't things that we brought up as specific issues to discuss. They just came out at different times, and we discussed them then. There were never any secrets.

"I also handle my own medical issues. My daughter works a full-time job, and so I don't ask her to be involved in too many appointments. I'm sharp enough to take care of my own matters, but if I feel she should be there to hear what the doctor says, I'll ask her to come, and she does. She's not bashful or backward about dealing with medical issues or asking questions if she is with me in an appointment. If I ever felt I couldn't manage keeping all the medical issues and appointments together, I would ask her for help.

"On the other hand, there are things my daughter has dealt with in her life, that she went through on her own, sharing very little with me. I would like to have been involved, at least enough to provide some emotional support. But it just didn't work out that way."

Cultivating the Art of Listening

Sometimes we don't have the option of listening with full attention to the person we're caring for, especially when they suddenly make a statement that sparks emotion and may be the tip of underlying issues. Caregivers often become a verbal punching bag, regardless of the topic of conversation. However, we have the option to choose how we listen and how we allow what is being said to affect us.

To learn the art of listening, first pay attention to the types of conversations you have and how they make you feel. By nature, we tend to take conversations personally, as if the person we're talking to expects or requires a response. That could be a judgment (agreeing or disagreeing with the speaker's opinion), an action, or an emotional response, whether positive or negative.

Applying the art involves actually hearing and making a point to employ a nonreactive mind-set. You can be active without being reactive. You can take notes, mental or actual, of what parts of the conversation stir your desire to react, but you don't have to do anything with them at that moment. The active part is where you repeat what the person is saying, validating what they're feeling, even if it's not what you're feeling. Repeating allows you to say something even if you really aren't ready to give a thoughtful response. This gives you mental and emotional space to deal with any hot spots later, rather than in the heat of the moment, when you might later wish you'd said something different.

For example:

Words from parent: "I'm so frustrated that you and Nancy don't come by more often."

Reaction from caregiving child's heart: "I'm here now and I'm here several times a week! How could you say that? I have a life of my own, and I'm doing all I can to love, honor, and support you. Nancy, however, lives nearby and comes once a month, if it's convenient. How could you possibly put us together in the same category? That really hurts."

Active listening response: "So you'd like us to be around more?"

At this point, Mama might actually tell you what she feels is missing from the time you have together. Perhaps she'll say that she just wants time to have fun time with you, or the conversation might just fade away. Then, you can shift the conversation to something different. You've validated what she said, honoring where she is in her mind, even if it really rubs you the wrong way and causes all kinds of anger. When you choose not to react, at least right away, you regain control of yourself in the situation. This often helps maintain personal balance.

Notes to self: What is Mama missing in her connection to me, as close (and demanding) as I feel it is, and how is that tied to Nancy, or is it? Maybe there are certain kinds of time together she needs. I have some unresolved issues about Nancy not being a part of all I'm going through with caregiving. Maybe it's time to talk to her about doing more. I didn't realize just hearing Mama mention her name would make me feel such anger.

Possible thoughts to dig through later: Most of what I do with Mama deals with necessities. Maybe she's missing less focused time such as going out to lunch together when everything isn't centered around a doctor's appointment. That's the kind of the time she has with Nancy. When Nancy comes, it's for something fun, like shopping. Would I like more time like that too? Maybe Mama would like the three of us to be together to do some things. Would I like that? Would I be comfortable with that?

Rationale: Here you have the opportunity to explore the possibilities, your feelings, and what actions you'd be comfortable with. You might decide to let it go or decide to bring the issue up again when you've formulated your ideas about it.

Follow-up conversation: "Mama, the other day you mentioned wanting Nancy and me to be around more. Nancy's schedule is pretty tight, but it made me think that maybe we spend all our time together on doctors' visits. We haven't had time for something fun. Let's plan something and invite Nancy. If she can come, fine. If not, we can have some cut-loose time together."

The compromise: You might actually prefer doing something by yourself or with someone else, but going with your mother is a valid compromise for meeting needs you both have for a change of pace and to ease the caregiving routine that has become wrapped around your relationship.

Living Water

"I am young in years,
   and you are old;
that is why I was fearful,
   not daring to tell you what I know.
I thought, 'Age should speak;
   advanced years should teach wisdom.'"
   (Job 32:6-7)

No matter how old we are, we're afraid to discuss certain subjects with our parents. Even as adults, we often fear their disapproval or anger. But effective communication requires us to push beyond fears and preconceived responses and to risk tackling potentially difficult topics.

In Matthew 10:19, Jesus instructed His disciples not to worry about what to say or how to say it when they faced opposition. He assured them that "at that time" they would be given what to say. It can be the same for us.

Sometimes we fret about communicating on certain topics, and magnify our expectation of the upcoming discussion into something much worse than it turns out to be in reality. Instead, we should approach the conversation with assurance that at the moment we speak the words, God will give us the right ones. Breathe a prayer— "Lord, let these be Your words to fit the need"—and trust that He is speaking through you.

James 1:19 provides a snapshot of effective communication. "My dear brothers, take note of this: Everyone should be quick to listen, slow to speak and slow to become angry." Memorize this verse. Meditate on it and incorporate it into your communication style. It is sage advice for any personality, at any age.

Additional Information

Online resources:

The www.gilbertguide.com site offers a "hot topics" section on communicating with loved ones as well as articles on other hot-button topics.

Books:

Personality Plus: How to Understand Others While Understanding Yourself, Florence Littauer (Grand Rapids, MI: Revell, 1992).

How to Get Along with Difficult People, Florence Littauer (Eugene, OR: Harvest House Publishers, 2006).

Chapter 9

Confronting High-Tension Issues
Addressing Difficult Topics

I've heard speaking in public is the number one fear of all adults. However, I think our number one fear is of each other," a speaker said to a large audience.

When it comes to family, you can just take that fear factor up another notch, or ten, depending on your circumstance. No matter how close you are or think you are to the heart of communications, tough issues trigger archived emotions for each person involved. When it's our loved ones sharing their thoughts and desires, we fear even more because we don't want the tender balance and relationships we've built over the years to change with the answers.

Numerous issues need to be sorted out as caregiving unfolds. Many of these are tension builders that pop up at times when a caregiver is already thinking enough is enough. Being proactive on these issues makes life easier.

It doesn't feel good to ask parents about their finances, insurance policies, and other details of life and death. High-tension issues cause us to feel the friction between the adult role we must now take and the childhood role we sometimes struggle to retain. It's equally as hard for our parents to give up their independence. Margaret, who entered the caregiver role when her father was hospitalized and her mother needed help managing details he had been handling, said:

> I really don't want to know that my parents want to be cre-
> mated and have their remains "planted" in the Memorial

Garden of Grace Episcopal Church in a little town two states away from where we all live now, but I must if I truly want to honor their wishes. The little girl in me still wants to believe her parents will live forever. Dad will be there with that twinkle in his eye that's just for me, and Mom will want to go shopping for another pair of shoes she really doesn't need. But the adult in me knows that when all is said and done, I do want to know their wishes so that I'll have the peace of knowing I've honored them and given them what they wanted.

High-Tension Issues

Money

How secure are your parents financially? Will other members of the family ever have to step in to provide for basic living expenses? If so, isn't now the time to realize this? Social Security isn't a life plan for financial security and doesn't support most lifestyles. Who has money and in what forms (savings, investment accounts, certificates of deposit, stocks), and how do they want it to be spent toward family healthcare? How, when, and by whom would your loved ones want those resources accessed if they're incapacitated?

A responsible party, in addition to your parents, should be listed on all accounts, or at least hold power of attorney to allow access to those accounts. The power bill comes and must be paid whether your parent is hospitalized or not. Someone should be able to handle those details, even if it is not the primary caregiver. Perhaps there is a sibling who cannot do other things but is willing to manage the bill paying. Set up a weekly plan for picking up and paying bills, and arrange for account access with banks, if necessary. If you or your brother are suddenly writing checks from your parents' account, it is wise to inform the bank, even if your names are already listed on the account.

Additionally, primary caregivers should have access to a debit card or standard checking account to pay for incidentals. Just make sure the primary caregiver saves receipts from purchases and passes them along to the bill payer or shoots him an e-mail with the information. Including an expense sheet in THE NOTEBOOK also helps.

When caregivers are listed on bank accounts, paying attention to how they are listed can limit probate issues later. Co-owners of accounts, who are authorized to write checks and perform transactions, may be responsible for taxes. However, the designation of "transferable upon death" may limit tax liabilities depending on the state laws involved. A primary caregiver needing to write checks might not be listed as a co-owner, but may be able to handle bill paying if she or he has a durable power of attorney.

Form Alert. The power of attorney (detailed in chapter 23) is a legal document that authorizes a person to handle finances and other legal issues on behalf of another person. Someone needs this authority, but let your parent choose who that person is. Usually that authority falls to a child, but sometimes a parent doesn't think that's the best choice and selects a financial advisor or close friend to be the agent. Perhaps you live too far away to make this practical. Or maybe you don't want the responsibility. A sibling or another person may be better trained or suited for this job. Try not to take it personally if you're not the designated agent or attorney-in-fact. But do make sure you understand the agent's duties so you can offer support, if needed.

There is also a "Healthcare Power of Attorney" (called Healthcare Proxy in some states), which is specific to medical decisions. Again, someone who is close enough to a loved one, geographically and emotionally, needs the authority to see that parents' healthcare wishes are carried out if they're incapable of making those decisions themselves.

Insurance

Insurance coverage is closely tied to financial security. If you've looked at an insurance Explanation of Benefits (EOB) statement lately, you know what medical services cost. A vast difference exists between what doctors and hospitals initially charge, the amount insurance companies negotiate down, what insurance pays, and what the patient is expected to pay. There are uninsured and underinsured patients, and those just may be the loved ones under your care.

Insurance companies also have caps on payouts for certain types of expenses. One bout with cancer, which can include costly treatments, hospitalizations, surgeries, and assistance care, can max out those limits. With other caps, after reaching a certain out-of-pocket expenditure, the policy pays 100 percent. But even those have coverage limits. Some caps are simply maximum coverage amounts, and once that line is crossed, you are responsible for paying everything else. It's important to know the nuances in coverage.

Another area to know and document is the insurance company policy on hospital admissions and outpatient service. Many companies require prior notification and authorization before admission to the hospital or testing occurs. Penalties are incurred if these policies aren't followed.

Reality Check: *Must a primary caregiver become an insurance expert? Aren't the hospitals and doctors' offices supposed to take care of those things?*

Not completely. Insurance filing clerks want insurance companies to pay and work hard to utilize the systems in place for each patient. However, notice posted signs that remind patients they are ultimately responsible for remaining balances. Who is going to verify that insurance is paying the maximum allowable and that remaining balances are as small as possible? In some cases, it is helpful to hire an expert to navigate the complex language involved in medical expense management. But at the very least, it's not too much to expect a caregiver to know who is responsible for notifying the insurance company if preapproval or notification of admission is required.

On an Explanation of Benefits (EOB) statement Mary received, she and her insurance company were billed $5,848 for an outpatient surgical procedure. The charge acceptable by Medicare was only $654, of which Medicare paid $523 to the doctor's office. The balance of $131 was charged to and paid by Mary's second carrier. She was not responsible for any part of that bill. The doctors were paid, albeit much less than they'd hoped. But consider this: The person without Medicare or another insurance provider to negotiate better rates for services would receive a bill for the full $5,848 and be expected to pay it within 30 days.

Some people even have three insurance policies. But ideally, at least two companies are providing coverage. While Medicare coverage helps, it doesn't cover everything.

Long-term care insurance is designed to help when someone needs long-term skilled care outside a hospital environment. Care can be in-home or in a facility. It's essential to know the terms of these policies before purchasing or activating one. Sometimes, preexisting or self-induced conditions (such as illnesses related to smoking or alcohol abuse) limit or nullify the benefits of such policies.

Lifestyle

How do your parents want to live out their days? What do they envision for themselves in the next 5, 10, 15, or even 20 years? Do their resources match their vision? Perhaps they haven't thought about the future. You might be blessed to dream with them, encouraging them to fulfill goals they never realized they had or were afraid to voice. Having a "where there's a will there's a way" attitude can boost everyone's spirits. Plan and dream together and work to make those dreams realities.

While you may be aware of the big picture, don't overlook day-to-day lifestyle. Dirty clothes and dishes, unwashed bodies, and ignored incontinence can all become issues. It may be obvious to you that your dad's tie has three-months' worth of stains on it, or your mother is wearing the same dirty pair of pants she's worn all week, but parents seem oblivious and get huffy when you mention it. Your normally fastidious father may suddenly stop shaving, using deodorant, or getting a haircut. Your mother may have to be reminded to bathe and wash her hair. While bathing and brushing teeth are part of the everyday grooming routine for us, as our parents age, personal hygiene becomes a chore for them and is often ignored or put off.

Anne's father complained to her that he didn't have time to complete his tax returns because he had so much to do.

"Daddy, what do you have to do? You haven't had any doctor's appointments in weeks, and you don't drive anymore."

"I know, but I'm busy."

"Doing what?"

> ■ ■ ■
>
> Depression-era parents save everything. Encourage them to de-clutter by promising you'll purchase items with your money if they need them later.
>
> ■ ■ ■

"Taking a bath, dressing, making the bed, fixing meals, taking medicine, paying bills, and reading the paper and mail. It takes up my whole day."

Although you'll likely meet with resistance, continue to encourage your parent to make personal hygiene and living-space cleanliness a priority. It may involve hiring someone to help with cleaning chores. Sometimes our parents are more receptive to a nonfamily member cleaning their space and throwing out their clutter.

End-of-Life Care

End-of-life issues are a touchy subject, but they must be addressed. While a sudden heart attack, stroke, or other calamity may make this a moot point, with medical advances extending life, it's more and more an issue. One conversation about end-of-life care may not be enough as perspectives often change over time.

"Mom, Dad, if you could choose how you die, what would you choose?"

Some parents will joke about the question just to deal with their own fears. The answers that come out in your family discussions might surprise you, and so might your reaction.

Olivia, a very strong woman, terminally ill with ovarian cancer, told her family she did not want to die at home. She didn't want the memory of her death associated with the home where her family would continue to gather without her. But weeks later, she changed her mind and ended up dying at home, quietly and comfortably with family surrounding her. The memory left behind was that of loving support and one the family still treasures years later.

People can and often do change their minds about the answers to the big questions about life and death. However, when they are brought up for discussion, the darkness and fear surrounding them dissipates, and revisiting the issues becomes easier.

When broaching difficult subjects, try starting the conversation with "I heard about someone who…" Your parent's answers might cause you to panic or feel peace. It's okay to feel either. It's also fine to drop the discussion and pick it up later. The great thing about dealing with these issues when you're not in an emergency situation is that you can develop a sense of peace with the answers (see forms for managing tough issues in chapter 23).

The Business of Death

One of the most difficult factors to juggle along with managing a grieving heart is the business aspect of death. Budgets and finances, admittedly hot-button issues, can create further strain. The key to making these issues easier is preplanning and communication.

Unlike daily finances, funeral expenses are rarely thought about or budgeted for. Yet, aside from a home or car, a funeral can be one of the largest single expenses incurred. Costs for services vary from region to region but can range from a few thousand dollars to tens of thousands of dollars. The six thousand dollar national average does not incorporate many extras you might assume would be included.

Start looking at the finances now, planning for ways to accommodate your loved one's wishes. Insurance policies are available for burial, and some funeral/memorial service providers offer their own in-house payment plans. It is easier for your parent to be the one to make the choice of a less expensive option prior to death than to be faced with those decisions yourself when you are grieving.

Many people fall into the trap of equating final expenses with the life value of the deceased and therefore make financial choices based on emotion rather than reality. The key to making the business of death easier is to look at the issues before the need comes. All of the following decisions factor in:

1. Burial or cremation
   - Embalming
   - Cemetery plot, mausoleum, urn (and possible burial of urn/cremains)
   - Plot opening and closing fees
   - Liners (Some cemeteries require special liners, others do not. However, some funeral homes include liners in funeral packages regardless of whether the cemetery you chose requires them or not.)

2. Casket (purchased, rented, style)

3. Viewing and funeral service
   - Location fees
   - Bulletins
   - Flowers
   - Music
   - Photos
   - Honorariums for those officiating

4. Obituaries (length, photos, and the number of times and the number of newspapers an obituary appears in)

5. Markers (whether gravestone, plot markers, or those used on crypts)

6. Transportation (limousine, hearse, airfare)

PLANNING AHEAD: *Candy's Experience*

I remember how upset I was when I found out my father had "bought" his funeral the week after receiving a terminal cancer diagnosis. It was too soon! Why was Daddy looking at caskets when the doctor said he had six months to live?

However, when I heard the story of my father's funeral purchase from the cousin who took him on this excursion, all Daddy's wit and wisdom overshadowed the solemnness of the occasion.

My father approached his funeral purchase in a manner similar to buying a car. When escorted into a display room full of high-end caskets, he listened to the sales pitch, viewed the goods, and then looked the funeral director in the eye and said, "I've seen the Cadillacs. Now, where's your bargain basement?"

Momentarily stunned, the funeral director hesitated and then led my father through the embalming room to a large closet. There, he pointed to a lovely wooden box, devoid of ornamentation, and most often the choice of orthodox Jews. My father, a builder, ran his hand over the wood grain, asked the price, and with a lopsided grin tugging the corner of his mouth, announced, "SOLD."

Communication tip: A good time to broach the subject of final wishes is when you are attending a funeral with your parent or shortly after your parent has been to a funeral. Ask what parts of the service were special to your parent, what music was meaningful, and other questions to bring the idea of preplanning to the forefront of your parent's mind.

Five months later, my father died. There was great comfort in knowing he'd already made all the decisions regarding his funeral, and the bill was stamped "paid in full." It was his gift to Mama and me. He spared us the anguish of being about the business of death while our hearts were breaking.

Preparing for Probate

Probate is a process in which the court decides who receives assets of the deceased person. Assets are anything of value a person owns, such as property and cash. Death laws vary from state to state, but there is a time limit, often thirty days, between a person's death and when that death must be reported to probate court and a will filed. If not done within the time frame of state law, fees may result.

If a will does not exist, someone must be designated as personal representative. This is handled in the probate office. For example, if a husband dies without a will (intestate), a wife may assume she will inherit everything. That may not be true. Joint assets would be hers, but anything left in the estate, if valued over the state's limits, may have to be divided. In some states, the wife automatically inherits only 50 percent of assets and children divide the remaining 50 percent. Having a will in place, understanding the basics of your state's regulations, and making everything clear is the easiest way to avoid confusion and potential family turmoil.

It can take a year or more to clear an estate and disburse certain assets because rules require placing notices in newspapers and allowing time for any creditors to come forward to claim money owed. Some assets may be accessible during that time. Others may not. Every probate case is different, but most people come into a probate office clueless about the process and its potential effects. Gaining knowledge ahead of need will help you cope during the process of settling the estate while grieving.

Probate is not always necessary to disburse everything of value. If the deceased person had bank accounts or owned property with another person, the surviving co-owner will then own this property automatically. Banks require a death certificate to remove a person's name from an account. If a person dies leaving very few assets, such as personal belongings or household goods, these items can be distributed among the heirs without the supervision of the court. States have limits on the value of estates that need to be probated. Find out the state limits affecting you and your family.

If the value of the estate is above these limits, someone will need to be designated as a personal representative, either through a will or by the court if a will has not been executed prior to death. This person works with the court to make sure all bequests are made and that debts are paid and collected. Talking with a loved one about who they want to handle these issues is important. Having an attorney involved before death occurs is helpful, especially when a primary caregiver or personal representative is present.

If you have been handling day-to-day care of your father, and your brother Joe has agreed to handle estate matters, plan a meeting with your father's attorney when Joe is in town. Make sure necessary documents (depending on your state) are registered with your city or county clerk.

Knowing the Location of Important Papers

Whatever your parents' current health status, it's never too soon to locate their important papers. Following is a checklist:

- *Bank accounts*—Make sure you know all the banks and account numbers for your parents, including banks where they may have certificates of deposit.

- *Social Security numbers*—Be aware that you will need to notify the Social Security Administration immediately upon a parent's death. Checks or deposits received after death must be returned.

- *Insurance policies*—Your parents may have a number of life insurance policies, through employers or former employers, and privately purchased policies. Make sure you know the locations of the policies and have contact information for the companies. Your parents may also have credit card insurance or loan insurance.

- *Veterans Affairs (VA) benefits*—Anyone receiving VA benefits should have a current Benefits Summary. If not receiving benefits, you should keep a copy of discharge papers and other verifying documents in case benefits are applied for at a later date.

- *Will*—Know the location of your parents' wills. If they don't have wills, remind them it will be much easier for a surviving spouse, and you and your siblings, if a will is in place.

- *Marriage certificate*—A surviving parent needs a copy of a marriage certificate in order to file for life insurance benefits. If your parents can't locate their marriage certificate, a copy can be obtained through the county clerk's office in the town where the original license was issued and may also be available through the county or state website.

• *Birth certificates*—If your parents don't know where their birth certificates are, get copies from the records office in the county where your parents were born or through the state's vital records office which may be accessible online.

• *Death certificates*—If one parent pre-deceases another, you should get several certified copies of the death certificate in order to finalize the estate, get life insurance benefits, and remove the name from accounts. Death certificates are available through county or state vital records offices.

• *Liabilities*—Try to get an idea of the amount of debt your parents are carrying. Ask them about mortgages, promissory notes, credit card debt, and any money they owe family members or others.

• *Assets*—This includes deeds to real property, vehicle and boat titles, stocks, bonds, mutual funds, retirement accounts, checking and savings accounts, and contact information for banks, financial advisors, or brokers. Don't forget hidden assets. Sometimes our Depression-era parents don't trust financial institutions and squirrel away cash or other assets in unusual locations.

After Lyn's grandfather died, her grandmother sent her great-grandsons into the backyard with metal detectors to search for buried treasure. When the digging was done, they had uncovered $56,000 in gold and coins!

Ask your parents now if they've hidden money or other valuables in locations you're not aware of (behind mirrors seems to be a favorite location). They may even have a bulging safe deposit box in a bank in another state. Now is the time to find out. Otherwise, these assets may never be found.

Teaching Old Dogs New Ways

"But I'm accustomed to writing a check. If I get a debit card, I'll spend too much money, or someone will steal my identity."

Shelly took a deep breath and explained to her mother, again, how a debit card works. She had been trying to convince her mother to apply for a debit card for months, so that when she shopped for her mother, she wouldn't have to use her own money, wait for her mother to write a check, and then swing by the bank to deposit it.

To Shelly, it made perfect sense to get a debit card for her mother's checking account that she could keep in her purse to use only for her mother's purchases. Finally, because Shelly's name was also on the account, she decided to get the debit card and tell her mother later. At first, her mother was resistant. Eventually, when Shelly began referring to it as a "check card," her mother understood it was the same as writing a check. Sometimes, Shelly has to remind her mother to subtract the debit receipts from her account, but for the most part, forcing the debit card issue worked out well.

The old adage of being "set in their ways" frequently applies to aging parents. Sometimes, it's difficult to introduce new ideas because our parents refuse to acknowledge we are adults and capable of having more knowledge or wisdom than they do.

Some new ideas are easier to introduce than others, but if you meet with resistance, don't give up. As a caregiver, you need to make things as easy as possible for you. Although parents initially may be uncomfortable with new ideas, you aren't being bossy or difficult by encouraging them to exhibit some flexibility.

Because Bree's mother had always grocery shopped every day, when she stopped driving, she expected Bree to continue this habit. At first, Bree tried to accommodate her mother's five- to ten-item daily grocery list, but quickly found herself irritated, exhausted, and spending an exorbitant amount on gas to make the 25-mile round-trip each day.

One day, Bree showed up at her mother's house with a grocery list pad.

"Mom, from now on, I'm shopping for you only twice a week. When you start running low on an item, write it on this pad right then. I'll call, get your list, and shop for you on Tuesday and Friday. It's up to you to think ahead, plan meals in advance, and stock up."

Although Bree's mother grumbled, after a few weeks she learned to think beyond her daily grocery needs.

Keeping an accurate calendar may also be something you need to push your parents to do. Make sure your calendar's days of the week coincide with your parents. Most calendars begin with Sunday, but a few begin with Monday. This can cause confusion if you and your parents are looking at calendars formatted differently and you slot an appointment on the wrong date.

Also, it doesn't hurt to follow up with a medical provider when your parent informs you of an appointment date and time. Sometimes they get it wrong and are too proud or embarrassed to admit their mistake, blaming the mix-up instead on the office scheduler. If you verify with the provider a day or so in advance, you'll avoid unnecessary trips.

Procrastination becomes a hurdle many of us face when caring for our parents. Because they often delay tackling things that require effort, it may be necessary to remind them of the benefits of not waiting to do things. Often, it's tempting to take charge and do it for them because it's easier than arguing over when it's going to be done and how. But resist the urge to take over and do too much for them. While parents still want some independence, allow it. The day will come when you're doing it all.

■■ Through the Looking Glass ■■
A proactive approach to dealing with sensitive issues.

In the mirror: Edna, author, educator, widow, and mother of adult children

> "My husband handled our finances and was an excellent manager and steward. He kept a monthly roster of bills in a ledger

book, recording everything, including the tithe. I checked the ledger book with him.

"My husband died suddenly many years ago when my son was 19 and my daughter was 15. After his death, I continued to go over the ledger book with the children just as I had with my husband. I did this so they would learn and also so they would understand our cash flow. That way, when things were tight, they understood. It also helped them see the importance of saving.

"We had a footlocker with all the important papers. Even before my husband died, my children knew that box was important. Now, those papers are in a designated filing cabinet drawer.

"Once, when I was away from home, I fell and was taken to the hospital. When my daughter was notified, she knew the exact location of my living will and insurance information because we had talked about what to do if anything happened to me. I don't have a fear about dying because I know where I'm headed. I don't want to be plugged into tubes to stay alive.

"I was fortunate in that both my adult children offered to let me live with them when I was ready to give up the hassles of maintaining a home of my own. Though I'm independent and driving, I live with my daughter and her husband now. It's nice to be in a situation where I don't have to deal with things like gutters and the lawn.

"Even though we live together, we have our own space. We have the type of relationship that includes respect and openness. This openness has allowed me to state what I'd like to have happen if I'm not able to care for myself. I've mentioned various assisted living facilities that I like. I want my children to know I realize and accept this as a realistic option for us all someday.

"Being open about everything with my children from an early

age has kept us from having friction over what others may see as high-tension issues. I'm so thankful we've handled things together so that when challenges come later, we can focus on the joy we have in each other, not the difficult issues. If you haven't addressed these issues, it's not too late to start talking. It's much better than waiting until you're faced with an urgent need."

Viewpoint:
What Kim didn't want to know!

I was only 12 when my parents began showing me the location of their important papers when they'd go out of town. About two days before, they'd ask me to sit down at the dining room table. After sighing heavily, Mom launched into "the speech," while Dad sat quietly by.

"Now, if anything happens to us while we're gone, the lockbox with all our important papers in it is in the bottom of the hall closet. Aunt Jane will help you go through them, if you ever need help. Do you remember where the key is?"

Although I'd say yes, Mother always took me to it anyway. Sometimes, I even had to practice opening the box. All this scared me. I didn't want to think about an event happening that rendered my parents no longer in charge of "the box." I didn't want to know what was in that box!

All those feelings came back when I actually had to go through that very same box when we knew my father's last days were imminent. My mother couldn't see well enough, so the job fell to me. As an adult caregiver, this was something I had to do, despite my feelings.

Now, I have a box of my own. It contains our important papers. Some people keep copies of their life insurance policies, wills, and other important documents with them, while storing the originals in a local bank vault. Someone has to know about these papers and where they are located. It's more than common sense. It's security for all involved, even if you really don't want to know.

Living Water

> So do not fear, for I am with you;
> do not be dismayed, for I am your God.
> I will strengthen you and help you;
> I will uphold you with my righteous right hand.
> (Isaiah 41:10)

> Do not be anxious about anything, but in everything, by prayer and petition, with thanksgiving, present your requests to God. And the peace of God, which transcends all understanding, will guard your hearts and your minds in Christ Jesus (Philippians 4:6-7).

Fear can be one of the worst enemies of a caregiver. We allow our minds to what-if and predict until we create a whole set of worries that probably will never come to fruition. Fear often leads to procrastination. We delay tackling touchy subjects for fear of upsetting our parents. We avoid discussing financial issues because we're afraid our parents will get mad or think we're meddling. We don't press our parents to seek healthcare for recurring complaints because we're afraid the outcome will catapult us into an even more demanding stage of caregiving. We fail to tackle other high-tension issues because we fear emotional ghosts from other attempts to discuss difficult subjects.

Fear is an emotion that weighs us down, causes needless worry, and paralyzes forward motion. The opposite of fear is faith. If we believe that God is in control and take our concerns to Him in prayer, then we can rest in the knowledge that He'll provide strength, help, and freedom from anxiety. The by-product of faith is peace. And peace is something we desperately need while balancing the caregiving role with the rest of life.

Ask God to free your mind from all the worries you've projected onto future potential caregiving circumstances. Ask Him to strengthen and uphold you. And then allow Him to do so.

Additional Information

Online resources:

Understanding wills and probate—http://wills-probate.lawyers.com/ and http://law.freeadvice.com/estate_planning/probate/.

Estate planning—http://www.estateplancenter.com/.

Funeral planning—www.funeralplanning101.com/.

The Centers for Disease Control and Prevention (CDC) web site has a vital records homepage through which you can connect to vital records contact information for your state. http://www.cdc.gov/nchs/w2w.htm.

Books:

The Emotional Survival Guide for Caregivers: Looking After Yourself and Your Family While Helping an Aging Parent, Barry J. Jacobs (New York: Guilford Press, 2006).

Wills, Probate, and Inheritance Tax for Dummies, Julian Knight (Hoboken, NJ: John Wiley and Sons, 2008).

The Complete Probate Kit, Jens C. Appel III and F. Bruce Gentry (Hoboken, NJ: John Wiley and Sons, 1991).

Chapter 10

Mobility Assistance and Obstacle Courses
Aiding Safe Ambulation

Janet opened her eyes, stretched, and saw the pale rectangle of light on the wall. She slid out of bed, slipped on her robe, and opened the curtains. A panorama of autumn colors glistened in the early morning sun. Today would be a lovely day for an invigorating walk. But a familiar tension settled in her chest as she pondered the pitfalls of trying to formulate a plan for the day. In this stage of life, it was almost laughable to utter, or even think, the word *plan*.

Janet made her way to the kitchen and poured a cup of coffee. She scanned her planner. Hope bloomed as she realized this had the potential to be a day free of errands and obligations. *Better not get my hopes up,* she thought, as she reached for the phone.

"Good morning, Mom." Janet forced a cheerfulness she didn't really feel. It was a little game she played with herself—beating her mother to the morning's check-in call.

"Hi, um, I think we need to go to the doctor," her mother said.

Usually such a declaration took a few minutes of conversation. *This must be bad,* Janet thought.

"Okay, what's up?"

"It's your father. He's having a problem with his temporary catheter. He's in pain, so I need to go with you to explain the situation. Sometimes your daddy doesn't give full details."

Janet paused, calculating the logistics for this trip—her father in pain, both parents' rolling walkers, her mother's oxygen tank, not to mention getting in and out of the car, across a parking lot, through hard-to-open doors, and up the slowest elevator in town.

Thoughts of a leisurely walk on a crisp autumn day evaporated.

Mobility Aids

Various mobility issues come with aging. Some caregivers notice a need to offer a hand to steady a parent or to slow their own step. There are, however, many useful devices to support safety, which is a key issue for all caregivers.

Some aids are prescribed for your parent when case managers discharge them from the hospital. Others come from just realizing a need or from recommendations offered by other seniors.

For most assistance devices, it is better to head to the medical supply store than rely on catalogs or large-chain discount stores. Costs may be higher at a local medical supply store, but you'll benefit by receiving instruction and guidance from a well-trained staff.

Canes

Standard Cane. A hand rest and a single stick works well for the person who needs just a little extra stability. But even the shape of the handle can affect a cane's effectiveness for support. Perhaps Dad is sensitive about the occasional wobble in his step and needs his ego boosted, so a fancier model will make him feel the Dapper Gentleman. For safety reasons, canes should be measured by a professional, and Dad may need training on how to use his new cane. If he gets in the habit of putting his cane too far to his side now, he's not likely to want to learn the correct way later. Getting some training before buying or using a cane can make a huge difference in its effectiveness. An adjustable model helps as Mom's osteoporosis worsens and she's hunched over more than before. As her height changes, her cane should match.

Four Prong. A four-prong cane has the basic handle and is adjustable, but at the base, it branches into four feet, each tipped with rubber. It provides even more stability than the standard cane.

Walkers

Walkers are a bit more complex as insurance issues may need to be considered. Insurance companies may pay for a walker, so if you can get medical staff to guide you to the right one based on your projected long-term needs, you may avoid needing and possibly paying for several different types.

Basic Walker. A standard model has arms that wrap around the person's hips at a distance from the body. It has four straight legs with rubber tips. It's often the first type of walker brought in by rehabilitation staff in the hospital. Because they do not have wheels, these provide the greatest stability and can be sized to fit. Tennis balls are often added to the leg tips, which help the walker legs slide when the user wants to have more flow of movement.

Wheeled Walker. This model has wheels on the front legs and rubber tips on the back legs. Pushing the wheels often drags the rear rubber tips and provides resistance, which can prove both a blessing and a curse. The resistance helps the user not move too fast, but the rubber tips wear out quickly and sometimes provide too much resistance. Plastic slides can be purchased to replace the rubber tips to provide less resistance. If the user doesn't need resistance, consider a three- or four-wheeled walker.

Three-Wheeler. These walkers are triangular in shape and smaller when folding for storage. Options include a traveling bag but not a seat.

Four-Wheeler. Each leg of the walker has a wheel on the end. The more expensive models offer wheels of different sizes and include brakes.

Hand brakes are important as are the locking mechanisms. A good rep at a medical supply store can make sure the user understands how to properly utilize both.

Locking mechanisms are necessary to stabilize a walker any time it is to be used for stationary support. This is where "Mr. or Ms. Independent" can incur serious injury from a fall if brakes and locks aren't used. Brakes should be checked often. They may need tightening, adjusting, or even replacing.

Wheelchairs and Scooters

A wheelchair is useful, but again, there are different types and needs to consider. The weight of the chair and how easy it is to fold and place in a vehicle are all factors in the decision. Seat covering is also an issue. You're likely to want to get some extra cushioning if the wheelchair will be used for more than short-term transfers.

■ ■ ■

Tips

- Make sure the walker will fit, even folded, into the car(s) being used to carry it.

- All sorts of add-ons can transform the basic walker into the wheeled walker (without the brakes) at most medical supply stores; just bring your wallet as they can be expensive.

- Walker baskets can get filled with junk in no time, just like your kitchen counter at home.

- "Papa's wheelie," a term coined by one four-wheeler's grandson, can be the source of some entertaining, moment-lightening jokes to ease tensions.

- Just for fun, consider decorating a cane, walker, or wheelchair to match its user's personality.

■ ■ ■

Many people buy a wheelchair after a hospital stay, don't use it very much, and end up storing it in a closet for years. Insurance will often cover the cost of a wheelchair, but you might want to borrow or rent a chair for short-term use. Medical supply stores can help with rentals, or you might find a local church or senior center that could loan you one, though the result may be an older, bulkier model that is harder to manage.

Purchasing a transport chair, a lightweight, compact wheelchair designed for short excursions rather than constant usage, is also an option. Transport chairs are less expensive than a standard wheelchair and will be an out-of-pocket expense unless you can borrow one.

Waiting to use the wheelchair insurance benefit makes sense because most seniors, especially those in retirement communities, prefer a scooter if long-term mobility issues arise later. Insurance companies are unlikely to cover both a wheelchair and scooter. Many scooter companies handle the insurance paperwork, and depending on your coverage, offer "no cost to you" service. If the need is there, let insurance cover the thousands of dollars for the scooter rather than the hundreds for a wheelchair. There are also motorized wheelchairs, a good middle ground and more useful in a house or apartment than a fancier scooter.

Another option is to buy used. When a user dies, or as needs change, wheelchairs and walkers that have been stowed in closets and attics can find new owners. Checking for safety is just as important as if purchasing new. Insurance will not pay for anything used.

Before you get your parents involved, try out any mobility device before purchasing or borrowing. You can even take the kids along and practice "driving" a wheelchair in and out of buildings. The kids will have fun going for rides, and you'll make lasting memories.

Paperwork note: When it comes to getting insurance assistance for mobility supplies, you may have to sign a load of forms with the medical supply company that look suspiciously like rent-to-own deals. This happens for a reason. For several months, the insurance company will be billed for partial, rental-type payments on the wheelchair. If the chair is returned during that time period for lack of need (or a death), the insurance company could stop paying the supply company and save money. It really doesn't affect the buyer, but that's the way some insurance companies work.

In most cases, mobility assistance tools are paid for and help on a number of short-term occasions over the years. If and when anything happens to one parent, should the other have that kind of mobility need, the needed assistance might already be in the closet.

Traveling Through Obstacle Courses

It takes only one trip, even locally, with an aging loved one to realize logistics and navigating obstacles pose problems, particularly when you are using tools to increase a parent's stability. Often those around us aren't considerate or tuned-in enough to help by even opening a door. So how can you circumvent hazards and make locomotion as easy as possible?

The key is to know the lay of the land before you get started. You may think you remember the best side of the building to park on for that appointment, but when you're visiting perhaps a dozen offices, some only twice a year and others twice a week, you'll benefit from taking notes.

If new locations have been added to your destinations, take time to drive to these places a day or so ahead of the appointment to scope things out. When the inevitable question, "Do you know where we're going?" comes up, you'll be more confident answering yes.

Even with this level of forethought, unexpected things happen. For example, what do you do when all the handicapped spaces are filled? Even if you arrive early, waiting for someone to vacate a handicapped spot eats up the clock quickly. You may find yourself faced with either leaving your parent on the sidewalk or just inside the door while you find a parking place, or parking remotely and expecting your parent to walk the distance. Either option is fraught with potential dangers.

The main thing to remember is—just as with a child—you can't trust your parent to remain where you've instructed him to stay, and you shouldn't "assign" your parent's care to strangers, no matter how nice and accommodating they seem.

For these occasions it might be worth the expense to purchase a lighter weight wheelchair and stash it in the back of your car, even if your parent is adamantly against it. Given the option of walking a quarter of a mile or riding "this once" in a transport chair, parents can often drop their pride long enough to accept this help. And it prevents you from having to leave them unattended while you find a parking place and walk back to the building.

Reality check: A woman was ticketed for parking in a handicapped space after letting her mother out at the door. The officer stated the handicapped person must be in the car at the time the car is parked. Check your state law for handicapped parking regulations.

Elevators

One walker or wheelchair added to a crowded elevator causes stress. Here timing is important. Arrive early enough for appointments to allow waiting for the next elevator. It is your right to squeeze in, and others on the elevator should be sensitive enough to make room, but you've been on the other end of that too. Consider waiting and making life easier on all.

Revolving Doors

> I will never forget the first time my mother headed straight into a revolving door with her rolling walker. Immediately the image of her 92 pounds squished between the moving doors and metal bars of the walker caused me to panic. She wasn't moving in the right direction, nor was she walking fast enough. Surely tragedy was on its way, and the car wasn't even parked yet!—Kim

Most revolving doors now have a "slow" button on the wall beside them, or better yet, a separate access door that doesn't revolve. You may need to go through the revolving door to get to the other door and open it for your loved one, but using the nonrevolving door will eliminate the perils of those moving towers of metal, glass, and fear.

If you find you must navigate a revolving door, position the walker as close to center as possible and gently instruct your parent to walk as straight as possible. Following the curve of the motion is harder and wheels tend to get stuck. This also works for moving wheelchairs through a revolving door.

Escalators

KIM'S EXPERIENCE

While at the airport to greet a friend, I suddenly saw my father,

■■■

Honoring Perspectives—Kim

Do you remember your first time through a revolving door? It's like a ride at a carnival and a rite of passage all wrapped in one. You're suddenly big enough not to have to hold someone's hand as you go through, and amazingly, you come out the other side in a whole new world.

It took some time, but I finally understood why my parents were so determined to use that revolving door at every opportunity. It was one more sign of independence. It took me so long to realize it because it seemed such a small issue to me. "To me" is the key here. It wasn't about me; it was about them.

■■■

"Mr. Independent," ascending the escalator. He'd propped his four-wheeled walker on the step above and was teetering on the moving stairs. Mom lifted her eyes heavenward and shrugged. The scenario of what could happen rolled through my head like a warped horror flick. Feeling helpless, I prayed.

This was one of those times that taxed my patience to the max. I wanted to yell at Dad about his lack of judgment and common sense. He frightened me. But somewhere from the traumatized depths came the voice of reason, "But he's your dad, the one you love, who's fighting for his independence and sense of self."

Reason intervened, preserving both our dignities, and I quietly told him that the escalator wasn't safe to navigate with a walker.

Doorways

A woman, obviously a senior herself, was adamant about holding the door for my father, a very proud and chivalrous man. They did not go through the "No, I'll get it," battle, and he graciously walked through. Seeing it though gave me a jolt of sympathy for him as I knew his ego had been struck yet again.—Kim

All sexism aside, a pride issue will often become evident around the most innocent of things—even a door. Some men still want to open the door for ladies. However, when an aging father with mobility and strength issues tries to hold a door open, he then may have difficulty navigating through the door with his walker or cane. The door often bangs hips, legs, walkers, or a cane creating a hazard.

Caregivers must deal with this situation by situation. Sometimes getting just enough paces ahead so that you arrive at the door first will make it a non-issue. Other times, someone else in the area sees you coming and holds the door. Whether you are a primary caregiver or not, hold the doors for anyone who even remotely looks like he needs it.

■■ Through the Looking Glass ■■

Making the best of mobility aids

In the mirror: Carol Ann, who started using a cane at the age of 54 when she began having stability challenges from neuropathy in her legs.

> "I'd fallen several times but just did not want to get or use a cane. To me it signaled that I was giving up or giving in to what I was dealing with physically. If I gave in, I might as well quit. But when I fell and knocked my teeth out, my reality was obvious. I had to change how I was thinking, but it was very depressing.

> "I know now that it doesn't signal giving in, but it took a long time. Actually, it was my mother, who had never had mobility issues, who helped me with the transition.

> "She knew I'd been falling quite a bit, and we had a family wedding coming up. She saw a beautiful cloisonné cane in a Smithsonian catalog and sent it to me. She said it would match what I was wearing. Mama made almost all my clothes when I was growing up, and she always made them to match. In my mind, having everything match was important. Mama knew that having a beautiful cane that would match my outfit would mean something to me, and it did.

"Of course the cloisonné cane didn't match everything, and I finally accepted that using a cane was the smart thing to do. So I decided that if I had to use the stupid things, then I was going to make them cute. Now I have all kinds of canes decorated in many different ways to match my outfits and my personality.

"When I've had to use a walker, also given to me by my mother, I dress it up with flags. I just take some sticky Velcro and put it on the front bar of the walker. Then I take the other part and attach it to a decorative flag. I now have them for every season and for my favorite football team. I've done that for my daughter-in-law's mother too. I know it makes her feel better about using a walker.

"When you decorate, people smile at you. It's a way to show my personality despite the challenges. It's like thumbing my nose at these legs of mine that don't do what I ask them to. I'm doing my best to make lemonade out of the lemons."

Viewpoint:

It's the little things that trip you up.

Ten days before Candy's father died, he fell out the back door, tumbled down the steps, and landed on the hard cement garage floor, where he remained until her mother finished her shower, dressed, and found him.

"What were you doing, Daddy?" I asked as I applied ice to the lump on his head.

"Aw, I just wanted to go outside. I've been in the house for weeks, and I wanted to go out and see the trees and hear the birds, and I didn't want to wait. I wanted to do it myself."

Thankfully, aside from soreness and a few scrapes, he had no major injuries. Whether the tumble hastened his death, we'll never know.

While my father literally tripped over nothing more than an elevated doorsill or his own feet, as a caregiver, you'll probably discover it's the little things, often unrelated to caregiving, that trip you. While you may not splatter on hard cement, you can expect your feelings and emotions to sustain some major bumps and bruises.

You may find your tripping spot occurs in a place you least expect it, perhaps in an area of life you perceive as most stable. Suddenly, a volatile issue erupts between you and your spouse, or you receive a call that your teen, who has never been in trouble before, is camped in the principal's office for an infraction that requires your presence, or an unforeseen financial issue materializes, or someone needs surgery. The list could go on and on. But when these unexpected situations crop up, it's then you realize the delicate balance you're maintaining on the tightrope that is currently your life.

When these trip-up moments happen, realize that God isn't pouring on more to see if you can bear it. It's just life, and so much is beyond our control. The one thing we do have control over is how we respond. You have the option of deciding if you're going to vent your anger on an unsuspecting salesclerk, wear a perpetually grim expression, or tell everyone who will listen how challenging your life is.

While it's good to have someone to talk to occasionally, be careful not to make caregiving the only subject you discuss with people. Otherwise, they'll scatter when they see you coming. And let's face it, incontinence and dementia aren't exactly stimulating dinner conversation, even if it's with your spouse and children.

My father had a saying that pretty well sums up the need for flexibility in life, whether in a caregiving role or not. He said, "You've got to roll with the punches."

That means although we're going to take a hit or two—unkind words that emotionally wound or unexpected situations that blindside us—we have the choice to roll away from the trauma, hop back on our feet, retreat to a neutral corner for a few minutes, and then get back into the ring. We have the option of choosing whether we let this season of caregiving change our personalities and outlook on life, or whether we move forward and deal with situations as they occur, while praying for grace, and patience, and wisdom.

Living Water

> Strengthen the feeble hands,
>> steady the knees that give way;
> say to those with fearful hearts,
>> "Be strong, do not fear;
> your God will come."
>> (Isaiah 35:3-4)

Encouragement. We all need it, especially when all that we consider stable in life is knocked out from under us. While we can acquire the physical support our parents need, we sometimes overlook the areas of encouragement and spiritual support. During your caregiving journey, don't forget to pray for your parents and to provide opportunities for them to attend worship services or Bible studies, if possible. It may mean being creative, like having the Bible study group come to them for a few weeks. Also, look for ways to encourage your parents by pointing out positives or reminding them of blessings.

You need encouragement and spiritual connection, also. While it's tempting to haul out the "I'm too tired" excuse, don't cut yourself off from your church and neglect spiritual renewal through organized Bible study. You may discover that your greatest source of emotional and spiritual support comes from those in your Sunday school class or small group. And when people offer to help you, let them! Their offers don't indicate you're doing a poor job caring for your parents. Their willingness to help is the body of Christ in action.

Additional Information

Online resources:

www.specialtymedicalsupply.com; www.1800wheelchair.com; and www.improvelife.com; offer extensive listings of mobility and home care aids. They offer free catalogs and phone support. You can also find gift ideas such as talking calculators, aids for buttoning clothes, and other items for supporting independence.

Chapter 11

Navigating the DMV and
Avoiding Treacherous Travel
Transportation Challenges

Susan's very independent father, Frank, had recovered from cancer surgery and was managing treatments fairly well. His wife didn't drive because of physical limitations. Susan coordinated the schedules of her own family and that of her parents and served as chauffeur.

Susan and her mother, Olivia, knew Frank was not likely to be strong enough to drive again, but it wasn't long before he started mentioning the subject. Although he relinquished his keys with the initial diagnosis, now that he was feeling better, he missed that jingle in his pocket and the freedom it represented.

Susan sidestepped the issue as gracefully as possible, but eventually it had to be discussed. Frank ignored the doctor when he advised against resuming driving and brushed aside his wife's concern.

Susan looked to the Department of Motor Vehicles for help. After multiple calls, Susan discovered the office for Driver Improvement and was able to talk to the director.

"I know where you are. Believe me, I had to do the same with my father and it was the hardest thing I've had to do," he said.

Susan almost cried. This man understood and perhaps could actually help.

"My dad insists he be allowed to take an on-the-road drivers' test. Is such a test offered?"

Instead of offering the test, the Driver Improvement office sent

Frank a pile of forms, which mainly required medical status verification by doctors. One question on the form asked if the doctor would be comfortable riding in the car with this person at the wheel. Of course, Susan never knew how her father's doctors answered this question since the form was sent directly from the doctors to the DMV.

The next letter that came was a surprise. Instead of offering a date and contact for the requested driving test, the letter suspended Frank's license pending improvement.

"What improvement?" Frank wanted to know.

Frank vowed to write the DMV to find out what he had to do next, but before he ever got around to writing that letter, his wife had to have surgery. A projected four-day hospital stay turned into twenty-eight days in two different hospitals and an additional week at a healthcare center.

"Susan, I think I could drive over to visit your mother today," Frank said.

Susan finally snapped. She'd done all he asked in an effort to protect his ego and give him the chance he needed to prove himself, but he just wouldn't accept the inevitable answer.

"Dad, let it go, okay?"

"But I want to relieve your burden."

"It's not a burden, and please let's not go there. I'm not up to it."

"But—"

"Okay, you know what? I can't do this anymore. So here it goes. You respected our wishes while you recovered from surgery and having treatments, but now that you're feeling better you want to drive again. I understand that. I don't want to hurt your feelings, but I truly believe you have no business on the road, and I wish you'd just drop the subject. Your health makes it difficult for your hands and feet to feel the wheel and pedals. Your response time is compromised. The pain in your hips makes it hard for you to move suddenly. You're in a new town. The roads are unfamiliar, and the drivers around here are not anything like you're used to. You can't hear well, and your ability to comprehend what you are hearing is limited because you're only catching parts of it. Drop it, Dad, please."

"Okay," he said.

Surprisingly, Susan's dad didn't appear beaten down by what she'd said, just thoughtful. Perhaps he was relieved that what needed to be said finally had been.

Seniors and Driving Limitations

Driving is the number one issue for seniors and has been called the nuclear warhead of caregiving.

"It's their last bit of independence and something they've been doing nearly all their lives," said one AARP 55+ Safe Driver instructor. At 78, and retired from the insurance industry, he is still able to drive, but from his training and experience with AARP, he knows seniors face issues that can limit their driving skills.

For example, the safest way to avoid blind spot collisions is to turn and glance over your shoulder to verify that your blind spot is clear. When backing up, it is safest to steer with one hand and look out the back window, not just the rearview mirror, to navigate. But for many seniors with arthritis, such movement is awkward if possible at all.

In some areas, independent driver evaluators can give an objective look at a driver's abilities and safety on the road. However, evaluators are not easy to find, and doctors are often unwilling to put the brakes on driving for a senior. They know what it does to a patient's self-esteem, and despite realizing the potential hazards, the doctor may not be willing to issue the hang-up-the-keys order.

"You'd be surprised how many 70+-year-olds have survived cancer, but come right back in this hospital through the ER just because they didn't stop driving when they should have," said one oncologist.

Driver safety courses, specially designed for mature drivers, are available all over the country, often at no charge. Some are even offered online. The courses get seniors looking at the issues surrounding their driving and how those issues have changed over time. Can a driver really handle driving 75 mph down a major interstate, changing lanes, and navigating exits with a cell phone ringing?

Drivers often forget the rules of the road they learned decades ago. As part of the class, drivers learn that the main mistakes seniors make are "failure to observe right of way" and "improper left turn." Participating in a class is a good way to look at the issues with others to avoid finger pointing or having it become a power struggle within a family.

If there is driving tension between a husband and wife, then having both take the class provides objective insights and perspectives to help the decision-making process.

Whether a class will work to help your senior make the decision to limit or stop driving depends on the person. Sometimes it's a gradual process. The first step could be no driving out of state. A second step, no driving in bad weather. A third may be staying in the county on familiar roads. And another, only to very local destinations, such as the post office or the grocery store. Be prepared, that final step of actually handing over the keys is the hardest.

After driving for 50 or 60 years, giving it up is hard. It's often the last independence seniors feel they have to hold on to. Even when seniors limit driving, accident rates increase with age. AARP reports that compared to drivers in the 35-54 age range, seniors have more accidents per mile driven. Age-related physical limitations and medications impact safe driving. Fatalities in drivers over age 75 jump due to an increase in the body's inability to withstand trauma, reports The Hartford.

Some seniors refuse to acknowledge their limitations. In such cases, family members spend countless hours worrying. Stop the inner turmoil and look for solutions. If you reach the point where you have to lay out the issue firmly, have some solutions for transportation needs already in place or thought out.

Consider the following conversation starter:

> "Dad, I know you believe your driving is just fine, but we
> disagree. We know you have worked very hard to provide a

lifestyle of comfort for you and Mom. But if you are in an accident and there is proof that you shouldn't have been driving, then you could be held liable for more than just what your car insurance covers. You don't want to lose the financial security you've worked so hard for. I'm concerned, too, that we as your family could be held liable for letting you be on the road."

Having alternate plans is an essential element when encouraging seniors to hang up the keys. If they see no other way to get where they want or need to go, then they'll be reluctant to let go of the keychain. Look into local transportation systems, and as a caregiver, your own ability to help. It may be easier to shop for Mom's groceries, but delivering bags to her door doesn't meet the psychological need to get out of the house occasionally. Try role reversal here to gain perspective.

If Mom and Dad are accustomed to traveling to Aunt Sue's two states away every summer, have an idea of what other options are available before you issue the edict of impossibility.

ID Cards. Sometimes the matter of pride can be handled with a DMV-issued identification card. The ID card looks just like a driver's license, photo and all. Carrying it in a wallet and being able to use it when asked for ID eases self-esteem issues.

Consider resources in your parent's home community or church family to meet their changing needs for transportation.

In a situation with two parents, one may be an advocate for hanging up the keys and willing to manage schedules so family members can help with transportation. Having an inside informer can help, at least for a while.

Identify local driving services. Many counties provide free transportation to and from doctors' appointments. Having this information handy or helping a parent schedule a trip will make it easier to utilize the service in the future. These services aren't like city buses, but for a parent who has never used public transportation, this concept might be daunting. Go with your parent the first time to determine for yourself if this is a good option. If it doesn't work for you or your parent, mark it off your list as a potential resource. Either way, knowledge is power.

Consider hiring a driver to give your parents a night out. This isn't a limo situation. More likely it will be the high school or college student who lives down the street who needs to earn a few extra bucks. Once your parents have a taste of having a driver in a non-need-based situation, they'll be more likely to consider similar options when there is a need.

The driving ability of seniors varies not only by age but also by basic physical limitations. Some seniors may be very capable drivers who can help their friends and peers. This gives the driver a sense of being needed and available to offer help. The caution is to find the truly able drivers in your parents' social group. Perhaps in your church there are older adults who don't have physical limitations and can offer driving services. Another possibility is grandparents who cared for their grandchildren, who are now school age. They are displaced caregivers and often want to fill time and provide a service to others. Widows and widowers who miss companionship might be a perfect fit.

When developing these types of relationships, remember it is a process. You might try out several contacts before finding one that works. Or you may have to coordinate with several different drivers depending on driving needs. Some drivers may be available only for limited time periods.

Potential Issues with Drivers

Your parents have that cream puff in the garage. The engine should be started occasionally. Should a driver you hire use their car? If it's someone who will be driving your parents regularly, it's worth considering. If it's only for the rare trip to town, it's generally better to use the driver's own car.

When recruiting friends, neighbors, or others to assist with transportation, consider how to handle payment. Offering an hourly rate may not be feasible if your mom wants to spend the entire day at the mall. You end up paying for eight hours of a driver's time.

Determine an hourly rate for services. Check out what baby sitters in your area earn and then add some for the cost of gas if you are asking the driver to use his or her own car. Other options are a per-trip or per-day rate. This might work if your mom wants to visit Aunt Sue for a couple of days, and it takes a full day to get there and back, followed by the return trip to pick her up. If it takes all day to get to Aunt Sue's, arrange for the driver to spend the night before she heads back with Mom. Be willing to negotiate fees, but let your budget be the guide.

Some friends may refuse pay for helping out. This is where a caregiving child can step in and talk to the potential driver. It might be a pride issue. Your dad insists on paying, but your driver may be a longtime friend who wouldn't think of accepting money for helping. Perhaps the person doesn't need the money, and your parents are on a limited budget. Being open is the best way to proceed, even if discussion is uncomfortable. It may be that despite their protests, you leave an envelope in the car after each appointment or send thank-you notes with gift cards in them. Working with friends can be a blessing and a challenge, but the benefits easily win.

Longer Distance Travel

Can trains or buses take your parents to visit Aunt Sue? Can you incorporate your vacation into their plans? If you don't want to visit a whole week with Aunt Sue, look nearby and find out what things might be of interest to your own family. If taking time off from work is not a good option at the time your parents want to travel, then negotiate with them. Perhaps putting off the trip a couple of months would enable you to help them travel, while meeting your own family's needs. Or maybe the distance is close enough that you can drive them back and forth and come home in between. That's the toughest option.

Another option is to pay a friend or college-age son or daughter to chauffeur. Remember, most kids love to drive, and they'll have the whole way back to listen to whatever music they choose. Just check out the insurance issues.

Trains and Buses

Train and bus travel often mean multiple stops. Some train schedules, especially those for train tours, involve odd hour departures. This can disrupt sleep cycles and body rhythms, and factors in when determining the pros and cons of any travel plan.

Some tour companies offer special trip packages just for seniors, whether for day trips or longer vacation-oriented travel. With these packages, the staff, drivers, and guides are accustomed to offering door-to-door service and meeting special needs of senior travelers. Included in the trip are things like frequent leg-stretching stops and baggage handling. If the trip isn't a tour event, both rail travel staff and bus drivers should be informed of a passenger's special needs.

For caregivers and their loved ones, local church-sponsored trips may provide a nice break from the routine. Often, churches allow nonmembers to participate in trips. But before sending your parents on these types of trips, know their limitations. Let courtesy toward others guide the decision to send your parents on a group trip. Obviously, a weeklong bus trip to tour the Grand Canyon is not a good option for a parent with severe incontinence issues.

A caregiver may need to go on the seniors' trip, too, depending on the care specifics. However, short day trips may provide enjoyment for your parent. Even in the most loving parent-child relationship, a caregiver benefits from a needed break. Trips for special shopping or to see shows or plays can provide both parties a chance for independence.

Air Travel

Air travel has its own set of challenges, but can be a viable option. Security issues cause potentially long waits for checking in and boarding aircraft. Delays can be very difficult for seniors with mobility problems. Some seniors don't use a cane, walker, or wheelchair, but have arthritis that makes standing, sitting, and movement painful. When using air travel, be sure to request special service. Airlines are most willing to accommodate.

> In the early days of my parents' mobility challenges, I actually encouraged them to fly up to vacation with my sister. They had been world travelers, but it had been years since they'd navigated the "friendly" skies. They took the trip, and came home vowing never to do it again. Oops. We chalked it up to a learning experience. The vacation was fine, but the travel stress took away a great deal of the overall pleasure.—Kim

Tips for Air Travel

- Since family members aren't allowed beyond security checkpoints, call ahead to request special services or guides for seniors at both departure and arrival airports.

- Booking online or through a travel agent offers an option of requesting "special assistance," which can apply to mobility, hearing, or vision impairment.

- Upon arrival at an airport, ask for "wheelchair assist" (this doesn't require a doctor's order).

- Let the airline know your parent uses a cane, walker, or wheelchair. If your parent can get in and out of the plane's seat unassisted, then the airline staff will stow the chair or walker in a special section of the plane. Canes can be stowed under the seat. If a trip to the restroom is necessary, having familiar support will be safer than relying on soft, moveable seat backs.

- Discourage drinking caffeinated drinks during or before travel. They increase negative effects of air travel, such as aching, sinus trouble, and jet lag, and stimulate the bladder.

- Drink water to aid hydration.

- Sit as close to first class as possible. If your parent has a mobility issue, it is likely she will be allowed to use the first-class restroom rather than having to struggle to a rear section of the plane.

- Look for seat break sections or emergency exit seating. If your senior has an able-bodied traveling companion, then you're not likely to be asked to move from this location. These spots have more legroom and allow passengers with circulation issues to stretch often and be more comfortable.

- Check with doctors before planning air travel. Ask if medications need to be administered differently or if medicine is available to calm flight anxieties. It is better to ask a doctor who understands all the medical issues involved rather than just heading for an over-the-counter fix at a local pharmacy.

- Be sure to take only enough medications for your trip, in the proper prescription bottles in your carry-on. Medications packed in luggage can be stolen during the luggage screening process.

- Small pillows and light blankets can be found on most airlines, but parents may prefer to bring their own.

- Dress in easy-to-remove layers.

- Save time with baggage check-in and retrieval by packing just a carry-on.

- If you have to check bags, use the curbside service offered at many airports. The staff at curbside check-in can also call for the wheelchair assist. If a senior is navigating airports on his own, make sure bags have wheels and are easy to manage.

- Magnify any safe driver concerns before considering a rental car for your parent. Dad may be fine driving his car in his hometown, but managing a different car while navigating unfamiliar roads could prove hazardous.

- If your parent does rent a car, consider a GPS or other navigational system. It may be helpful to rent or borrow a navigation device prior to the trip and teach your parent how to use it. Check to make sure the system you let them practice on is the same offered by the rental car company. Or prepare a list of destination addresses and ask the agent to program in the addresses.

■■ Through the Looking Glass ■■
Traveling despite mobility issues

In the mirror: Betty, 75-year-old RV enthusiast

"As a result of an accident at our home, I broke both bones in my lower right leg. Following surgery, I went into a nursing home for rehabilitation therapy. When I went home, I progressed from wheelchair to walker to cane. I had to use the motorized carts to go shopping, but none of this bothered me. I was willing to do whatever helped keep me going.

"Long before the accident, my husband James and I planned to join an RV caravan tour that took us through Mexico. We've been RVing for more than thirty years and camping for around fifty years. I wasn't going to miss that trip. My doctor said I could recuperate in the RV as well as at home. There were a couple of things I couldn't do—a hike and climbing into a boxcar for social hour before boarding the train for the Copper Canyon—but I attended pretty much everything else.

"There were always people ready to help.

"I had lived 74 years and never had a broken bone, so I did not anticipate this. I've always been a strong-willed person, up and on the go. I wasn't going to let this hold me back, and it still isn't."

Viewpoint:

Knowing when to hang up the keys—Mary's perspective

My sister Louise experienced a retinal hemorrhage, but was still able to see well enough to drive. However, one day she walked in the back door, hung up her keys, and announced, "That's my last time to drive."

When I asked what prompted her decision, Louise said, "I realized on the way home from my appointment that I couldn't see the center yellow line and all the lane markers were hazy. I prayed and promised the Lord if He would get me home safely without my hurting someone else or myself, I'd never drive again."

I was relieved she made the decision on her own without my having to encourage her to stop driving.

Living Water

> This is what the Lord says:
> "Stand at the crossroads and look;
>   ask for the ancient paths,
>   ask where the good way is, and walk in it,
>   and you will find rest for your souls."
>   (Jeremiah 6:16)

Years ago, my husband and I enjoyed a trip to Scotland. We rented a car, drove on the wrong side of the road, and traveled up through the highlands. I'd made reservations ahead of time at inns along the way, breaking the trip into what seemed like manageable chunks of driving time. But when we got to the western isles, everything took longer than expected. We had to make a ferry crossing, and the schedule was different from what was posted on the Internet.

Once on the other side, the road was literally a rutted cow track. We bounced and jostled through fields and over hills, often pulling aside to let other vehicles pass on the narrow lane. At one point, I was almost in tears. It felt like we were lost. I begged my husband to turn back, but he said we'd gone too far to give up. We knew we had a place to sleep once we arrived.

Night descended, and at last, a light glowed in the distance. When we finally reached our destination, exhausted and weary, the innkeeper greeted us warmly. Although we went to bed hungry, rest was sweet.

We are all pilgrims on the journey of life, and we often stand at a crossroads and wonder which direction to take. Sometimes we embark on a path that isn't the best direction. Then we're faced with whether to turn back or continue on. But like the words of Jeremiah 6:16, the Lord instructs us to ask for direction, walk in the good way, and find rest.

As a caregiver, you will often stand at a confusing crossroads. Don't be afraid to ask for directions, to seek help from those who have answers. Look to God for wisdom also, and find rest for your soul.

Additional Information

Online resources:

The Hartford Insurance Group offers advice for having "the discussion" with senior family members: www.thehartford.com/talk-witholderdrivers.

The American Medical Association offers the *Physician's Guide to Assessing and Counseling Older Drivers:* www.ama-assn.org/ama/pub/category/10791.html.

Also check out www.seniordrivers.org and www.aarp.org for additional information specific to senior drivers.

Chapter 12

Finding Healthy Perspectives
Nurturing Emotional Stability—Yours and Theirs

Often the stresses of caregiving negate joy for the caregiver. That's why it's important to be intentional about finding avenues of joy and keeping a global perspective on life. Although there is no way to predict how long you'll be in this situation, don't put the enjoyment of life on hold while you fulfill the caregiving role.

In any stage of life, we tend to adopt the attitude of enjoying life once a current hurdle is over, rather than finding snippets of joy now. Contentment comes in tiny nuggets through small victories in daily struggles or private moments of thankfulness. On the days your parent is mentally alert and happy, give thanks. If your parent is able to sit on the porch on a warm day, enjoy the tranquility. When a friend offers to stay with your parent for a day or a few hours, seize the opportunity and do something just for you. It may be a walk or a nap, a shopping trip or a game of tennis—whatever lifts your spirits and makes you happy.

Renovating Attitudes and Actions

It's easy to fall into a pattern of negative thinking and adopt a woe-is-me attitude when you're balancing caregiving with the other demands of life. So it might be helpful to honestly assess where you fall on a positive/negative continuum. Often our attitudes, actions, and reactions need a little refurbishing. While an extreme makeover might not be in order, following are some areas to consider:

Readjust Your Outlook

It's easy to get into the habit of criticizing others or viewing everything negatively. Negative thoughts create a sense of defeat. But you have the option of changing your outlook and your attitude. Perhaps the tone of voice you use with your parents, spouse, children, coworkers, or service personnel could use a spit shine. Or maybe your self-perception and self-talk needs a good dusting. God created each of us with unique gifts and talents. Wipe away the layers of doubt regarding your worth. Adopt an attitude of thankfulness for the positive elements in your life.

Revamp Your Actions

When our attitudes stink, our actions often follow along. Sometimes we drop into a pattern of behaving certain ways without even thinking how our actions affect others. Does your body language project an image of superiority, arrogance, or impatience? If you get angry easily or make decisions impulsively, slow down and think before acting. Imagine the results your actions will have on you and those around you. It may take great effort to behave differently, but give it a try and notice the resulting improvement in your life.

Reconsider Words

Many of us consistently wound others with our words. On some level, this may be intentional, but it is more likely because we're simply stressed, in a hurry, and oblivious to how what we say and how we say it affects others. Our aging parents are particularly sensitive to tone of voice, and impatience is frequently the emotion that zings through our words. It will take a conscious effort, but you can work on verbally conveying love and care rather than impatience and annoyance.

Refocus Your Vision

It's easy to get self-focused and fail to see the hurts and needs of those around us. Yet there are times when we could offer a few words of encouragement that would make a huge difference in the life of someone who is struggling. Despite the busyness of your schedule and the demands of caregiving, be available to listen to others. When focused totally on our own situation, we lose touch with others and forget we're not the only ones with challenges. We all need motivation to look beyond the tiny boxes of our own lives and reach out to others. Interaction with others helps gain perspective and bring moments of revelation and joy.

Restore Relationships

All of us have difficult, high-maintenance people in our lives. Conflict feeds on reruns of old offenses. Constantly dwelling on past controversial incidents leads to more conflict. None of us like to admit we might be to blame, even partially, for problems in relationships. Sometimes, restoring a broken relationship seems to involve more effort than it's worth. But if you're willing to take the first step, you may be able to rebuild that relationship. Offer an olive branch. Don't try to rehash the whole incident. Just tell the person you're sorry for the rift and would like to move forward. If the other person is unwilling, this may be as far as it goes, but at least you've made an effort at restoration. While you can't change others, you can change your response to conflict, and you can choose to forgive.

Reconnect Spiritually

Frequently, our spiritual lives are the most uncared for area. We get so caught up in what seems urgent that a thick layer of dust forms on the spiritual element. Now is a great time to reconnect spiritually. Start by asking God to show you areas in your faith walk that need renovation. Attend a Bible study. Make worship a priority. You'll discover that remodeling your spiritual life brings a more positive perspective to other areas as well.

By giving attention to these aspects of your life, you can successfully restructure your attitudes and actions, thus enhancing the overall quality of your life.

Self-Care for Caregivers

If you're the primary caregiver, you know it. Unfortunately, most of the time you don't have or recognize what you desperately need—a caregiver! And in some cases, no one is going to rush to your aid.

Even if relationships with your parents and extended family are good, caregiving strains even the best relationships. Feelings get hurt. Miscommunication happens. Someone invariably feels left out of the loop. There will be days or weeks when you think one more tiny comment will send you over the edge. That's why it's important to make self-care a priority. Here are a few ways to do that.

Understand the Guilt Factor

Guilt is often the stressor that drives us to do what we do in the caregiving role, and in life. And let's face it, no matter how kind our parents are to others, they often are experts at playing the guilt card—hauling it out at unexpected moments and trumping you to defeat.

Because this is an uncertain time of life for your parents, you can expect them to fluctuate between expecting you to handle everything and wanting to exert their independence. Parents still want to be "in charge," and once you've established a routine, be prepared to have that routine interrupted or turned upside down when your parent forces a power struggle.

While it's normal to crave parental approval, you may find you can never seem to be enough nor do anything well enough to please your parents. Try not to let guilt or feelings of failure rob you of realizing you need to take some time for yourself. If no family members are available to help, check with your local council on aging, or similar organizations, who can recommend qualified persons you can hire to provide care for your parent while you take a few days off.

Set Boundaries

While challenging, it's essential for you to set up and enforce some boundaries with your parent. Role reversal makes it difficult for your parent to view you as capable and not in need of coaching. No matter what our age, we're still "little Susie" or "Johnny" to our parents.

With the aging process comes a shift to a more self-centered mind-set. Your previously thoughtful parent may become overly self-absorbed, obsessing about medical issues and demanding immediate action by the caregiver on chores or activities that aren't as urgent as your parent perceives them to be. It's essential to construct boundaries. Just because your parent is out of two grocery items doesn't mean you have to jump and run. Let parents know you'll shop once or twice a week for them, but everyday trips to the store aren't possible. This will require your parent to think ahead and keep a running list—something you may have to train and remind them to do. Realize, also, that sometimes these urgent requests for items are merely a veiled attempt to get you over to their house. Loneliness is a major issue for senior adults, but you can't be a constant companion for your parent and maintain a semi-normal life of your own.

Time boundaries are necessary but difficult to enforce. Realize your parent is probably unable or unwilling to understand the scheduling hurdles you face in tacking caregiving onto your activity load. No matter how many times you explain reasons for doing things in a certain time frame or pattern, the reasoning will be forgotten in light of what your parent perceives as urgent.

Many of us experience the "tack-on" phenomena, whereby you've allotted what you think is the necessary amount of time to accomplish various tasks for parents, only to discover when you get them in the car that they've added numerous items to the list that they didn't bother to mention to you beforehand. To minimize tack-ons, start asking ahead of time all that your parent expects to accomplish with this trip or, if you are going without the parent, all she wants you to do for her. The list may be too long for one outing, so help your parent prioritize. Again, their sense of urgency is often overblown. The bill that isn't due for 15 days doesn't have to make it to the post office today.

Emotional boundaries are perhaps the most difficult to establish and maintain. Anxiety accompanies aging, and you may find your parent continually spills his anxiety onto you. This is an area where you especially need to learn to disconnect, or the pressure you already feel from balancing your own life and caring for your parent will increase exponentially. Many seniors worry constantly, verbalize those concerns, thrust their emotional burdens in your direction, and expect you to ease their uncertainty or solve their problems. Remind your parent there is peace in giving those cares to God and leaving them with Him. He is the only one capable of totally meeting all their needs.

Reject Critics

If you haven't learned by now, a critic is always waiting in the wings with an in-depth critique of all you're doing wrong or have failed to do. Frequently, your chief critic is an extended family member who does little to help, but can dish out the criticism and mess with your mind. These are the folks who have lots to say about a yard that needs mowing or carpet that needs vacuuming. It never occurs to them that you are just barely managing to tread water in a sea of responsibilities or that they might be able to assist you rather than slathering you with criticism.

Your critic may be the aunt who makes a perfunctory visit following her bridge game, or the sister who still harbors a grudge because Dad gave you his mother's locket, while she got only the photo album. Or it may be the neighbor who's never been in a caregiving role but has a plethora of advice for how you could be doing the job more effectively. No matter who materializes as your chief critic, learn to close your ears. Don't allow criticism to cause you to question yourself. You're doing an excellent job, despite the critics. Look to God for your affirmation. His approval diminishes critical voices.

■■■

Caring for You

Here are some ideas for finding peace amid your tasks.

- Hire a service to clean your home, your parents' home, or both.
- Take a nap or sleep late.
- Escape to the gym or take a walk.
- Go fishing or swimming.
- Discover a museum.
- Research dream trips on the Internet.
- Sing out loud.
- Be silly and laugh.
- Try aromatherapy to lift your mood.
- Indulge yourself with a massage, facial, or manicure.
- Find music that calms or energizes you and play it soft or loud.
- Hire a sitter to stay with your loved ones while you take a day off.
- Take up a hobby that is doable for your available time.
- Go to the movies by yourself. Eat popcorn. Relax. Recruit a friend to care for your children. This is not being selfish. It's self-preservation.
- Run away, even if it's a last-minute decision when you see a couple of days with no appointments and the availability of others to help with your parents and children.
- Talk to someone outside your family. It may be a pastor or professional counselor, but find someone who is not involved in your household or hasn't been your best friend for years.

■■■

Your Parent's Emotional Stability

The Need to Be Needed

While self-care is extremely important, realize that your parent is also struggling to adjust to this phase of life. One of the hardest parts of aging is accepting role reversal. No longer feeling needed by their adult children is a dagger to the self-worth of most seniors. Keep this in mind as you handle the details of your parent's life. A good way to tap into your parent's need to be needed is to ask him or her to pray for other people or situations. A word of caution, however. If your parent is a high-anxiety person, temper these prayer requests so they don't cause your parent to have additional mental anguish. And don't forget to tell your parent about answered prayer. Some actually keep a list and check off the request when an answer comes.

> ■ ■ ■
>
> "Leviticus 19:32 instructs us to show respect for our elders. Let them know they are important and valued. Look at the person and think, *This is my daughter or son at age 85.* That will give you a soul connection."
>
> —Rev. Sal Barone,
> Pastor of Senior Adult Ministries
>
> ■ ■ ■

The Power of Touch

Our parents, especially those who have lost a spouse, are hungry for physical touch. Part of their loneliness comes from not experiencing the touch of another human. We need to remember this as we minister to our parents.

Jesus is our example for physical touch. He welcomed little children into His presence and into His arms. He touched those He healed. He offered a helping hand to those struggling along the way. We can be His hands and convey His love with hugs, pats, and hand-holding.

Our mothers may enjoy having their hair brushed or having lotion applied to their backs, a place that is impossible for most to reach. Dad may appreciate a neck massage or a foot rub. Either may want you to sit beside them and just hold hands for a while or link arms and take a stroll.

The Importance of Nostalgia

When you're sitting quietly, holding hands with your parent, don't be surprised if you hear a story from bygone days. It may be a story you've heard a hundred times before, but resist the urge to say you don't want to hear it again. It gives your parent joy to remember happy times from the past. With a little interaction, you may coax out a story you've never heard before. You may find out your grandfather was a poet, and his poetry journal is stored in a plastic bag in the old cedar chest under the attic eaves. Or you may hear an interesting tidbit in a variation of a much-related tale that causes you to ask questions and discover a kernel of family history never revealed before.

The main thing is to enjoy these nostalgia moments with your parents. Allow them to take a sentimental journey and slow down long enough to hop on the train with them. Go through boxes of photos with them and let them tell you all about Uncle Joe, his wooden leg and dry sense of humor, or the "Sunbonnet Grandma" who made the best blackberry cobbler in the world but wouldn't share her recipe. Your dad may reveal a World War II story you've never heard before. Make notes or record the story. Years from now you may feel the urge to compile a family history, and these stories will provide important content.

Nostalgia may also come in the form of remembering your childhood or your children's early years. Sometimes it's harder to listen to stories about our childhoods because the cute little things we did make us feel juvenile or stupid. It's okay. Your parent enjoys reliving these stories in the same way you love to remember your son calling instructions "constructions" or your daughter calling her purse a "moose."

At first you may think you are indulging your parents by listening to their stories, but ultimately, you'll find you enjoy these nostalgic moments as much as they do.

▪▪ Through the Looking Glass ▪▪

Maintaining joy

In the mirror: Dorothy, 86, lives independently in a retirement community in the same town where her daughter lives. Her son and another daughter live a few hours away.

"I believe that joy is ours already. We do not need to look for it or work for it, simply accept it as the gift that has already been given to us by God through our salvation. It has nothing to do with age and what some see as physical limitations or challenges.

"There is a difference between happiness and joy. Happiness depends on circumstances, which change. Physical abilities are one of the things that change as we age. I've learned to stop looking at what I can and cannot do. Focusing on my own abilities (or lack of them) is self-centered and limits my ability to find peace. Focusing on things we have no control over takes us away from our joy.

"If we don't live our lives for self, then we take the circumstances in each day as they come and retain our sense of joy in living for God. By surrendering myself to God daily, I can be a vessel for His use. My age doesn't prevent God from using me. Sure, my age and body have stopped me from playing tennis and waterskiing, but every day is still filled with purpose. It may be the opportunity to talk with my grandchildren or to share with a prayer partner, or any number of things. Each day is different. Being a Christian is exciting. I get up in the morning thanking God for another day in which I can be available for the doors He chooses to open for me. I feel His presence always."

Viewpoint:

An Anniversary to Remember—Donna's story

Daddy and Mama always did something special on their anniversary. Often, my sisters and I played a part. Sometimes they'd arrive at their getaway destination to find we'd paid for their hotel room. Other times, we'd surprise them in other ways.

Mama had always talked about wanting to renew their vows. After Daddy received a lung cancer diagnosis, his decline was rapid. We knew that next anniversary was probably their last and wanted to make it special, even though Daddy was at home and unable to get out of bed.

We took them 38 balloons and 38 yellow roses. We got Daddy up and into the wheelchair so he could see the balloons, roses, and the wedding cake with their photo airbrushed on top. Then we brought in the big surprise—the minister.

Daddy and Mama renewed their vows, and afterward, they enjoyed a special dinner for two in their room. Later, we helped them cut the cake and served them coffee. Then we turned on their song, "Look at Us," by Vince Gill, and closed the door. We wanted them to have that special time together.

The next day, Daddy went back to the hospital, and died a week later. But they had the opportunity to celebrate their anniversary by renewing their vows, and it made them so happy.

Living Water

> A cheerful heart is good medicine,
> > but a crushed spirit dries up the bones.
> > (Proverbs 17:22)

On the tenth day of a hospital stay, my mother celebrated her eighty-eighth birthday. We tried to have a little party, but she felt so awful it was hard for her to do much other than blow out a candle on a cupcake. Our present to her was a neck pillow, a gift that would, we hoped, make her more comfortable.

The next morning when I arrived at the hospital, she pointed to the foot of the bed and said, "Please hand me my *horse collar*. It got away from me during the night."

Momentarily confused, I finally realized she was referring to her new neck pillow. I burst into laughter and laughed until the tears spilled down my cheeks. Mama joined in. Standing beside that sick bed, the words of Proverbs 17:22 came to mind. After days of drugs, shots, IVs, and pain, in that moment, joy truly was the best medicine.

The writer of Proverbs knew that the ability to find humor in unexpected places brings joy to the soul. Likewise, a crushed spirit has physical side effects.

Choose joy.

Additional Information

Though valuable for many links, articles, and food for thought, the www.matureresources.org site has unique columnists that offer insightful perspectives, not just facts.

Chapter 13

Which Hat Are You Wearing Today?
The Flexible Mind-set of Multiple Roles

Honey, have you taken your meds yet?" Jayne asked.

Ed took his wife by the hand and led her to their toy-littered living room.

"What are you doing?" Jayne asked.

"Look around."

"I know, it's a mess, the kids have their stuff everywhere, and I haven't had time to pick up yet," Jayne snapped, reflecting the pace she'd been keeping for days and her irritation at Ed for pointing out the obvious.

"No, honey, just look. You're not in a hospital or a nursing center. You're at home, with our kids, and I'm your husband who loves you. I'm not your dad, and I'm not old enough for you to refer to my cold medicine as my meds. You're home, so relax."

■ ■ ■

Caregiving requires a closet full of hats and an understanding of which ones to wear, when. In Jayne's case, she'd left her nurse's hat on even after getting home from taking care of her father. Her husband helped her remember that she could take it off.

There's the nurse's hat, worn when providing for physical needs; the case manager hat for juggling all the information; the adult loving-child cap; the chauffeur's chapeau; the listening best-friend visor;

the psychologist cap; the beret for hearing about trips to Paris taken 50 years ago; and the wide-brimmed bonnet for when the need to get away from it all finally takes priority.

Putting hats on and taking them off provides an essential measure of control and boundaries for any caregiving situation. The person wearing the hats remains the same no matter which hat is worn or for how long. In order for a primary caregiver to hold on to sanity in the most trying of circumstances, time has to be spent hatless as well.

The Hats We Wear

The hat analogy can be useful in delegating duties to family members. Looking at the different hats provides a way to spread caregiving tasks to other family members or friends who volunteer to help. The chauffeur's chapeau is one that can be handed off from time to time as can the nurse's hat.

Nurse's Hat

A primary caregiver is likely to don the nurse's hat often. The caregiving nurse learns through on-the-job experience that details count. Managing medications is a large part of this job. It includes monitoring allergies, dosages, refill dates, side effects, and contradictions between medications. When multiple doctors are prescribing for different conditions, having one person keep up with medications can circumvent problems. Some medications can't be taken with food or within certain proximity to food or other medications.

Nurses also deal with taking temperatures and blood pressures and monitoring these closely to determine if a call to the doctor or a trip to the emergency room is necessary. The caregiver wearing a nurse's hat notices skin color and temperature, breathing changes and mobility struggles that may indicate a new condition for observation or treatment.

When a loved one is hospitalized, the nurse's hat is not turned over to the paid staff. Showing knowledge and a willingness to help when those professionals are around makes a difference.

Hospitals are short staffed, and nurses, however well trained, have ridiculous patient loads, so it's advisable to have a family member or other caregiver available for hospital duty. It's even more important in a hospital setting, when patients are recovering and often well medicated for comfort, to have an extra set of eyes and ears to gather information and translate doctor lingo.

Reality Check: Hospital Advocacy. While we like to think our loved one's care is well covered while in the hospital, in reality a caregiver's job expands when hospitalization occurs. Realize that your parent will likely see numerous doctors, and each of these doctors can order tests and change or discontinue medicines your parent has been taking for years. Speaking up about drug and food allergies and keeping up with medication changes requires vigilance that often extends long past visiting hours.

Many times the word never makes it to family members that medicines have been discontinued, so if your parent has a sudden change in behavior or mood, don't assume it's just the illness or the pain medication. If possible, have a family member present each day when the hospitalist (often an internal medicine doctor) and specialists make rounds. Ask questions. Take notes. And don't assume every doctor assigned to your parent's case has a full vision of everything going on. If your parent moves to a care facility for rehabilitation following a hospital stay, ask to see the list of medications the hospital sent with your parent.

Tip: Don't assume your parent leaves the hospital on the same medication she was taking when she entered. Several days after my mother moved to a care facility, I (Candy) became concerned that she had so much edema (swelling). In discussing the situation with the nursing supervisor, I learned the medication she normally took to control fluid was not on the list sent from the hospital. Although the nursing supervisor at the care facility immediately called my mother's cardiologist and got her back on the medication, it took almost a month to get the swelling under control.

Bedpans and Baby Wipes

Kate's Story

"I'd cared for my father in every circumstance, and we'd long moved beyond anything that could be considered father-daughter modesty. I thought we'd gone through it all, but just days before he died, he was obviously uncomfortable. He'd needed diapers only for a couple of days, and he was having trouble relaxing enough to use them. He got more and more agitated.

"'Kate, could you please clean out my rectum?'

"In that moment, my inner little girl shattered. No daughter should have to do that for her father. But the adult loving child who wanted only to bring him peace reached for her nurse's hat, took a deep breath, put on gloves, and did the best she could. Afterward, the adult loving child took her other half, "Little Katie," out onto the porch to have a good cry.

"Much later, I was able to see the grace in those moments. His request was honoring both the love he knew I had for him and the resulting closeness of the long journey we'd traveled together. That he allowed himself to need me in that way was a gift to me, even though I couldn't look at it that way for quite some time."

Linda's Story

"'There isn't a part of my parents I haven't seen or washed. It doesn't bother me anymore,' I told my friend.

"While my friend was horrified, that was our reality. At the time, I was surprised by her shock, but realized that I'd come far in my emotional ability to handle the situations inherent with caring for my parents. I'd emptied catheter bags for each of them, wiped their bottoms, applied cream for hemorrhoids, and given suppositories. I didn't have nursing training; it was on-the-job training. You just learn to do what needs to be done."

If you know you could never get to the point where you'd handle what Kate and Linda have, find someone who can. Learn what care levels and quality standards you can live with and what you can't. Don't feel bad if it's not you. You're doing all you can. Realizing your limits is a sign of grace.

Jenny's Story
"It really bothered me that care staff didn't think it important to wash my mother's hair during a 28-day hospital stay. So I figured out what I needed, found towels and a foaming cleanser for hair and body that requires no rinsing, and washed her hair. We both felt better. Using the cleanser isn't the same as washing with water, but under the circumstances it was a great substitute."

Personal care is a dignity issue for all of us. If your parents don't want you helping with personal care issues, respect that and ask who they're willing to have help them. Personal care isn't optional for you and shouldn't be for them either, even if dealing with the corrective action involves ruffling some feathers.

Perhaps your parent is incontinent due to a virus or a longstanding condition. At this point, you're in a situation similar to having an infant or toddler again. Whether the condition is temporary or permanent, this mind-set is important, so be prepared and have supplies handy. Keep a bag of pads, baby wipes, and even extra clothes with you. Just don't pack one with pink bunnies on the outside! Remember it's essential to maintain dignity.

Amy learned to keep certain supplies in her car after a nasty virus and chemo took their toll on her mother while they were driving across town. The situation was embarrassing for everyone in the car, and Amy was forced to stop and buy underwear, wipes, and pants and put them to immediate use.

Keep Listerine handy, too, not so much for bad breath, but because it is a miracle deodorizer. Put a little on a tissue and wipe it across a surface. It sanitizes and freshens the air immediately.

■■■

Case Manager Hat

Wearing this hat often requires a quiet place, a phone, pen, calculator, calendar, and pencil with eraser. A copy machine and fax are also useful. An all-in-one machine that copies, prints, scans, and faxes can more than pay for itself in reduced hassle and trips to office centers.

The case manager deals with insurance, scheduling, appointments, and treatment glitches, of which there may be many. Case managers must be prepared to make a simple phone call and have it lead to ten more in finding necessary answers. Make notes about your conversations in the doctor's log or incident log in your notebook. Expect frustrations. Occasionally, you may have to take the case manager hat off, go outside, and yell into the wind, releasing some of the pressure.

Another key to management is budgeting plenty of time. If, ideally, one 15-minute call would result in a solution, allow yourself a couple of hours to deal with the issue. You won't feel as much pressure when one call becomes six and you're still struggling to get needed information. Overbooking tasks is the biggest problem when wearing a case manager's hat. The related stress filters down to all the other aspects of getting through the day's challenges, so do yourself a favor and allot extra time.

Adult Loving-Child Cap

This is the one you wear underneath all the others, although you may not recognize that you've slipped it on.

When Elizabeth's father asked about her mother's physical condition for the fourth time in as many weeks, she pulled into a parking space when they reached their destination, but didn't unbuckle her seat belt. Elizabeth knew she needed to calmly and clearly explain things to her father, yet another time. She also realized the importance of curbing her impatience at the repetition. It was a conscious decision on her part—the adult in her taking over for the child inside who wanted her father to be the omniscient one and the comforter. She tucked the little girl away and accepted her role as the adult.

When you realize this hat comes on and off and that you're putting the "little girl" or "little boy" inside you away, you actually start to grieve for the real loss you are experiencing in the relationship you have with your parent (see the Caregiver's Grief section, chapter 21).

Chauffeur's Chapeau

If your parents once enjoyed attending events in tuxedos and glittering gowns, you may want to be chauffeur for a night on the town that lets them get dolled up again and remember the good old days. Find a fancy restaurant, help Mom brush the dust off Dad's good jacket, and drop them off for a good time. They may want you and your spouse to join them, but remember, they dated and dreamed and enjoyed time with each other before you came along. They might like to do it again, even if you help a little or they feel silly at first.

If your parents aren't the type for fancy restaurants, find out what works for them with their health, medical challenges, and finances. It'll be encouraging for you to facilitate some fun at a time in their lives when their bodies often deny them even the simplest pleasures. Perhaps setting up a dinner with friends they haven't seen for a while will do the trick. It really can bring a boost to everyone involved.

Listening Best-Friend Visor

Perhaps you slip into this role when driving your parent to an appointment or having a casual phone or waiting-room conversation. Suddenly you're laughing together over silly things or finishing each other's sentences. You'll find you're talking about things the way you do with friends, even sharing things you may never have thought you'd share with a parent. You might even confess "wild-oat-sowing" stories together. It's amazing to realize that your parent can be a friend too. For the moment, they finally see you as more than just their child. And you are.

Psychologist's Cap

When you suddenly realize that you're thinking of how to deliver certain news because you know how a parent's mind works, you've slipped this hat on. You time what you say and how you say it so information is received in the best possible way—not to manipulate but because you care about how the news will affect your parents. You're aware not only of their physical health, but their emotional health as well, and want to help them process issues or situations with as little anxiety as possible.

Parisian Beret

If Dad spent part of his life with the baguettes, wine, and cheese of Paris as his daily fare, travel those streets with him again. Wearing the hat he gives you with his stories will provide an opportunity to see the man behind the father role in which you know him.

Or instead of the beret, maybe your mom grew up on a farm, milking cows and riding in rodeos. So be willing to pick up a cowgirl hat and head on down to the barnyard for some great stories.

These hats will become some of your most treasured in years to come.

Wide-Brimmed Sun Hat

This is the hat you wear to give yourself a sense of personal drama and a mental break from reality. You deserve a little sunshine and pampering, so take out your Southern Belle Bonnet, dip your feet in some water, and envision yourself dangling a foot over the side of the boat your Prince Charming is rowing across still, gentle waters. In actuality, you may be sticking your foot in the plastic pool in the backyard while the kids are squealing nearby. Or you might prefer a golf cap, tennis visor, or a hat with the insignia of your favorite team, but you get the picture.

The Parent Hat

Once a parent, always a parent, even when you're parenting your own parents.

I (Kim) remember realizing that, because I was spending so much time and energy caring for my parents, I hadn't been there for my kids. I didn't know whether to feel good or bad about it—good that I'd realized it or bad that it happened. But it did increase my awareness of how I needed to make each moment count.

We had an annual beach trip with extended family. But because I was knee deep in caregiving for my parents, it was hard to plan for the trip, let alone be excited about it. After much logistical juggling, we made it to the beach.

As I walked and talked with my oldest daughter along the shore, I noticed she was calling me Mama instead of Mom. A preteen, she hadn't called me Mama in years. The next day when we went for a walk, she opted for the more engaging term, Mommy, and held my hand. The realization of what had happened in those two walks crashed over me with more power than any wave could have. I wanted to cry when I realized with great sadness how few "Mommy moments" I'd had, and yet I wanted to shout joyful praise that my daughter had not forgotten that I'd always been her Mommy.

Amid the laundry, chores, carpool duties, homework papers to sign, and multiple aspects of parenting, exhausted caregivers have to interact purposely with their children on a more relaxed level. It's a necessity. There really isn't a downtime-with-your-kids hat, so maybe you should stop by a craft shop, purchase materials, and get your kids to help you make one. Involve them in the process of decommissioning your many caregiving hats, even if only momentarily. This can work for toddlers to teens. You might even make a full event of it, allowing your children to create a general mom or dad hat for time spent in family mode, and perhaps one designed by each child for your special one-on-one time with them. Even if you cannot wear them very often, knowing they're there will help you remember to make time for being a parent to your children.

The Wedding Veil

Married caregivers need to remember that they have a spouse. No matter what type of relationship you have with your spouse, it is a precious part of your life. Sometimes you lose sight of that when you arrive home after an all-day trip to the ER, and the first thing your spouse says is, "What's for dinner?" But dig that wedding veil out of storage frequently and put it on, even if only in your mind. It's perhaps one of the hardest hats to consciously pull out and put on.

We depend on our spouses and the relationship we have with them even if we, or they, don't acknowledge the bond, which often happens the longer we're married. That's why it's important to plan time alone with your spouse. Dating your spouse is more important now than ever.

A spouse can easily give in to insecurities if you're suddenly sucked back into nearly constant interaction with your parents. Marriage means you leave parents and cleave to your mate. But the lines of leaving and cleaving blur when parents suddenly need lots of your time, attention, and emotional support.

Even the most understanding, kind, and caring spouse needs to feel his role in your life and special connection to you is still important. So find space in your heart and mind to remember special moments, memories, and interests only the two of you share.

Time with your spouse can be as simple as dinner on the deck followed by a snuggle-on-the-couch rented movie. If you're resourceful, it may be a weekend away together. Ask your spouse to make the plans. He'll be glad you thought of it.

Too tired for the ooh-la-la that can become an expectation when time alone is planned? Talk about it. Being open helps desensitize the issue, especially if you talk about it before it becomes an in-the-moment issue. Some caregivers are so physically involved in their roles that they want time where they aren't touched physically or emotionally by anyone. It isn't a spousal issue; it's simply sensory overload on multiple levels.

Sometimes planning ahead for time together revives interest in physical intimacy. Even if it's just a Saturday night at home, you can sneak a few moments to feel womanly and pick up a new nightgown on the way home or have your nails done to spark your feelings of femininity.

Have the goal of maintaining intimacy that works for your relationship. It will be good for both of you to connect in ways that are sacred to you as a couple.

■■■

Not sure what hat to wear or when? Remember they're all with you all the time. Consciously choosing to take them on and off empowers the caregiver, the spouse, the adult child, the mommy, and you, the beautiful compassionate person underneath them all.

■■ Through the Looking Glass ■■

Lessons learned while caregiving

In the mirror: Lois, a 78-year-old mother of eight adult children, who works part-time

"I became my mother's caregiver when my father died suddenly. Mother was from Finland and very independent. When she was in her thirties, she was proactive about her health, but later in life, put off healthcare. By the time her ovarian cancer was discovered, it had metastasized. Although she didn't want to go to the hospital, we took her there when she became too weak for me to handle and for pain management. Then she went to a nursing home.

"Shortly after her death, my husband, who had been a smoker, started needing oxygen. Over five years his health declined. He was hospitalized a number of times for congestive heart failure. It was quite a task keeping track of his medications, his vitamins, inhalers, and managing his diabetes by monitoring his food and insulin injections. He was Scotch-Irish and very stubborn. He wanted to do things for himself, but began experiencing dementia. Little by little, I realized I had to take over the medications and the bills. He realized it too.

"Emphysema finally took its toll. He got to the place he couldn't walk even ten feet. By then I had home health nurses helping. Eventually his heart gave out.

"These caregiving experiences helped me decide that I'm not going to do the things my mother and husband did. I have checkups and preventative screenings and take care of health issues as they arise.

"To some extent I enabled my husband and mother because they didn't do anything for themselves, and I took care of them. But my goal is to make things easier for my children. I talk to them and express my preferences. I own my own home, but I realize I may have to sell it if I ever need assisted living. My kids know my financial status and can handle a budget.

"The Lord blessed me by giving me a glimpse ahead of time of the health and financial challenges that could come as I age. This has helped me prepare. I've made my wishes clear to the children too—don't make me hang on. The good Lord is my best friend. I'm not at all afraid to meet Him, and I don't want anything keeping me from that."

Viewpoint:

When big, strong Daddy needs very personal help
—Candy's experience

From the time I was a little girl, I'd always viewed my daddy as the funniest, smartest, sweetest, strongest man in the world. He could do anything, that is until cancer wrapped its tendrils around him, sapping his strength.

Several months into the caregiving journey, Daddy was having a relatively good day, despite the fact that he had been very ill days prior. I asked if there was anything I could do for him.

"I sure would like to get in the shower and wash my head," he replied.

While I knew it would challenge him physically, I wanted to grant his request. With effort, we made it down the hall and into the bathroom. I helped him get undressed and seated on the shower chair, then got him bathed, dressed, and back down the hall to his favorite chair before we both ran out of energy.

As I walked toward the kitchen to prepare lunch, Daddy grabbed my hand, looked in my eyes, and said, "Thank you. I feel better than I have in a long time."

Being this involved in a parent's personal care is not something you ever imagine having to do, but God equips you for these moments.

Living Water

> Let us not become weary in doing good, for at the proper
> time we will reap a harvest if we do not give up. Therefore, as
> we have opportunity, let us do good to all people, especially
> to those who belong to the family of believers (Galatians
> 6:9-10).

Do you ever get to the point you're so exhausted that all you want to do is stare? Many components combine to sap the caregiver's energy—processing churning emotions surrounding role reversal, lending constant encouragement to our parents, thinking on multiple levels for long periods of time, and desiring a different kind of "normal" all factor in. And let's face it, there are days when we go to bed weary and wake up the next morning still as exhausted as we were the night before.

Although the good that we're doing in caring for our aging parents has benefits, we may be too tired to notice. But while Galatians 6 encourages us not to totally give in to weariness, there comes a point when you need help.

Within the family of believers are those who are praying for you and willing to lend practical support. It's okay to call in reinforcements when you're weary and it's okay to admit you can't do it all. There's only so much strength and support you can offer your parents before you have nothing left to give them or your own family. Allow friends and family to help while you take some time to refresh, restore, and reconnect with others in your life.

Additional Information

From the Princess Margaret Hospital in Canada, the Caring to the End of Life website focuses on palliative care for cancer patients, but also offers concise definitions of caregiving roles and information on many care topics. Go to www.caringtotheend.ca/body.php?id=21.

Chapter 14

When Home Care Isn't the Best Care
Lifestyle and Care Options

I n general, the level or amount of care provided by a primary caregiver
increases along with the age of one's parents. Some periods may offer
a bit more reprieve than others, but as aging continues, the challenges
increase, so be prepared.

Perhaps your parents have been living independently in your hometown and doing just fine. Maybe a health scare or temporary condition
caused you to begin thinking. Roll with it. Investigate. The more you
know about the services available before you need them, the easier necessary decisions will be later. Tour communities near your home or
near the home of the ones in your family who will provide the majority of support care.

Whether or not you've tackled the subject with parents yet, you
can scope out potential alternate living arrangements before a change
is warranted. Constraints on the primary and supporting caregivers,
level of assistance needed by a parent, or a parent's long-term prognosis may all contribute to the decision that home care for your parent
isn't the best option, even if you wish it were.

There are more distinguishable levels of care offered by outside
sources. The majority are scaled or rated based on independence of the
patient. "Retirement Community" is the term often used for multi-
level care facilities. They often encompass a large campus, offering
different levels of care, usually in multiple buildings, and with a wide
variety of staff. You may see independent living, assisted living, and

skilled care (nursing) centers or any mixture of these in any one community. The amount of care given at each level varies and depends on the management. Many communities are owned by large corporations, so it is important to check the stability of the parent company when considering such alternatives.

Independent Living

This could mean living in a single-family home or apartment without assistance. As in any home situation, family members or paid caregivers can offer aid in this setting. Sometimes in-home help provides more care for a parent than he would receive if he moved into a facility. However, in-home care, especially to cover 24 hours, is more expensive.

Some communities have strict guidelines for determining resident placement, but health challenges and independence levels don't always fall on a straight continuum. The potential red flag is assessing independence. Some communities will not allow a person or couple to move into independent living unless they can walk independently or can verify that they will be safe using a wheelchair if they have been using one most of their lives.

When looking at a retirement community that offers multiple support levels, ask beyond the obvious questions of cost and amenities:

- What circumstances would require a move between levels of care?

- What temporary options are available if a short-term situation requires additional help, such as recovering from a hip replacement?

If you're looking at a community that does not offer multiple levels of care, see where additional support is offered locally. Discover what is available—how accessible it is (is there a waiting list?) and if it is affordable.

Within the realm of independent living within a retirement community, there are also several cost considerations. Some communities offer month-to-month apartment rentals. Others require an upfront fee and monthly rent. Still others offer the purchase of homes, patio homes, or apartments, which can be resold later. Each option comes with a monthly fee, called by a variety of names. Services may include meals, activities, transportation, utilities, general maintenance, and cleaning of the home. It takes time to go through all the options and match needs and potential use to find the best value.

Modifications to the House

If you're planning to keep your parent at home as long as possible, you may have to make some modifications for the sake of safety, ease, and navigability. These modifications may include widening doors to accommodate a walker or wheelchair, installing ramps or rails, making a shower handicapped-accessible, adding an elevated toilet seat, acquiring a shower/bath chair, removing thick carpeting and rugs, putting all lights in a room on a single switch, and rearranging furniture, closets, cabinets, drawers, and small appliances for easier access.

Seniors also need help with chores such as changing light bulbs, yard maintenance, and caring for pets. A good way to see where your parents need assistance or modifications is to spend the day shadowing them, watching what they avoid because it is too difficult and seeing things they attempt that could create a falling or tripping hazard or foreshadow other safety issues. By taking the time to observe and then make adjustments, you may be able to afford your parents the ability to live at home safely a little longer.

Emergency Link

You may want to investigate alarm-type services available for senior adults living independently that provide a "panic button" worn around the neck. While the level of service varies, most are for emergency purposes—a fall, heart attack, or breathing problems—rather than serving as a monitoring system. If you procure such a service for your parents, make sure they know the difference so they don't have a false sense of security. In other words, the service will respond only if they push the button. Also, make sure they comprehend that the service is for medical emergencies, not for help finding their glasses. Another thing to stress is the service works only within range of the monitoring box placed in their home. It won't work at the park down the street or at the mall cafeteria. Used properly, this service can provide an added level of confidence and security for aging parents and their children.

Nutrition

As parents age, proper nutrition may become an issue, particularly if they live alone. Medications and health conditions often change a sense of what tastes good, so foods your parent once enjoyed may hold little appeal now. And you've probably noticed they are much more vocal about their food likes and dislikes, which may change weekly or daily.

One thing to watch for is how much salt your parent uses. With changing tastes, seniors often try to compensate by salting foods excessively. This especially becomes a problem for those with heart conditions because of the potential for fluid retention.

Another concern comes when parents fail to get adequate nutrition because preparing a meal seems like too much bother. You may want to see if your community offers a program that delivers one meal a day to senior citizens. These programs are often free and provide your parent at least one nutritious meal each weekday.

Proper nutrition is especially important for parents with conditions such as diabetes or low iron. You may need to encourage your parents to drink canned supplement shakes if their eating habits are poor. Several brands are available, some with low sugar content.

While some seniors have a hard time getting enough calories, others need to watch calorie consumption because of a more sedentary lifestyle. Indulging in salty junk food or rich desserts seems to be the downfall of many and can lead to serious health complications.

If possible, encourage the incorporation of the following foods in their diets:

- Protein—egg whites, lean meats (turkey, fish, chicken), beans, and peas
- Fiber—whole grain breads, fruits
- Fluids—six to eight glasses of water, juice, or milk per day
- Good fats—nuts, olive oil, avocado
- Vitamins and minerals—green vegetables, raisins, cheese, and yogurt

Home Care

If a parent is in her own home or a family member's home, look into options regarding home health services and sitters. In certain situations, a person can receive support care in the home while recovering from a surgery or for a longer term depending on need. Guidelines for the length of time home health organizations can provide care vary. It is helpful to know how to contact these support agencies before the need arises.

Most hospitals offer discharge support, so if you are not knowledgeable about what is available or what you may need, counseling and referrals are available before leaving the hospital. There may not be time to investigate additional options other than those offered through the hospital, but at least there is help for such transitions.

Many home health organizations use an approach similar to physical therapy services. They see their job as one of education, teaching the patient what he or she or the family needs to do. Once home health discharges a patient, it's up to the patient whether to follow the instruction. The same is true for many related services. Limits may be placed on what services can be offered and how long you may receive them.

> My father loved the attention he received while in the care of a physical therapist, and the sessions were productive. But when he was discharged from the program, he lost interest and would not do the exercises he had been taught. Aside from tying those elastic bands on him ourselves and becoming

his personal trainers, Mom and I were at a loss as to how to motivate him to follow through.—Kim

In this situation, it's a case of choosing your battles. Find a way to re-qualify for the service, become the instructor, or accept that your parent isn't going to put forth the effort.

Sitters

Professional services and individuals offer specialized services for home care. These may or may not be covered by insurance.

Some sitters work for agencies, but many work independently. Sitters come into the home, apartment, or even hospital room to provide very basic services. Some home health organizations have a list of sitters available, but many can be found by word-of-mouth referrals. Typically, sitters have limits on the duties they will and will not perform. Some provide light housework and others just "sit," watching the patient and providing care when needed, much like a babysitter for children. Most sitters charge by the hour. Fees depend on duties, number of hours, and qualifications (see chapter 23, "Forms").

When hiring a sitter, a pre-service interview is essential. It's important to match personalities.

■■■

Situations where a sitter's service may be helpful

Vacation time with your own family

One day a week to provide you a break

Extra support (when caring for parents in your own home) at a time of day when your kids need help with homework and you're cooking dinner

Driving parents to appointments or handling errands

Extra in-hospital care, or care for the other parent while one is in the hospital

■■■

Expectations for services should be as clear as possible. Establish a basis for building trust. Approach hiring a sitter for your parents the same way you would find a sitter for your children. If you're completely in the dark when you start the interview process, allow the sitter to ask questions about the situation and offer suggestions for services he or she may provide.

Word of Caution: The majority of sitters will fall into the "gem" category, but it is crucial to check references, even if you feel an instant connection with a sitter. You're likely to be leaving them in a situation where important personal and financial information is easy to access, so references are important.

Reality Check 1: While it may seem hyper-vigilant to hire a sitter to watch a parent while he or she is in the hospital, sometimes having that extra pair of eyes and ears offers the best care and peace of mind. Some sitters work in teams or are willing to help you create a team to provide round-the-clock coverage for your loved one. You can hire sitters for hours, a series of days, or weekend work. Again, each sitter should be interviewed.

Paying a sitter on an hourly basis is much more expensive than assisted living and some skilled nursing care. The financial support for long-term sitter care needs to be factored into care planning.

In addition, some sitters prefer to be paid in cash. This is not a reflection on caregiving ability and it is not your job to monitor whether a sitter reports income. But it is well within your rights to ask for receipts, which are required for reimbursement from insurance companies that provide in-home care benefits. Make sure you know what information needs to be included on the receipt or make up your own form that covers insurance requirements. This is one hassle that using an agency may help you avoid.

Reality Check 2: If you are providing care for your parent in your own home, and you tend to be a neat freak, get over it! Accept that your house will be filled with supplies and equipment. For the time being, this is your new normal. Now is not the time to attempt to earn a Susie Homemaker badge.

Assisted and Skilled Care

Long-term healthcare insurance policies take effect when a parent needs assisted living. An assisted-living situation with the support of insurance benefits may be less expensive than an independent apartment or home with paid caregivers. But not many people have thought ahead to purchase this insurance.

One issue to be aware of with assisted living is the size of the living quarters. Moving from a four-bedroom house to a space barely large enough for two small bedrooms and one living area is not only dramatic but traumatic. Accept and understand the emotional trauma that can come from such a life change. Your parents need to have at least some of their own things around them for comfort. The same is applicable even if you're looking at such a transition for only one parent.

When evaluating living arrangements that involve staff member support, there are specific things to look for that would be valuable in both assisted-care and skilled-care situations.

What to Look For

First, of course, is to determine if the services provided meet your parent's needs. Assisted living in one facility may include bathing and laundry service, while in another, laundry service is not offered unless skilled care is utilized. For multi-care-level communities, looking at a list of services provided at each care level will help match need to placement. You are not likely to find a perfect fit, so prepare to make some compromises.

Investigate the number of patients or residents assigned to each staff member. But don't be misled by numbers. Facilities readily offer figures based solely on employee and patient numbers. Management may be included in these figures, yet these employees may not actually provide hands-on care. It takes time to evaluate how long it takes to provide the services your parent needs and whether there is enough staff to do so.

Find out how many residents one staff member is responsible for bathing in a day or on a given shift, and what that staff member's other duties include. The answers will let you know if the staff actually has enough time to do the job to meet your standards of care.

How does the patient/staff ratio change by shift? Many dementia and Alzheimer's patients have more difficulties at night, yet that may be when there are fewer staff members available.

How does the training level of the staff change throughout the day? Not all staff members have the same training, certification, and abilities. Who is on duty, and when, can affect quality of care. If no registered nurse is on duty at night, can certain medications be given if they are needed?

Additional things to consider:

Medication Management: Many facilities use their own pharmacies or have specific procedures in place for managing medications.

- What steps are taken to get, change, or refill prescriptions?
- How long does it take to get new medications started?
- What action is taken if side effects occur or are suspected?
- Who monitors whether a new medication seems to be working?

Bathing:
- Is bathing service offered?
- Does this mean a once-a-week trip to a communal-style shower room down the hall?
- Sponge baths only?
- If your parent has a room with a private bath, will someone come in and assist? If so, when?
- Bathing service schedules are common. Can you get Dad to compromise on having his shower at night rather than in the morning to fit the schedule?

Appointments and Transportation:

- How are doctor's appointments, physical therapy, and medical tests handled?

- How far in advance does staff need to be notified of your parent's appointment?

- Who makes the appointment if your parent becomes ill with a sinus infection or other ailment?

- Will the facility ensure patients get to appointments on time and that they don't have to wait a long time for return transport?

- Will a staff member be in the examining room and take notes?

- Will a staff member set up transportation to tests that the doctor orders?

A family member may be able to handle such appointments whether or not a care facility offers support in this area. But what if that caregiver has his own emergency? Whether you initially plan to use those services or not, find out what the facility provides. Knowing what support is available offers peace of mind even if it isn't all utilized at once.

Emergency Care:

- What steps are taken and who is available to handle emergency situations?

- Some facilities offer call buttons in assisted-living and skilled-care rooms. If so, who answers the calls, who responds, and what is the response time?

- Is there enough support staff to take over regular care of residents while emergency situations are handled?

- Falling is one of the most common accidents among the elderly. If a fall occurs (and it can happen even under the most watchful eye), what is the protocol?

- Is EMS called first to take your parent to the hospital? Or are you called first to make a decision based on staff members' initial assessment?

Laundry:

- Will all of your parent's laundry be done on site?

- Will linens be changed and washed as often as you want? You may have to provide your own laundry detergent or do your parent's laundry if you don't want items washed in the institutional products the facility uses. Your parent may prefer her own sheets to the ones available at the facility. Consider this: Your mom loves her 400-count buttercream-colored sheets. She's agreed to have them cleaned with the rest of the laundry done in the assisted living community she's chosen. Will they make it back to her bed and not her neighbor's, or is it better if you buy a second set and wash them yourself? If you do that, will someone change the sheets for her? Details matter when matching services to needs.

Facility Pharmacy

Many facilities use a contracted pharmacy in their skilled nursing center. All medicines must be purchased and dispensed through this pharmacy. The cost will appear on your parent's monthly bill from the facility or be billed directly to his drug insurance provider.

Skilled/Nursing Care

In a community setting, the skilled-care support needs to be investigated in the same manner as an assisted-living situation for patient/staff ratio and supervision. Here, too, insurance plays a major role. A majority of seniors utilize Medicare as their primary insurance. Medicare must approve the level of care and the facility in which it is given.

Medicare then pays the difference in amounts charged, negotiated, and covered by additional insurances. The remaining balance, if any, comes out of the patient's pocket. If a facility is not certified by Medicare, none of the charges are covered by Medicare and many secondary insurance companies will not approve payment either.

Patient/staff ratio and supervision are among Medicare's qualifiers for facilities. Though your standards are likely higher, having Medicare approval is a starting point.

It is more difficult for smaller skilled-care facilities to gain Medicare approval. If that's the case, find out why, and make sure the standards you set for your parent's care are being met.

Another issue with skilled and nursing care is the use of doctors and hospitals. Some facilities require their patients to utilize a staff physician and services provided by specific hospitals if hospitalization or outpatient services are required. This may or may not work within your insurance guidelines and may not meet your needs.

If Mom has a general physician she and you communicate well with, but the facility requires her to change to its physician, that may reduce her level of comfort and the continuation of care she receives from specialists she is currently seeing. Medication changes may also be a concern. While there may be no other option, be aware of what to look for and ask about before making a transition into skilled care.

Reality Check: Discussing life goals before challenges hit can help parents determine the need for long-term healthcare insurance. Even if you discussed issues a decade before you became more involved in their care, you may realize having your parents move in with you or another family member probably isn't going to work. In that case, at least look into long-term care insurance and weigh the costs. The younger your parent is when the insurance is purchased, the lower the premiums. Like all insurance you buy, you may never need it and may think you've wasted the premiums. But if utilized, long-term insurance could save you far more financially that you ever spend on premiums.

Understanding "Bed Hold" Fees

Many care facilities require a "bed hold" fee if your loved one is hospitalized. This is usually an out-of-pocket fee because insurance providers will not pay a per-day hospital charge and a care facility bed fee for the same dates of service. If you choose not to pay the fee to hold the bed at the care facility, most require you to clear out all personal items from the room, including furniture, by 5:00 p.m. the day your parent enters the hospital. And there is no guarantee a bed will be available for your parent at the same facility once he or she is released from the hospital.

Making the decision about whether to pay this fee is difficult because, more than likely, your parent is experiencing a health crisis, and your focus is on your parent's condition. To aid your decision, ask the ER doctor about a projected course of treatment and an estimate of the days required for diagnostic testing. Also, check with the admissions coordinator at the care facility regarding bed availability. If eight beds are available and the projected stay in the hospital is five days, it may be best to release your parent's bed at the care facility. Otherwise you may have to fork over roughly $1000 or more out-of-pocket. Conversely, if your parent's projected stay in the hospital is 48 hours, it may be worth the $400 so you don't have to remove everything from the room and have your parent return to a new room and roommate once released from the hospital.

Tip: If your parent is hospitalized for three days or more, not including time spent in the ER or the day of discharge, Medicare coverage for rehabilitative services kicks in again for twenty days at 100 percent once your parent returns to a care facility. After twenty days, Medicare pays 80 percent of the bed fee and supplemental insurance the other 20 percent up to day 100.

When There Is No Money

While skilled care and assisted living are wonderful options, unless your parent has long-term care insurance, money can become an overwhelming issue. If your parent doesn't have much in the way of liquid assets, you may find locating the cash to cover a $5500/month semi-private, skilled-care bed or a $3000/month semiprivate, assisted-living bed a major problem. (These costs vary greatly, of course, in different parts of the country.)

So what do you do when your parent has no money? If you're not careful, you'll quickly deplete your own savings, so now is the time to begin searching for hidden assets. You should consult your parent's tax preparer before doing anything, but here are a few options to consider with your parent or your siblings:

- Sell or rent your parent's house.

- If it seems likely your parent will come home at some point and you don't want to sell, look into securing a reverse mortgage or line of credit on her house.

- Liquidate antiques, jewelry, guns, cars, or collections.

- Sell rental property or land.

- Investigate in-home respite care (see chapter 6 under Additional Information).

- Determine if your parent is eligible for VA benefits.

In the Know Regarding VA Benefits

My (Candy's) father was a WWII veteran, but once he got home from years of service abroad, including a stint as a POW, he wanted nothing else to do with the military. He refused to apply for veteran's benefits. But now, 18 years after his death, my mother could use the help, so I decided to investigate. Here's what I learned:

- Who is eligible?—A veteran who has served more than 30 days or his current wife. (A former wife and a current widow cannot both apply at the same time.)

- There is no limitation on when a widow can file following a veteran's death as long as she hasn't remarried.

- Where/how do I apply?—The best way to file for benefits is to go to your local county Veterans Affairs (VA) office. You can file online, but each situation is different and reviewed case by case. A VA officer may ask questions that bring important information to light, information that is crucial to your receiving benefits.

- What documents will I need?—Military discharge certificate, picture ID of the person applying, Social Security number of the veteran and the person applying (if different), marriage certificate, divorce decree (if divorced), and information about financial assets. (Be sure to give accurate financial information to avoid overpayment, which you will have to later return.)

- What type of benefits are available?—Potential benefits include: disability compensation, pension, healthcare, vocational rehabilitation, education and training, life insurance, home loans, burial, and death pension.

- How will you receive benefits?—The VA prefers direct deposit to a checking account, but will also mail checks for those who do not have a checking account.

- How long will it be before I receive benefits?—You should receive notification within 30 days that your case is under consideration. This may be followed by a request for additional information. It could take up to 90 days or longer before benefits begin or your claim is denied.

- Don't believe myths about losing current benefits if you ask for a review of eligibility for additional benefits. Ask a VA officer for clarification.

Making Tough Decisions

While physical needs are usually the determining factor in deciding to move a parent to a facility, sometimes the emotional atmosphere is an issue for deciding when home care isn't best.

Several years after her father's death, Holly and her husband decided her mother should move in with them. Their decision was based on issues with medication and financial mismanagement.

They built a new house with a mother-in-law suite and established rules that allowed them to preserve some family time independent of Holly's mom. There were challenges, and often Holly's mother's old patterns of emotional and verbal abuse came into play.

Holly's siblings offered brief periods of respite by having their mother stay with them several weeks during the year, but ultimately, what seemed like a good solution years before began to deteriorate.

When Holly and her husband encountered a particularly challenging period with one of their teenagers, Holly's relationship with her mother was also strained.

"I knew when mother verbally abused me in front of my teenager that the time had come when I couldn't continue to care for her in our home," Holly said. "I begged Mother not to continue the conversation with my teen present, but she would not hush. I was faced with a very difficult decision. But after much prayer I knew that it was more important to work through issues with my teen and strive to make that relationship a quality one rather than allow my mother to stay with us, even though telling her she had to move out would risk making my relationship with her worse. There have always been issues with our relationship, and I knew I couldn't sacrifice my relationship with my child for my mother."

■■ Through the Looking Glass ■■

Leaving the security of home

In the mirror: June, age 80, living in a bedroom community outside Charleston, West Virginia

"Buck and I spent five years of our retirement in beautiful North Carolina. After his death, I remained there three more years, perfectly independent in our lovely home. But my children pressured me to move closer to them.

"Finally, I sold my home and moved, but I have spent much of the past eight years knowing I made a mistake and wishing I had stayed in North Carolina.

"I know there are many reasons for moving closer to family, especially health and financial considerations, but I didn't have those problems. Too many times children encourage a living parent to move away from everything familiar when it's not always the best choice. If a parent's mind is clear and she is able to take care of herself and her needs, then I say, 'Leave her alone.' Even though I didn't have family in North Carolina, I had my neighbors, friends, doctors I felt comfortable with, and my church family.

"Most of all, I could drive wherever I needed to go.

"I realize it eases the worry of children if their aging parent is closer, but it's important to look at the point of view of the parent. In my situation, I had more quality time with my children when I lived far away because when they came to visit for a few days, they left their other duties at home. But now, they are busy living their own lives and only call now and then. One of my children has actually moved several states away.

"Finding my place here has been extremely difficult, but I've adjusted. I've become an active volunteer in a local elementary school and was awarded the prestigious Jefferson Award, Hometown Hero, and special recognition by the board of education for volunteering more than most retirees do. I am a retired elementary teacher, love children, and have always volunteered in many ways. Some of my motivation has been trying to keep busy in a place where I felt strange.

"I've joined some travel groups, senior citizens clubs, and a church with lots of widows, so now I'm happier. But I know I would have been just fine, happier, safer, and more secure, if I'd stayed where I was. It's so very important to look at both sides of the issue of moving an elderly parent before encouraging a move before it's necessary."

Viewpoint:

When Kim's mother moved in

My mother moved in a year to the day after my father died. Mom's health challenges made it impractical for her to live completely on her own. The retirement community that met my parents' needs as a couple wasn't meeting hers as a widow. She paid for the addition of a room and porch onto our house, and we shifted the family around so she had her own apartment that combined the addition with our old master bedroom and bath. It gave her privacy, but also gave us all the benefit of being close. It worked out better than any of us imagined. She and I grew closer, and her grandchildren made connections with her they wouldn't have otherwise. But that doesn't mean everything was smooth.

When I was little, the kitchen was always her kingdom and she was its queen. When she wanted to help by doing some dishes or tidying up, I got jumpy. If she was in "my kitchen," I felt out of place or like I shouldn't be there. It was a territorial thing I never considered. Helping out with some of the household chores made her feel useful and needed, but it was hard for me to feel okay about not being the one doing them if she got to them first. However, I realized when she helped, I could get other things done. The key to making it all work was understanding our own control issues and need for boundaries. I can imagine how difficult it would've been if we hadn't been able to talk things out. It was a real learning process for both of us.

With her gone now, sometimes I still expect her to be rattling the dishes in the kitchen or walking around the corner. Though those memories cause moments of grief, they are fleeting. I treasure the time we had to be so close.

Living Water

> Now we know that if the earthly tent we live in is destroyed,
> we have a building from God, an eternal house in heaven,
> not built by human hands (2 Corinthians 5:1).

While I enjoy being outside, tent camping has never held much allure for me. When it comes time to go to bed, I'm ready for a nice bug-free, non-lumpy, cozy environment. And when you think about the safety and security of a house versus a tent, there really isn't much comparison. So when Paul talks about our bodies as earthly tents, I get the message—life, as we know it now, is temporary.

While it's not a very comforting thought, with every tick of the clock, our earthly bodies are wasting away. Our faces get more wrinkled, and it's a little harder to remember names. With each passing year, physical endurance wanes, and the enthusiasm we once had for endeavors diminishes. The tent is wearing out.

Because my father was a builder, I know how houses are constructed. From the time I was a small child, I watched construction from the ground up. When I think about the care my father took to build sturdy houses, I'm reminded that although my dad built the best houses possible, my heavenly dwelling is far more wonderful than anything my daddy ever constructed. What a comfort to believe and know the security of eternity.

If you're uncertain about life after death, take time now to investigate what it means to be a follower of Jesus Christ. Maybe you've put off the decision for some reason, or never taken the time to think about anything other than day-to-day urgencies. But right now is the right time. Today can be the day you nail down the security of your eternity. I encourage you to talk to the pastor of a Bible-believing church or to explore some good books, such as John R.W. Stott's *Basic Christianity* and Andy Stanley's *How Good Is Good Enough?*

Additional Information

Medicare benefits booklet: www.medicare.gov/Publications/Pubs/pdf/10050.pdf.

U.S. Department of Veterans Affairs Benefits: www.vba.va.gov/VBA/.

Home safety checklist: www.strengthforcaring.com/daily-care/home-safety-modifications-home-safety/home-safety-checklist/.

Senior housing options vary by community. The following two websites can help you find what is available where you need it: www.seniorhousingnet.com and www.myinhomehealth.com.

Chapter 15

Money Management

Becoming Involved in Your Parents' Finances

Jean and her husband, Mike, live independently. Their income is enough to cover expenses and have a little for an occasional trip.

When Mike had a sudden stroke and was in rehab for four months, their son Ed, who lives locally, came by every day and helped his mother pay bills. She'd never paid bills or handled insurance claims and payments before, so together they went through everything, balanced account statements, and got an overview of how Mike had things set up. Once a month, Ed's brother Evan reviewed everything with them so all had an understanding of the finances.

After six months, Mike recovered sufficiently to resume his former duties. Though hesitant to disrupt the smooth operation they'd put into place, Jean, Ed, and Evan knew it was important to allow Mike to take over the finances again, if he was able. Ed and Evan sat down with their father, explained what they'd done, and asked Mike to do the bills with Jean in the future so if another crisis arose, she'd know how to manage. They decided Ed and Evan would review things once a month so they'd stayed informed too. Additionally, Ed was added as a signatory on his parents' accounts so that he could provide immediate backup if needed.

■■■

Your assignment: Put yourself and your family into the above scenario.

Would it work with your family dynamics? If not, why? This is where you need to begin work.

Where to Begin

Money management is a hot button for caregivers. Issues with money often connect people to emotions, control sensitivities, and even insecurities for both the parent and the child. Desensitizing the money issue with communication is essential. We've addressed how to cool off hot issues in chapter 9, so let's get down to the basics with a series of questions to help you wrap your mind around this tough issue.

A crucial element for success is remembering to leave judgmental tendencies at the door. You're about to step into an area your parents have likely handled on their own for longer than you've been alive. And they probably handle their finances differently than you handle yours. Take out any idea of "right" or "wrong" and let the goal of security set the tone.

Gather information as objectively and openly as you can before deciding what, if any, action should be taken. Remember, your job is to help provide safety and security, not necessarily to take over.

The Basics

1. Are your parents capable of handling their finances? (Your opinion about that may be different from theirs!) What plans do they have for when they are not able to manage the day-to-day or monthly expenses on their own?

2. Who's in charge of what? Does Dad handle all the bills and your mom have a grocery allowance? If so,

   • What happens to the monthly bills if Dad is gone or incapacitated?

   • Are any monthly bills automatically paid from their bank account(s)?

3. Do your parents own their home? Is there a mortgage payment?

4. Medical costs: Some are fortunate to have enough insurance coverage that this is not a worry, but that is rare rather than the norm.

   • How are your parents equipped to handle medical expenses, particularly hospitalizations?

   • Have they planned for any long-term care expenses?

5. Is a monthly budget in place?

   • What is your parents' monthly income?

   • What are their monthly expenses?

   • If there is a shortage/overage, how is that handled?

   • How are bills handled that aren't paid monthly (things such as taxes and insurance premiums)?

   • How do they handle gift expenses? Do they budget or save for Christmas shopping, birthdays, graduations, weddings?

When you feel secure with the questions above, dig deeper and look at long- and short-term handling of money. Below are "watchpoints" for safety and security.

Banking

1. Do your parents pay all their bills by check and write a check for cash to have cash on hand?

   • Watch for visual or physical impairments that make writing checks difficult.

   • Watch to see that the checkbook register is kept current and that it is reconciled each month with the account statements.

   • Watch for automatic deposit/withdrawal transactions and verify.

2. Do they use a bank/debit card?

- Record PINs in a safe place.

- Make sure that purchases are recorded in the account register.

3. Do they use credit cards?

- Keep a record of the account numbers, PINs, and customer service phone numbers.

- Reconcile account statements soon after they arrive to guard against fraudulent use.

- Write down the number to call in case the card is lost or stolen (you can make a photocopy of the card, front and back).

- Verify who is authorized to use a card.

Investments

1. Do you know what long-term investments your parents have?

2. Do they count on interest or other income from investment accounts for their monthly budget?

3. Does this amount stay the same or fluctuate according to the stock market?

4. How long will the expected monthly income from these investments last?

5. Are there certificates of deposit (CDs) that need to be renewed and does your parent shop banks for the best rates?

6. Are there stocks or other investment portfolios?

7. Who is authorized to handle those accounts?

8. Have the accounts been set up to limit tax liability at time of death? Consider payable-on-death (POD) or transfer-on-death (TOD) options.

When to Take Over

Short Term

In times of medical crisis, you'll obviously need to take over money management. Don't wait until the crisis arrives to make sure you're authorized to do what you need to do.

1. Are you listed on the household checking account as an authorized user? Someone other than your parents should be. Whether you're caregiving from a distance or locally, this has to be someone who has access to your parents' mail and can actually handle the job.

2. Do you have enough peace within yourself and your relationship with your parents to take over this responsibility?

3. If you are not independently wealthy, will you feel comfortable accepting gas money from your parents for your extra trips or reimbursing yourself from their account? Is this what they'd want if you can't ask them?

4. Do you want or need a system of checks and balances to feel comfortable doing this? Do you want to do the bill paying and reimbursements once a week with your sister or someone else to help minimize future money issues? This isn't a do-you-trust-yourself kind of question but a personal limits-of-comfort question that only you as a caregiver can answer.

Long Term

Short-term money management often paves the way for the longer term transfer of these responsibilities to a caregiver. Communication boundaries are often broken, and a parent may decide, or it may become evident, that the short-term arrangement needs to expand into a regular caregiving duty.

Safeguarding from Telemarketers and Fraud

Lonely widows and widowers and the hard-of-hearing are likely prey for unscrupulous telemarketers. To protect your loved one, it is important to communicate concern without belittling their intelligence.

If you can't tell your father outright that you think he's been scammed into those two dozen magazines now cluttering his mailbox each month, then present your case to him as something that happened to a friend's parents and how your friend figured out how to cancel the mystery subscriptions. Let him give you suggestions for your friend.

> ■■■
>
> **Flexibility**
>
> In all realms of caregiving, flexibility is necessary. "Never" and "always" rarely have a place.
>
> ■■■

Suggest your parents add caller ID to their phone plan. Purchase a phone with a large display that is easily readable and teach them how to use it. Not answering the phone may be difficult, but if an "unavailable" or unfamiliar number appears, there's a good chance a telemarketer is on the other end. Those with high anxiety will have to train themselves to trust that every call isn't so urgent it must be answered immediately.

Register your parents' phone numbers on the National Do Not Call Registry to reduce the number of phone solicitations they receive. You can sign up for this free service at www.donotcall.gov. However, registering will not stop all solicitation calls. You may still receive calls legally from political organizations, registered charities, those taking surveys, bill collectors, and companies with which you have an existing business relationship. If you've purchased from, made payment to, or received a delivery from a company within the last eighteen months, you may get calls unless you specifically ask them not to call again. Some telemarketers create a loophole by conducting a survey and then requesting permission to call again, thus opening the door for sales calls.

Help your parents limit the number of credit cards they use. The more accounts they have, the more likely they are to be confused. Mistakenly pulling out a debit card when you think it's a credit card can cause havoc with the checking account. Also, when purchases are made via phone, online, or with mail order using a credit card, the purchaser's address often goes on a list that is sold, and a barrage of catalogs begin arriving.

Mail order is fun. Who doesn't like to receive a box delivered to their door with a surprise inside? Be watchful for the number of delivery boxes around the house. Your parent may be shopping wisely, but he might also be purchasing and hoarding the latest gadgets "As Shown on TV," hoping one day he'll be able to use them. Also, many older adults are taken in by shop-at-home programs on TV, believing every claim about the products. It's easy to call that toll-free number, talk to a friendly representative, and ring up a whopping credit or debit purchase for jewelry and clothing.

When one woman died, her family found a spare bedroom crammed with never-taken-from-the-box exercise equipment and a desk full of credit card statements with exorbitant past due balances.

Stopping the insanity. If your parent is barraged with junk mail, you can go online at www.dmachoice.org to get a name and address removed from many direct mail lists. The site offers directions for a Do Not Contact for Caregivers as well as a Deceased Do Not Contact list. Or you can write to: Mail Preference Service, Direct Marketing Association, P.O. Box 282, Carmel, NY 10512-0282.

Also, there is usually an "opt-out" phone number at the bottom of each preapproved credit card offer. Opting out will stop offers only from that particular company.

Charitable Contributions

Mail Solicitations

Seniors are targets for charity. Just one $10 donation given through a mail solicitation can bring dozens more to a mailbox. For a senior with limited contact with the outside world, feeling needed gives an ego boost. Sending even small contributions makes them feel they have something to offer.

Yet there are many red flags to look for. Some organizations send "reminder notices" of pledges. This taps a fear of cognitive decline, and some seniors would rather act on a reminder than question it or admit they don't remember making such a pledge. Other organizations send reminder notices of actual phone pledges, but send multiple reminders. Some seniors pay these "bills" without question month after month, thinking they've forgotten. They're loathe to tell anyone for fear their mental state will be questioned. If they don't record their checks carefully, looking back for confirmation of payment can be difficult.

> ■■■
>
> "For phone solicitations, I always thank the person for the offer, but tell them firmly that I do all my charitable giving through my church. This usually stops them."
>
> —Maribel
>
> ■■■

Ask your parents to put all mail solicitations in a special basket that you go through with them once a month. You may discover so many requests that had your parent contributed just $20 to each, it would have added up to a sizable amount without them realizing it. By handling these requests once a month, your parents can prioritize and keep donations within the budget they've set.

Phone Solicitations

Many phone solicitors push for an immediate commitment. Encourage your parents to always request that information about the charity be mailed for their evaluation before they make a donation.

■■ Through the Looking Glass ■■

Handling finances

In the mirror: Marian, in her 80s

"I'm on a fixed income with my Social Security. I lost the value of my home when I invested in a retirement community that went bankrupt. The new owners understood my situation and have worked with me. I now have my son-in-law helping me with my finances. I set up a debit account, and all my bills go to him. He pays them and makes up a statement for me that shows exactly what has been paid and what is left. His statements are easier to understand than the kind the bank would send.

"Where I live, dinner is included with our rent. I fix my breakfast and lunch in my apartment, and the cost for my groceries isn't much. I have some incidental expenses, but it all works out, and I'm able to make it on what I have coming in each month. Having my son-in-law help me handle the bills gives me real peace of mind."

Viewpoint:

Coffee, Conversation, and Cash Cards

Over precious mugs of coffee sipped without the presence of children or parents, Sally shared the following with longtime friend Meg:

"It's hard not to lose patience, particularly when shopping with Mother. Everything goes fine until checkout, when my mother fumbles with her wallet for what seems like ages. She can't decide whether or not to use cash. Then, if she decides not to, she fumbles again for her debit card. Without fail, she'll then look at me and with great frustration, say, 'Oh, can you do this please?'"

"Well, maybe you should just take charge," Meg said. "Get in line in front of her with her card in hand."

"She wants to keep up with her card herself, but she's always forgetting either her PIN or how to slide the thing through," Sally said.

"Then get a copy of the card issued to you. That way you can have it on hand for that kind of thing. That's what Mom and I did. She'd get so frustrated, but I'd hold back my offers to help because I was trying to respect her independence. Plus, I didn't want to embarrass her in line."

"Oh, wow, do I know about that. My mother rolls her eyes at me any time I suggest helping. Then, if I don't, she usually ends up asking and making me feel like a heel for not helping her before she got so frustrated!"

"I think having your own card will help. Consider talking to her about it when you're not shopping, when you're not in the heat of the moment."

"That makes sense. Maybe if I tell her I don't want the fun of shopping ruined for her by her getting frustrated by all the different machines out there, then she wouldn't think I'm saying she can't handle it."

"Sure. Then you could also ask her to tell you before you go into a store if she'd rather pay in cash or have you handle it. Then it would be all set before you get there, and you both can enjoy that time together."

Living Water

> Wealth and honor come from you;
>> you are the ruler of all things.
> In your hands are strength and power
>> to exalt and give strength to all.
>> (1 Chronicles 29:12)

Often we forget that everything we have belongs to God, and He's been gracious enough to entrust what we have to our safekeeping for a time. However, because many of our parents grew up during the Great Depression, they often have a more possessive attitude about money. Yes, they've worked hard for what they have, but all of it is a gift. By encouraging them to realize this, you may be better able to gain their blessing when you need to step in and take over their finances for a period of time or permanently.

Just remember, you are an overseer, not the owner, of their money. Keep their best interests at heart when making financial decisions rather than thinking about how things will best benefit you now or in the future. Ask God to keep you honest and faithful as you discharge the duty of money management for your parent.

Additional Information

A source for basic information, including a link to *Financial Caregiving: A Survival Guide* and basic budgeting worksheets: www. todaysseniors.com/pages/Money.html.

Chapter 16

Ear Trumpets and Spectacles
Hearing and Vision Changes

Hearing and vision loss top the health conditions that most affect a senior's quality of life. Yet these are often the most difficult for caregivers to offer support in managing. When vision and hearing are compromised, every aspect of daily life is affected. Left unaddressed, they can lead to depression.

Hearing Loss

Marie picked up her parents on the way to a doctor's appointment, eager to share her youngest daughter's newest interest.

"You know what Bella did the other day?" she asked as they headed across town.

"What?" her mother asked.

"She took every piece of jewelry out of all her little boxes and organized them in her new standing jewelry case that's just like yours. She's so excited."

"Bella gave you a show standing on a box? What kind of show?" her father asked.

Marie's mother gave her a look that read, *See what I deal with every day?*

After a few moments of stunned silence, Marie realized her father had caught only a few words of the conversation, even though he was sitting in the passenger's seat. Knowing that Bella was a little drama queen and hearing only snippets of words, Marie's father reacted as most do when they begin losing their hearing—they fake it. However, faking leads only to misunderstandings and delays in addressing the problem.

After years of accommodating her husband's gradual hearing loss, Marie's mother had come to the conclusion that he simply had "selective hearing," a passive-aggressive, controlling behavior. Think of the three-year-old who can hear the word *dessert* from two rooms away, but "didn't hear" your direct request for him to pick up his toys.

Types of Hearing Loss

There are several types of hearing loss. With *conductive hearing loss*, sound does not move effectively through the outer ear canal to the ear drum and the bones of the ear to the middle ear. Usually, perception of loudness or softness of sound is what is affected. This type of loss can sometimes be medically or surgically corrected or augmented with hearing aids.

Sensorineural hearing loss occurs when there is damage to the inner ear or to the nerve pathways from the inner ear to the brain. It cannot be medically or surgically corrected. This type of hearing loss involves more than volume. It affects clarity of sound and the understanding and interpretation of sounds and speech. It may or may not be helped by a hearing aid.

Presbycusis is a sensorineural hearing loss attributed to changes in the middle ear and increases with age. It affects the interpretation of high pitched sounds. Though usually occurring in both ears at the same rate, there can be variation.

Tinnitus, a ringing or roaring in the ears, is also an issue faced by many seniors.

Central hearing loss involves damage to the central nervous system and cannot be helped by hearing aids.

Hearing loss may be more severe in one ear, which creates additional problems, particularly when hearing aids are used to maximize remaining hearing.

Each one of these hearing issues poses challenges. When they are combined, they can seem monumental. The degree of hearing loss is something an audiologist can measure using a scale based on sound perception at various decibels (dB).

Normal range or no impairment = 0 dB to 20 dB

Mild loss = 20 dB to 40 dB

Moderate loss = 40 dB to 60 dB

Severe loss = 60 dB to 80 dB

Profound loss = 80 dB or more

Hearing loss is a real issue and one that may not be solved easily. Get a professional involved who can offer coping strategies as well as ideas of what can be done to improve hearing.

Unfortunately, a delay in seeking a professional evaluation and diagnosis often leaves either the caregiver or the one receiving care feeling a mental lapse is involved rather than merely hearing loss. You may find the problem can be solved with an easy fix such as the removal of excess wax in the ear.

Hearing aids are not always a one-time purchase, and they require frequent battery changes and regular cleaning and maintenance. When purchasing, check to see what the return policy is in case they do not help or are uncomfortable. Spending thousands of dollars on hearing aids and then having them sit in the box because they're uncomfortable will only create frustration.

Be wary of evaluations by companies that specialize in hearing aid sales. Ads for free hearing tests are often just glorified sales tactics by hearing aid companies seeking only to sell a product.

Tips for Managing Hearing Loss

- *Reduce background noise.* Choose quieter restaurants or a less busy time when going out to eat. Be aware of such things as proximity to a noisy kitchen or doors opening and closing.

- *Talk about it.* If your loved one has a problem hearing, ask him or her to let you know when they haven't heard what you said. It is a matter of practicality, not pride. You care enough to want to communicate well. Having your father tell you he didn't hear what you said might remind you to face him or lean toward his "better" ear when speaking. Some people don't even realize they've picked up lip-reading skill as part of their natural accommodation for hearing loss.

- *Write out key information.* If you're not sure your mother heard which doctor you asked her to call to verify an appointment, write her a note (or send her an e-mail) asking her to confirm.

- *Be patient.* Persons with hearing loss have to concentrate harder when conversing, so avoid having a long conversation in new locations or when there are noises that might cause distractions and make concentration even more difficult.

- *Accommodate.* When your parent reveals communication styles that work better than others, listen!

Vision Loss

The mountains Evelyn and her husband, Jack, could see from their kitchen window came closer with each new curve in the road as they headed for a weekend getaway.

"It's been so long since we've taken a vacation," Evelyn said.

"Retirement is a vacation."

"Come on, you know what I mean. We're only a half hour away from the house, and I feel like we're in a new world."

Jack and Evelyn checked into Pine Valley Inn. After enjoying a walk through the wooded grounds, they sat on the old-fashioned front porch to read.

"Jack, either your arms are going to have to grow or you're going to have to get glasses."

As usual, Jack's only reply was "Humph."

When Evelyn awoke the next morning, she saw a shadow and thought it must be the angle of early morning light slanting through the window or Jack moving around the room. But when she stood, she quickly realized she was unbalanced and the shadow was in her vision. More than half of what she could see through her right eye was shadowed.

■ ■ ■

Vision changes can be gradual or sudden, correctable or not. In Jack's case, he'd put off getting reading glasses for some time, and it had become somewhat of a joke. But Evelyn's vision loss was sudden, proving to be a partially detached retina, a condition that is more common with increasing age, has no warning signs, and requires immediate attention. Some conditions, like Jack's, require small adjustments. Others, like Evelyn's, require medical intervention.

Lighthouse International (www.lighthouse.org), a leading non-profit organization that conducts research and offers services to help people overcome vision challenges, notes that by age 75, one in four people will have some form of visual impairment, the most common causes being cataracts, macular degeneration, retinopathy, and glaucoma. Some vision problems can be controlled through diet and lifestyle changes, while others can't. The key to all is detection. Caregivers may notice a parent wanting more lights on in their home even before that parent complains about difficulty seeing.

Diabetes, high blood pressure, smoking, high cholesterol, and nutritional deficiencies or excesses can contribute to visual impairment. Medication, even nutritional supplements, can cause changes in eyesight. Vision changes are not always listed as a possible side effect from medication, so make sure your parents' eye doctor has a copy of their medications list.

Poor vision can range from low vision to blindness. Being vigilant about regular eye exams can help slow or halt degenerative conditions. Correction usually involves glasses or contacts, but multiple forms of correction may be needed depending on your parents' activities.

Consider the many ways you use your own eyes—for driving, reading, general navigating, or for detailed computer work or crafts. If you pick up a pair of reading glasses at the drugstore, they may help with the daily newspaper, but not at all if you're e-mailing friends.

Normal vision changes associated with aging include:

- Decreased focus
- Declining sensitivity to details, even color
- Need for more light

The good news is that technology offers a variety of tools, often inexpensive, that can help offset the effects of poor vision. Consider trying out tools at a local optometrist or ophthalmologist's office to see what works for your situation.

Snapshot of Common Eye Conditions

- *Cataracts* are among the most common eye issues seniors face. They cause cloudiness in overall vision similar to driving in a fog. Vision difficulties from cataracts can be aggravated by changing light. Cataracts can be removed, but doctors may suggest waiting a period of time before surgery until the cataract reaches a certain level of development and impairment of functional vision.

- *Macular degeneration* affects detailed vision and can cause spotty vision. The most common type develops slowly and affects vision in the center of the eye. Straight lines may look wavy. Side or peripheral vision is not affected.

- *Glaucoma* is a condition in which the optic nerve is damaged by pressure changes in the eye. Glaucoma is irreversible, but some factors that affect the pressure are controllable, limiting the damage if caught early.

- *Diabetic retinopathy* is caused by blood vessels that leak within the eye due to long-term damage from diabetes. Laser treatments can halt or slow damage.

- *Floaters* are tiny clumps of fibers or cells inside the clear gel-like fluid (vitreous) filling the eye. They can appear as little dots, circles, lines, clouds, or cobwebs. Floaters can be a result of the normal aging of the vitreous, but they can also indicate more severe eye conditions.

▪■ Through the Looking Glass ■▪
Coping with hearing impairment

In the mirror: Gibb, a senior living in a retirement community

"Nearly in my eighties, I can do much less than I did in my early seventies when I could still climb around on ladders and scaffolding while pounding nails into Habitat for Humanity houses.

"Now, I have trouble hearing what my wife says while the TV is on. I invested in hearing aids, and now I hear *everything.* My ability to eliminate what I don't need to hear is impaired, and a cacophony of noises interferes with what I need to hear to understand what's being said. When we eat in a large dining room, I hear all the people talking everywhere in the room, but I have difficulty understanding my wife next to me.

"Even the way a wall is made and the finish on it (like wallpaper in a doctor's small exam room) can change what I can understand.

"When I chew raw celery, I hear a noise inside my head that sounds much like a group of soldiers marching in step over a wooden bridge. If someone nearby sneezes or coughs, it sounds like a minor explosion. A car honking its horn is cause for alarm. Crumpling a piece of paper near me sends my nerves into overdrive. Water running in the sink sounds like a minor Niagara Falls.

"The fancy hearing aids I bought adjust to things like running water, and then change again when I step out of the bathroom. But with that kind of sensitivity, there seems to be no balance I can count on."

Viewpoint:
Technology offers positives and negatives.

Obviously, hearing aids don't work if you don't put them in or turn them on. One grandfather took great delight in turning his "ears" off while his three grandchildren ran squealing through the house. He sat in his recliner, saw their joy, and smiled as his wife chased them.

Another grandpa enjoyed taking his "ears" out while watching television, relying instead on a pair of remote stereo headphones to hear programs. The large headset allowed him to block out all other sound, and tune-in only to his favorite show.

Another set of grandparents found that technology simply wasn't enough. Even the highest-powered, most expensive hearing aids barely helped, so Grandma started amplifying her voice using a paper towel tube directed right at Grandpa's hearing aid. It was hilarious to watch, but worked for them!

Living Water

> I will lead the blind by ways they have not known,
>   along unfamiliar paths I will guide them;
> I will turn the darkness into light before them
>   and make the rough places smooth.
> These are the things I will do;
>   I will not forsake them.
>   (Isaiah 42:16)

My dearly beloved aunt sees only shapes and also has almost total hearing loss in one ear. Her vision impairment often causes her confusion about what time it is or what day and her location. Her hearing loss means she sometimes makes a statement that repeats what has just been said, or she misinterprets the subject being discussed. Both impairments are sources of frustration for her, but she copes by relying on her unshakable faith in God to see her through each challenge.

While visiting her recently, she joked that she guessed we just needed to take her out and shoot her. "Or maybe there's something else they do to infirm humans," she said. Although we laughed with her, we assured her that her infirmities render her no less valued and loved.

Even those of us with full sight are often blind to various facets of our lives. We don't see blessings, or we hear negatives instead of positives. We forge ahead, blindly, without praying for direction. But if we'll ask, God promises to guide us when we're traveling unfamiliar paths, to illuminate dark and shadowy areas, and to smooth out the difficulties. We can count on God not to leave us defenseless or forsaken.

Mark 8:22-25 records the story of a blind man Jesus healed at Bethsaida. He spit on the man's eyes and then touched them. He asked if the man wanted to see, which may seem an odd question to us, but sometimes we're so comfortable and accustomed to current situations that we don't want things to change. When the man opened his eyes, he saw people that looked like stick figures. Jesus touched the man again. This time, his vision was totally restored.

Perhaps today you need a second touch from Jesus. You need healing for wounded emotions or physical pain, or a sense of peace about your current circumstances. Do you want things to be different? Ask Jesus to touch you.

Additional Information

The National Institutes of Health offers information for seniors and their caregivers at www.nihseniorhealth.gov. The site comes with a speech option and an easy way to get larger fonts on the page so seniors with hearing and vision problems can still access the information.

Chapter 17

Cognitive Decline
Facing Fears and Learning Facts

W hen is Anne-Marie coming?" Henry asked Hannah, his wife of 42 years.

"She'll be here in about an hour," Hannah said, looking up from her sewing.

"Hannah, didn't you say Anne-Marie is coming today?" Henry asked a moment later, glancing at his wife from over his newspaper.

"I just told you, she'll be here soon," Hannah said, barely masking her irritation.

Henry wondered why his wife seemed so annoyed this morning. She'd been irritated with him a lot lately, and he couldn't imagine why.

The Monster in the Closet

Cognitive decline and memory loss are the biggest fear factor for seniors and their caregivers. Frustrations, miscommunications, and strained emotions further cloud an issue characterized by mental haze.

Determining if "senior moments" are consistent enough to affect quality of life and whether something should be done requires communication. It may be failure to pay attention that first raises concern and prompts the need for discussion.

Sometimes seniors become so accustomed to others planning their days that they don't take much time to focus on the details. A senior may ask a question and then not pay attention to or not retain the answer. Determining the difference is important. Talking about cognitive decline can bring to light what kind of intervention works. It may seem that just encouraging a parent to pay more attention to conversations would fix the problem, but often it helps to check what the senior actually heard by asking, "What did you hear me say?"

If Henry knew that Hannah's irritation came from what she perceives as his lack of attention to what she says, he might be able to make adjustments. Often it takes a third party to address such situations, because after years together, a couple may not realize complaints and irritations have a strong measure of fear behind them. But when fears of cognitive decline are brought into the open, they're a little less like scary monsters hiding in the closet of the mind.

> ■ ■ ■
>
> "Sometimes a caregiver tries to fill in the blanks when the senior lapses into silence [because of] word finding deficit or memory problems. The best approach is to help the senior get back on track by supplying a key word or phrase but avoiding totally filling the blank space. Even in the face of frustration in not finding the words, the senior takes pride in maintaining verbal fluency and should be encouraged to speak up."
>
> —Robert Ferrell, M.D., M.S.,
> Director, Elder Life Solutions
>
> ■ ■ ■

Assessing Cognitive Abilities

Now, doctors are able to better assess cognitive issues, and medications are available that offset the effects of brain shrinkage that naturally occurs with aging. Other conditions or medications may be part of the problem. Once determined, they may be easily remedied, thus allaying fears of the dreaded Alzheimer's disease.

The following tips will give you a starting place for assessing your parent's abilities and a way to monitor changes with less fear and more facts when deciding to involve a doctor.

Organize

While you may organize your life with your cell phone or computer, buying Dad a BlackBerry might not be the answer for many reasons. First, many seniors are not willing or able to manage new technology. Perhaps some kind of book-style planner is a better option. Or try a large wall calendar.

Your father's seeming disorganization may revolve around the fact that he never did the planning. Now that Mom's gone, he has no skill base to rely on, and he calls you instead to find out his schedule for the week. He's not losing his mind; he just has no tools for organizing.

Hint: Urinary tract infections (UTIs) can cause confusion and disorientation in the elderly. If your parent suddenly becomes confused and withdrawn, have her checked for a UTI. Once on an antibiotic, the confusion will usually dissipate.

If you call to check on your parents each night, ask them what is on their calendar for tomorrow. Your question and their answer give you confirmation they are aware of upcoming events, and that gives them a sense of control.

Don't Try to Mind Read

Caregivers often develop expert mind-reading skills. They know their loved one so well they anticipate a need or desire ahead of the request. At times this can be great, but encourage your parent to be aware of his needs, particularly for errands or transportation. This offers a sense of control and the use of practical life skills. You may know that Mom likes to go to the bank once a week, and if she doesn't mention it, you know to ask. But encourage her mental processing of such tasks.

Plan Ahead

Don't expect your parents to read your mind and follow your mental plan for the day. While your schedule seems logical to you, their brains may not follow your path. Keep a list of planned stops in the car so your parent can look at it as you head across town for the first doctor's appointment. Or you can post your list on Mom's calendar a day or two ahead of time. If Mom sees that you plan to stop by the post office while the two of you are together, then she's more likely to remember she needs stamps, too, and won't have to call after she's back home to ask you to take her to the post office when you were there only a couple of hours earlier. It's not that she has lost her mind or has no consideration for the time you've taken to transport her; she just may not have had enough time to wrap her mind around the plan you created for the day.

However, if Mom suddenly remembers she needs stamps and you're nowhere near a post office during a day's sojourn, ask her to write it on her list for your next planned outing, if there is no urgent need. This also helps with prioritizing and maintaining boundaries with your own time.

Use Lists

Women are often more adept at list-making than men because they traditionally keep up with grocery lists and have a skill set that can be applied in new ways even if their grocery shopping days are rare. Find out what worked for them before, and build on the existing skills.

One woman always wrote her grocery list on an envelope when she was younger so she could tuck coupons inside it. At 85 and living in a retirement community, she rarely buys groceries now, but her daughter keeps a box of envelopes beside her mother's favorite chair so she can make lists on familiar writing material of things she wants to accomplish.

Be Consistent, Develop Patterns

Keeping list-making supplies and the calendar in the same place will ensure that your parent has tools readily available. Referring often to these and their location develops a pattern of behavior to fall back on when "senior moments" happen. This can also apply to certain errands. Retirement communities often have specified days and times for trips to the grocery or drugstore. Residents pattern their other activities around these days. When in charge of transportation, caregivers can establish similar patterns for their parents. This is also a good tool for evaluating when cognitive decline may need intervention.

When you notice that for the last three weeks your father has forgotten Tuesday is grocery day, then you have a sign that a reevaluation is needed. That is better than all of a sudden realizing Dad is unaware of the days of the week because you've just been shopping for him each day, as needed.

Acknowledge Differences

Remember your parents' world is different from yours. Repetition, for some reason, doesn't seem to bother most seniors. It's as if seniors cross an invisible line where reviewing the same topics is no longer a point of irritation. Most caregivers haven't crossed that line, so repeated references to the price of gas, the color of a bush at a particular intersection, old news about a friend, or a report of the quantity and consistency of bowel movements that day may drive you slightly crazy.

But your parents haven't lost their ability to think. During the aging process, your parents' minds follow stream-of-consciousness thought patterns each day. While your mind follows new highways opened daily by interactions with other people at work, with social groups, or children, theirs may not. Their world is simply getting smaller. Unless they're interested and willing to push their thoughts by reading and discussing current events, their minds will take the established routes. But concerns arise when those well-worn paths become foreign lands. Being aware of these normal routes your parents' minds follow may seem boring to you, but if you pay attention, you'll notice when they change.

When the Monster Growls

But what if your analysis of daily tasks and small-world syndrome

> ■ ■ ■
>
> "We have to rethink every single component of how we're caring for our elders because the people they were are still in there."
>
> —Nancy Wolske,
> staff member of a residential-care
> facility near Portland, Oregon[4]
>
> ■ ■ ■

raises red flags? What if the calendar, organizing, list-making, and planning ahead are not bridging the gaps, and Mom's small world is like a different planet to you?

There is hope. Though it is difficult for physicians to diagnose cognitive impairment, evaluation tools and medications are available.

With brain shrinkage common to aging, or with diseases such as dementia or Alzheimer's, neurological pathways that carry messages around the brain and to the body can be damaged. But medication can limit the effects.

Side effects and other conditions may rule out medication as an option, but having a set of strategies you've used, along with a picture of how they've worked and when they stopped working, can help physicians guide you.

Even when memories and cognitive abilities fade, it is vital for caregivers to remember dignity. Talking down to your parents or speaking angrily to them can bruise hearts, even if they don't seem to register

> ■ ■ ■
>
> "I've always said that if I lose my mind I want to lose it all at once so I don't know what's happening to me."
>
> —a senior adult
>
> ■ ■ ■

offense by your tone. Just because the brain begins shutting doors to the outside world doesn't mean the heart and soul of a person is absent.

When glassy stares replace sparkling, engaging eyes, remember that your parent is still there, wanting to love and be loved, even if in new ways. Eventually, a head turned toward you may be all Mom can manage when she hears your voice and the only indication that she loves the fact you are there. While you may long for more interaction, accept that this is all the body allows you both to have, and treasure it.

Viewpoint:

Robin, a young mother of three living in Wisconsin, whose mother lives in Florida.

Robin's mother confused her doctor's verbal direction to double her dose of blood thinner. Not only did she double the amount, but the number of times she was taking it as well. Within two days, she was hospitalized in serious condition from the overdose.

Prior to this Robin had been concerned because her mother seemed mentally foggy. Now Robin wondered if this mental haze was the result of a drug interaction. She called her mother's doctor and asked her to review her mother's medications.

In talking to the doctor, Robin learned her mother had refused to comply when the doctor suggested a change in medication some months before. With the two medication issues causing concern, the doctor offered Robin a possible reason.

"I really think your mother is suffering from moderate to severe Alzheimer's," the doctor said. "She doesn't seem to understand what I'm telling her enough to follow up properly once she's back home."

But during their conversation, Robin picked up on the doctor's brusque personality, very unlike her mother's gentle nature, and realized these differences could be the culprit in miscommunication. The doctor expected Robin's mother to comply with her directives, although she didn't give reasons for them. Her mother didn't see any reason to change a medication she'd been taking for a long time, and thus was resistant.

The current confusion with doubling the dose of blood thinner came when the doctor failed to clarify what she meant by "double."

With the question of Alzheimer's in play, Robin made a suggestion to more clearly ascertain her mother's mental capacity.

"If anyone wants to determine my mother's comprehension level, just ask her about art," Robin said.

■ ■ ■

Was Robin's suggestion odd? Not really. It's all about reality. Keeping up with medication and drug interactions had never been part of Robin's mother's reality. The concepts were far removed from her world. She had no interest in understanding much more than the basics of the medical care she required. Why should she change medications that had been working all these years? If they were working, then that was all she needed to know.

The doctor's use of a misunderstanding of dosing instructions and a resistance to change in medication as clear indicators of cognitive decline was unrealistic. Robin suggested art, the topic of her mother's highest knowledge and interest level, because she knew that was a more accurate window to cognitive function.

This highlights one of the problems with modern medicine. Specialists have limited interaction with their patients. They do not have the benefit of having had a patient in their care for decades. Combine this with the personalities involved, and there is plenty of room for misunderstanding.

It is also an indication of one mind-set that many seniors have. They were raised in an era where doctors took care of everything. Their own parents may have had the same doctor for his entire career. But the doctors who, from years of watchful care, knew every medical issue their patients faced, are long gone.

In the era of records sent digitally from one specialist to another, it is often hard for seniors to understand that they have only a limited time frame to connect with their doctor. A fifteen-minute consultation and exam, a ten-minute pre-op visit, two five-minute follow-up visits in the hospital, and one fifteen-minute follow-up in the office may be all. Less than an hour is hardly enough time to really get to know someone.

Living Water

> [David] gave [Solomon] the plans of all that the Spirit had put in his mind for the courts of the temple of the LORD and all the surrounding rooms, for the treasuries of the temple of God and for the treasuries for the dedicated things (1 Chronicles 28:12).

Our brains are incredibly complex and amazing. Human minds created equipment to catapult people from one side of the globe to the other and into outer space—minds that discover cures for disease, compose music that swells our souls and makes us weep, minds that write stories that transport us to other worlds, or design structures that seem to defy gravity and imagination. All of this creativity and knowledge is God-given and inspired.

When a loved one becomes disoriented, confused, and seems to lose that mental spark that makes him unique, we panic. It feels like too much to have the person physically present but mentally absent. But remember, your loved one is still "in there," despite the befuddlement. Cherish moments when he reconnects and remembers. Praise God for the intelligence and humor that makes your loved one the person God created him to be. Then, pray for God to sustain you, mentally and emotionally, as you deal with the reality of today.

Additional Information

When cognitive issues come to mind, the biggest fear factor is the dreaded Alzheimer's disease. Check out www.alz.org to get the facts and their 24-hour hotline number.

Chapter 18

Social Needs

Understanding Your Parents' Need for Companionship

Elle raced home from the grocery store, thankful she didn't pass a radar checkpoint. Entering the house, she glanced toward the back-yard, where she and Dan had created a wooded oasis they could enjoy. She longed for just a few minutes of time alone there. Words from Robert Frost's poem came to mind: "The woods are lovely, dark and deep, / But I have promises to keep, / And miles to go before I sleep."

And it would be miles before Elle slept, with groceries to put away, follow-up appointments to schedule, and ball games for the kids.

The phone rang, startling Elle from her two-second mental trip to the backyard.

"Hi, Mama, you okay?" she asked, with more interest than she felt.

"I'm fine. Just lonely and thought you'd want to talk," her mother said.

After three conversations already that day and with two appointments scheduled for her mother tomorrow, Elle's day off, she wondered why her mother couldn't leave her alone for the evening.

Loneliness and Your Aging Parent

Caregivers, particularly those raising young families, are often so imbedded in the stage of life where every minute seems scheduled they find it difficult to realize Mom or Dad is lonely. Caregivers are looking for even a moment where no one is pulling on their time and energy.

Loneliness is something people try to avoid; solitude is enjoyable and fulfilling. When you discover that your parent is spending hours on the porch hoping a neighbor will see her outside and come over, then you can be pretty sure she's having trouble viewing alone time as something positive.

Because caregivers crave even the smallest amount of solitude, they frequently find it difficult to understand loneliness. But it's all about perspective. Going to the grocery store is not likely an event offering social stimulation for a busy caregiver. Yet for a senior, who spends most of her time alone, an outing of any kind can fill social needs. A trip to the store or mall, even just to window shop, provides needed stimulation, while the harried caregiver views a trip to the mall as one more thing on a long to-do list. What fills the social needs of a senior adult is not the same as what fills the needs for a 40-year-old mother of two.

Elle may love having a cookout with the neighbors where all the kids can play together, but for her mother, coming to such an event would be too stressful. The loudness of the children, food her delicate digestive system can't tolerate, and navigating the treacherous back-yard with her cane are all concerns.

But there are ways to compromise. A couple of hours in the peace and darkness of a movie theatre provides Elle a reprieve from the busy-ness of her life while giving her mother a great outing.

Caregivers can bridge the gaps by realizing the lives they and their parents lead have totally different landscapes no matter how close geo-graphically or emotionally they may be, or how often they are together. Social networks shift. Whether it's neighbors moving in and out of a development filled with young working couples or friends in a retire-ment community passing away, connections change. Building new ones can seem more difficult for some seniors because connections offered by work, kids, and carpools are no longer part of their lives. Church often fills the need for seniors to have their own social group. However, some seniors withdraw even from that outlet.

As one caregiver explained, "Mama taught the youth Sunday school class for more than 50 years. But when it became too hard for her to move between buildings to get to that class, she stopped teaching. But that isn't all. She stopped going to church. It was as if she felt she didn't have a place there anymore."

Opportunities

Many opportunities for social interaction for seniors require little, if any, caregiver involvement. There may be some initial coordination, but after that, a caregiver can let go of the reins. If you are short on ideas, think of all the things you might like to do if you had an extra few hours every week or two. And sleeping isn't on the list! Would you like to take an art class, join a bridge club, participate in a knitting guild, a book club, or a community choir? Build on your parent's background. What did your parent enjoy years ago, even if she never used it in a career field?

Consider the following possibilities:

Bible study groups—transportation may be available.

Senior activity centers—there are several types, some offered by county agencies and others with churches or colleges.

Senior day care—your parent may be willing to participate if the activities match his interests.

Volunteering—even when seniors have disabilities, they can become active in their communities. Opportunities include:

- After-school centers or day cares—serving snacks, reading, or helping with homework

- Local nonprofits—Perhaps she could offer her background with interior design for a local nonprofit planning a fund-raising event. Mom can't drive? No problem, she could call to offer her expertise and likely find people willing to pick her up on their way to the meetings.

- Arts agencies—costume-making, phone-calling for auditions, stuffing envelopes for mailers

Is Shopping a Social Outlet?

When you have errands to run and Mom wants to go, take time for a mental check of motivations. If you have six other errands and Mom just wants to get out of the house, consider whether she is willing or able to sit in the car so you can keep the pace you need for the day. While she may expect a leisurely lunch to be part of the outing, is it going to cause more pressure than your schedule really allows?

While it sounds simple to do your miscellaneous shopping when Mom does, it may be more prudent to separate your errands from hers. You'll only end up frustrated when her needs draw you away from your agenda. Sometimes it lessens the stress level to focus only on her shopping. She's accustomed to your being there to fill her needs. It's the pattern you've set as her caregiver. Her expecting that pattern to continue is natural. For her, being out or shopping (even if it's for something you think could wait a few weeks) fills a need for her to feel part of the world at large, not necessarily a connection with a specific person or place.

Pairing Up

Remember the days when seeing your parents kiss turned your stomach? Or perhaps you plant a loud kiss on your spouse in front of your kids just to hear them say "Eeeeww!" Intimacy is an issue at any age. Some caregivers have trouble with the thought that their single parent might want to start dating.

■ ■ ■

When Lacy arrived to pick up her mother for an appointment, her mother didn't answer the door. Lacy let herself in and called for her mother.

"In here at the computer," her mother called.

Lacy stepped into her father's study. Although he'd been dead for five years, she could still smell his cologne when she walked in the door.

Her mother was sitting at his desk with a large-screen computer monitor in front of her. The screen revealed an Internet dating service.

"Could you help me get signed up for this before we leave?" her mother asked, wondering why her daughter suddenly paled.

■■■

Some seniors say it is only companionship they seek when looking to connect with members of the opposite sex. And that can be true. However, what starts out as friendship can develop into more. You just may not want to believe that can happen to your parent!

Sometimes, a previously married senior loses the moral code of conduct once held regarding sex outside of marriage. While it may be a sticky conversation, ask your parent if he intends to be sexually active in a new relationship and suggest he have an open discussion with his potential next wife about her previous sexual activity. Your parent may need to be reminded that there are more risks now from sexually transmitted diseases and that his actions serve as a role model for grandchildren.

Talking to a parent about sex is probably harder than talking to your teens about the subject, but it really is a conversation you should have.

Viewpoint:

A Pastor's Perspective—Dr. Wayne Hyatt, minister to senior adults

"Seniors' social needs are extremely strong. We were created in the image of God to be in a relationship with Him, but He created us with the desire to be in relationships with others also. We are relational people. While age doesn't negate that, the circumstances of our relationships often change.

"Some seniors find themselves living in isolation as they care for a sick or dying friend or spouse. When they've lived this way for a long time, it's hard for them to realize they need social interaction. After the person they are caring for dies, they get back into the active world again and acknowledge their needs. They start having fun again, but are still dealing with grief issues, so sometimes feel they shouldn't have fun.

"Similarly, the sudden death of a spouse causes feelings of guilt for the survivor who is again enjoying life. As time goes on, with more socialization, seniors realize they are living normally and that their need for relationships, in whatever form they take, is normal too.

"When senior adults start dating, I'm frequently amazed by the reactions of their adult children. While some adult children have divorced and remarried and been through that process of loss and reconnection with relationships, many of them have a problem with their single parent dating or remarrying. They think it isn't right, but why isn't it? Their parent has a need for companionship, too, but it's hard for some adult children to accept that their parent could fall in love with someone other than the parent who died. Sometimes a new relationship gives adult children the feeling that something was wrong with their parents' relationship. Children have to work through these issues and realize that a new relationship is a different relationship.

"Some adult children have concerns about having a stepparent. But with older parents, the issue is not about someone taking a parenting role as much as simply having a quality relationship.

"Inheritance is another issue that can cause problems. It's amazing how people fight over possessions when someone dies. Adult children get defensive and want to know what a parent's remarriage means for their inheritance.

"There are additional emotions involved. When a parent dies, it can be difficult to see the surviving parent moving on, especially if the parent and child are at different stages of dealing with their loss. And moving on can mean creating a life and lifestyle that a child doesn't recognize. All of a sudden, Mom is traveling, doing things she never did with Dad. While travel wasn't a part of their parents' time together, life is different now.

"We're living in a society where stereotypes are being challenged by the fact that people are living full lives longer. 'Wait a year before you date' is one common stereotype. But it's not about a time factor imposed by others as much as it is about what feels right and works for the individuals. And it's all about companionship in whatever form it takes to meet needs. Some will date but never remarry. Others will.

"Aside from the fact that seniors sometimes surprise themselves by having these feelings again, they tend to accept their need for relationships very well, but tend to be more cautious and choosy. They aren't in any big hurry. It means so much to them when they do have quality relationships.

"If seniors or adult children are having trouble with these transitions, they can talk to others, a counselor, or pastor. Talking to someone who has helped others sort through these issues can make transitions easier."

Living Water

> Your love has given me great joy and encouragement, because you, brother, have refreshed the hearts of the saints (Philemon 1:7).

As Paul writes this letter to Philemon, he is an old man, imprisoned and in chains. Yet what clearly comes through in Paul's writings is his love for his fellow workers in the faith and the sustenance he gains from his memories of relationships with them. With a little imagination, we can catch a vision of Paul as a social creature.

We all crave relationships, whether with a lifelong friend or a newfound one. For some personalities, relationships are as crucial to sustaining quality of life as air is to breathing. While you may be more of a loner, your parent may desperately need companionship and social interaction. And that parent may feel like a prisoner in his home, chained there because he is no longer able to drive.

Our parents need encouragement, interaction with others, and refreshment. Their bodies may be wearing out, but the spark that makes their personalities unique is still aflame. Remember this, and do what you can to ensure your parent has some relational interaction aside from the family.

Additional Information

The www.eldercarelink.com site offers a free online assessment of social needs for a senior as well as "caregiver pages" that offer a communication link to keep family and friends in-the-loop and a caregiver/ helper link for additional resources.

The www.healthandage.com site provides resources for medical and social issues for seniors as well as caregivers.

The Senior Meeting Place—www.healthandage.com/html/res/meetingplace/index.htm.

Chapter 19

Mental and Spiritual Health
Dealing with Depression and Encouraging Spiritual Connection

I wake up every morning wondering what bad thing is going to happen that day," an 87-year-old widow said. Her statement conveys more than a negative attitude. It is a warning sign of depression.

Mental Health

Millions of Americans are affected by depression. Those 65 and older often have an increased risk for depression because of multiple medical conditions. Financial concerns are also a source of depression for seniors. Simply put, their money is running out, and they are too embarrassed to tell those who could help. Many feel they've failed to provide for their spouse or fear becoming a financial burden to their children.

Depression, Suicide, and Senior Adults

Suicide is a subject most often whispered behind cupped hands. But because of the high rate of suicide among senior adults, it's a topic that demands awareness.

On average, a senior adult commits suicide every 90 minutes in the U.S. The highest suicide rate of any age group occurs in those 65 years of age and older.[5]

Depression is almost always a factor in a senior's decision to take his life, with those who are either widowed or divorced accounting for a high percentage. Depression often stems from regrets over past failures or goals not accomplished, failed relationships, chemical changes in the body, substance abuse, or debilitating physical conditions.

With increasing frequency, reports surface of senior adults who opt to end their lives because they see no solution to current circumstances. One man killed his wife, an Alzheimer's sufferer, and then himself after he received a cancer diagnosis. His suicide note stated his fear that no one would adequately care for his wife if his disease caused him to die before she did.

If you suspect your parent is depressed or if you hear statements such as "I'm just living too long" or "I just wish I could end it all," don't take them lightly. These pronouncements could be your parent's cry for help.

As a first step, remove firearms from your parent's house. Then encourage your parent to seek medical intervention. Often our parents have a distorted view of mental illness, but help your parent realize there is no shame in admitting depression and getting help for it. Taking medication for depression is not an indication of personal failure. It's a smart thing to do to improve quality of life, and it's no different from taking medication for heart disease, diabetes, high blood pressure, or any other illness.

Also, realize that as a caregiver you shouldn't take sole responsibility for trying to alleviate your parent's sadness. Those who are clinically depressed can't be cheered up, and caregivers who try to take on the task are fighting a battle for which victory is impossible without a doctor's help.

Depression Is a Two-way Street

If a doctor knows a patient is a caregiver, he often voices concern about who is caring for the caregiver. This is a valid concern. And when a person serves as caregiver for a parent with Alzheimer's or other forms of dementia, caregiving duties are more intense and last for years. Depression becomes even more of an issue because a parent could outlive the person who is providing care simply because the caregiving process is so strenuous.

Caregivers need support as do seniors who are facing the fact that their physical abilities may not match their mental abilities. Depression may be a temporary issue based on difficult life circumstances, but it may also be clinical, meaning that it involves body chemistry and requires medical intervention.

Warning Signs for Depression

- Loss of interest in usual activities
- Feeling sad, down, or hopeless
- Easily annoyed or irritated
- Restless
- Crying spells for no obvious reason
- Unable to see the brighter side
- Loss of interest in intimacy
- Trouble sleeping
- Difficulty focusing or concentrating
- Difficulty making decisions
- Feeling fatigued or weak
- Unintentional weight gain or loss
- Suicidal thoughts or behaviors
- Unexplained physical problems

Looking at this list, you can probably identify some for both you and your parent. While these are warning signs for depression, many are fairly normal for everyone experiencing a bad day. Some are normal side effects of medical issues or medications, but when grouped together or not temporary, they need to be addressed.

If the caregiver is having trouble sleeping, the simple answer may be too many churning thoughts rather than depression. If your parent just doesn't want to be involved in normal activities, it may be boredom and a need to try something new for social interaction. But when

Dad stops telling his "good ol' days" stories or suddenly doesn't feel like playing pool with his buddies anymore, take note. If he refuses to talk to you, find someone he will talk to and at least alert a physician to the change.

Sadness can occur for anyone, but when moving past the issues at hand seems impossible, seek intervention. Depression is a not a normal part of the aging process, but life circumstances seniors face can contribute to depression. Consider the following:

- Transition from full-time productive careers to retirement (feelings of uselessness)
- Forced retirement due to chronic health issues or disability (feelings of uselessness, lack of purpose)
- Medical bills (threat to financial and long-term security)
- Loss of a loved one (grieving)
- Serious illness in lifelong friend or spouse (will this happen to me?)
- Lack of mobility (willing mind but incapable body)
- Driving restrictions (loss of independence)

As the aging process continues and seniors' worlds become smaller, any incident that happens to someone in their world can become personalized whether it's happening to them or not. They begin to take ownership of other people's worlds to expand their own. This can bring a sense of urgency, worry, or in extreme cases, obsession over things that have nothing to do with them. Cause and effect may not line up for easy understanding.

When Mom is suddenly possessive of her keys and wants to drive more, you may assume she's trying to assert her independence. A week later, when you hear from your cousin that Aunt Cheryl had to give up driving, you wonder why Mom didn't tell you. Then you realize your mother's sudden need to prove herself comes from fears triggered by what happened to her sister. After all, she's older than Cheryl, and she's afraid others, particularly you, her caregiver, will decide it is no longer safe for her to drive.

Spiritual Health

Some seniors have lived their faith all their lives, supporting family and friends through crises and mentoring others in their spiritual walk. The foundation of their religious beliefs carries them from cradle to grave. Yet even for those grounded in their faith, there will be times of questioning.

As your mother's friends die, she may suddenly begin questioning why she is still alive or wonder when debilitating illness will become her reality. Often church is the major social outlet for our parents, so be aware when church connections change or become limited. Changes may result from the inability to drive or a move to a new town to be closer to caregiving children. You may need to nurture your parent's walk in faith at a time when she needs it more than ever. Keeping or finding connections to match beliefs is essential.

Sometimes, when seniors move to a new community, they discover the church where they find the most connection isn't necessarily the denomination they've always been a member of. One woman expressed such unhappiness to her children and friends in her former community that they thought she was suffering from depression. Instead, she was grieving the loss of her established church family. Eventually, she branched out beyond her denomination to try other churches to fit her spiritual needs. Once she found a spiritual home, her unhappiness lessened, and she became more active socially. But what if she'd had a disability that prevented driving? Then she would have needed help to nurture new spiritual and social bonds.

If a parent moves closer to caregiving children, the family needs to recognize and help build social and spiritual contacts.

■ ■ ■

A wise senior said, "Growing old just ain't for sissies."

He was right. Caring for someone growing older isn't either. Maintaining social and spiritual connections can help avoid depression and keep seniors and their caregivers happy and healthy.

Viewpoint:

Kim's identity crisis

I left my teaching career so I could spend more time with my husband and children. But while caring for my parents, I was rarely home.

When Dad died, I found myself wandering around wondering what to do next. I knew Mom was doing the same thing. We'd both been so wrapped up in his needs that we'd forgotten who we were. But that realization didn't dawn immediately because it was easy to transfer all that caregiving energy into planning the service, handling the estate, and anything else that came up. It was actually quite some time before I asked myself, *Well, what do I do now?*

I'd lost my focus. And, at least for a time, I'd lost sight of the goals I had before becoming a caregiver. It was as if I'd pressed the pause button on my life, and for a time, I couldn't find the play button again.

This can happen to caregivers at any age. It happened to me, but it can also happen to the 69-year-old woman caring for her 72-year-old husband dying of a terminal disease. Caregivers are prime targets for an identity crisis. Finding time for yourself and nurturing yourself as a person and a member of society at large is essential.

Living Water

> [Elijah] came to a lone broom bush and collapsed in its shade, wanting in the worst way to be done with it all—to just die: "Enough of this, GOD! Take my life—I'm ready to join my ancestors in the grave!" Exhausted, he fell asleep under the lone broom bush (1 Kings 19:4-5 MSG).

Many people are ashamed of depression, refusing to acknowledge it or get help. But the Bible provides evidence that depression has always been a part of human existence.

In his psalms, David cried out for deliverance from false accusations, the oppression of enemies, and the weight of his sin.

King Saul appears to have been manic-depressive, alternating between egocentric highs and nearly inconsolable lows. When faced with capture, torture, and death, Saul chose suicide.

Elijah was tired of it all and begged God to take his life.

Depression is not a sign of personal weakness. Health conditions, grief, and chemical changes in the brain all factor into the depression equation. And when there seems to be no relief in sight for current situations, people often view suicide as the only logical means of escape. Nothing could be further from the truth.

If you notice any of the warning signs of depression, don't hesitate to seek medical attention. Prayer helps, but medication and counseling may also be necessary. There is no shame in getting help.

Additional Information

Information about depression's causes, symptoms, identification, and treatment—www.nimh.nih.gov/health/publications/depression-listing.shtml.

For additional information on suicide and senior adults, visit: http://mentalhealth.samhsa.gov/suicideprevention/elderly.asp or www.healthyplace.com/depression/elderly/depression-in-elderly/menu-id-68/.

Online screening test for depression: http://psych.med.nyu.edu/patient-care/depression-screening-test.

The HELP program (www.hospitalelderlifeprogram.org) provides specific information about hospitalization sensitivity common to seniors. It offers guidelines for older adults and caregivers regarding in-hospital care and safety at home.

Chapter 20

Seeing a New Horizon
Coping as Death Approaches

Caregivers who have been on the job solo for weeks, months, or years are often reluctant to call in assistance when it becomes evident that their duties will be coming to an end. Why stop now?

But asking for help doesn't signal you've stopped offering care. It's merely an expansion of care. Though calling in added support can be done at any point in the caregiving path, when end-of-life issues rise to the surface, the time has definitely come to let others join the journey.

In this day of rapid medical breakthroughs, new treatments, and a never-say-die attitude from physicians, patients, and family members, there is a general reluctance to choose comfort care. Many fear *hospice care* or *palliative care*, yet those who have experienced what they have to offer often say they received more peace in that stage of caregiving than in any other.

Palliative and Hospice Care

Palliative and hospice care are available to patients with a wide range of medical conditions. *Palliative care* is offered for people facing severe chronic or terminal illnesses. It is designed not for finding cures but for securing comfort in dealing with the symptoms as the disease progresses toward a natural end. The idea is to prevent suffering while caring for the living in a loving, compassionate manner.

Hospice care, a form of palliative care, provides comfort when an end is in sight. Insurance companies may not pay benefits for hospice care unless the doctor verifies details of prognosis, such as a six-month or less life expectancy. However, that does not mean that six months is the limit to services. The doctor may use the term "palliative care" instead if he questions whether his diagnosis will meet the insurance company rules for paying hospice benefits.

Hospice care can be given in the hospital, in a person's home, or in specially designed hospice homes, often affiliated with hospitals or other care agencies. Patients can move between the different types of care.

A person may move to a hospice wing or floor of a hospital after being released from another unit. He could then move to in-home hospice care or a hospice house situation. Perhaps he and his family decide to have in-home care, but he later says he doesn't want to die at home. So he is moved into the hospice house for his final days. Help is available to coordinate any changes, thus relieving a caregiver to spend quality time in that role.

One woman had several conditions that were life-limiting, and her doctor, believing her life expectancy was six months or less, ordered hospice care. However, she ended up receiving hospice services for more than eighteen months. Hospice didn't discontinue services at the six-month marker; they continued to offer care support according to her needs. One myth associated with hospice care is that it hastens death. But hospice care often relieves the patient's emotional concerns and physical struggle, thus extending life beyond initial expectations.

Time frames for life expectancy aren't set in stone. Hospice providers are not callous and do not abandon patients who live longer than expected.

On the other hand, patients can be discharged from hospice care if conditions improve or a life-limiting disease appears to be in remission. These patients can return to aggressive therapy under their physician's care and go about daily life. If a discharged patient later needs to return to hospice care, it's still available. A case manager can help coordinate continued care through other agencies such as home-health providers.

Hospice care also extends to the family of the patient and does not end at death. Bereavement counseling is available for up to thirteen months after a death, depending on the needs of the family.

Hospice is not one single, large company that offers services across the nation. Many organizations, some for-profit and some nonprofit, use *hospice* in their name, but each may provide different types of care and benefits. As in other elements of caregiving, it's important to match the needs of your situation to available care. Many communities have multiple agencies offering hospice care, so research is necessary.

It's normal for caregivers to be discouraged when hospice care is needed. When you've already learned more than you ever wanted to about your loved one's medical conditions and treatments, and you've put so much of your life on hold to accommodate them, the idea of researching how to let your loved one die seems a greater burden than any caregiver should have to bear. But it's worth it.

> When your parent begins seeing heaven and talking about long-dead loved ones, don't try to stop him from doing so. While this may be upsetting for you, it's a natural part of the "going home" process.

Doctors usually avoid suggesting one hospice company over another, but may be able to help you formulate a list of anticipated needs. This list then becomes a tool to match services to those needs. As primary caregivers arrange for hospice care, they can find peace in knowing this is one of their final tasks and they are selecting with as much care as they have given in other areas. Other family members and friends can help with this also.

Often caregivers believe they can't afford hospice services because of already excessive medical bills. However, regardless of ability to pay or insurance coverage, hospice services are available to everyone. In fact, once hospice is on the scene, additional financial burdens may be lifted. Hospice can provide care supplies and medicines. Part of the "intake" evaluation into hospice care is an evaluation of whether a patient is using all available coverage, benefits, and services available.

Some providers actually have a "no expense for the patient or family" policy. However, that doesn't mean services aren't processed through insurance. Just watch for any gaps and clarify who pays for what and how. This is when researching what services providers offer proves beneficial.

In addition, hospice providers manage paperwork, and doctor and hospital visits are often reduced while in hospice care. While hospice providers work closely with physicians, they also have their own medical staff. In one case, when the hospice nurse made her daily visit and suspected that her patient had developed an infection, she was able to take the appropriate specimen directly to a lab and obtain doctor-approved medications without the patient ever having to leave her home.

On the lighter side: A senior with dementia kept asking where her mother was. Each time, her caregiver replied, "She's with Jesus." After several weeks of hearing this answer, the senior finally said, "Mother's been going out a lot with him lately, hasn't she?"

When it comes to the nitty-gritty details of care, both caregivers and their loved ones have often developed such a bond of trust that they do not want others to participate in their struggle or challenges. If you've changed Mom's diapers for the last eight months, it's difficult for both of you to realize someone else can do that.

Hospice caregivers are a special breed. The nurses and nursing assistants providing the bulk of patient care become like family to their patients. They're trained to learn, understand, and accommodate each patient's and family's needs, medically and emotionally, whether hospice services are accessed months or only hours before a patient dies. Often, families who utilize hospice services only for a short time wish they'd done so earlier because the support was so beneficial.

The amount of time a hospice care provider is in your home depends on the patient's stage in the life-releasing process. Once hospice nurses and aids come, family members may be reluctant to have them leave.

Hospices provide service and support on a 24-hour basis. Nurses are on call even in the middle of the night or if more visits are needed than initially scheduled on the patient care plan.

Hospice care eases patients' worries, allowing them to let go. A patient may actually be struggling to live, fearing the effect letting go will have on his caregiver, often a beloved child. When someone else offers support, fears are relieved. Hospice manages pain—physical, emotional, and spiritual—and provides comfort and symptom relief. The goal is to allow a patient to be pain-free but alert so that any interactions with loved ones are of the highest quality.

Hospice as a category of care is not affiliated with any religion. Some churches and specific religious sectors have started hospices, some in connection with hospitals, but care is given to community members regardless of beliefs. Some hospice caregivers will pray with their patients, but only if those doors are opened by the patient or family. Hospice organizations often have chaplains visit as part of a care team, and they too are available on call, not just for the patient, but for the family members as well.

■■■

Home Health is not Hospice

Home healthcare is an entirely separate type of in-home service than hospice. Depending on their medical conditions, patients may be eligible for home health through different agencies and providers. Home healthcare providers tend to work with a patient or family member for a limited time to educate and teach home skills to better manage care. In some cases, home health provides daily or weekly services for extended periods of time.

■■■

Viewpoint:

A Hospice Nurse Speaks

Connie Bethea is a certified hospice and palliative care R.N. with Agape Hospice in Anderson, SC. When her husband died at age 36 from cancer, she saw him through his last days not only as his wife, but as a nurse and mother to their three-year-old daughter. Her father died a year later, also with hospice care. She became a hospice nurse in 1995.

"I wanted to be able to give back what I had received to others facing the loss of a loved one. This is not just a job. It's a mission. God has placed us hospice nurses in this position to do His work. Though we don't push religion, our clients know we are a faith-based service provider [not all hospices are faith-based]. We are dedicated to showing God's love and what can be accomplished through that.

"Over the years I've had patients who were atheists. We respect their opinions and minister to their needs as we do everyone. The beautiful thing is that I've never known anyone to die an atheist.

"Hospice care is not just the work of one individual. We work as a team and see our patients as unique persons with goals for their lives. It makes us so happy to help a patient reach his goal, whatever it is.

"Some of our patients just don't want to feel alone or abandoned in their final days. Sometimes they need help with their family connections and finances. This is something doctors can't do. Our team works with physicians to bring nurses, social workers, chaplains, and volunteers together to address a person's life, not just their physical condition.

"We offer comfort care for the body, but emotional and spiritual support too. Emotional pain is just as bad as physical pain. Sometimes it is hard for doctors to recommend hospice care because they don't want their patients to think they are giving up on them. But they realize we have something more to offer.

"When a person enters hospice care, it's not about giving up or dying. It's about living your best life. We often bring family members together so that everyone is on the same page, working together toward that common goal. It is such a reward for the family to know they have upheld the wishes of their loved one, and for us to be a part of the process.

"If you are there with a person at the very end of life, and you just listen—hear them talk of others who have gone before them—you may see a real glimpse of heaven as they begin to see its doors open for them."

Connie's advice: So many people look for big miracles. Take time to see the little ones God offers us every day.

Living Water

> Abraham was now old and well advanced in years, and the LORD had blessed him in every way. He said to the chief servant in his household…"Go to my country and my own relatives and get a wife for my son Isaac."…Then [the servant] prayed, "O LORD, God of my master Abraham, give me success today, and show kindness to my master Abraham" (Genesis 24:1,2,4,12).

Abraham was a venerable old gentleman who knew his days were numbered, and he wanted to take care of important business before he died. His greatest wish was to see his son Isaac married to an Israelite rather than a foreigner. So he sent his most trusted servant on a mission.

Perhaps the servant didn't want the assignment or the journey, but as caregivers, we can learn a lot from the servant's approach to his task and about honoring the wishes of those who are about to die. Here's what the servant did:

- *Prayed specifically*—The servant prayed for success with his task. His request was specific and he asked God to guide him.

- *Expected an answer*—In this instance, the servant's prayer was answered before he'd finished praying. While all prayer doesn't garner an immediate response, look for answers.

- *Reflected and observed*—Even though the servant had what appeared to be the answer, he took time to be certain he understood God's answer.

- *Gave thanks for answered prayer*—The servant bowed and worshiped the Lord, acknowledging His provision with praise and thanksgiving. It is important for us to remember to do the same.

- *Didn't get sidetracked*—Sometimes we second-guess answers to prayer. Abraham's servant didn't allow anyone or anything to deter him from completing his mission.

Prayer is a vitally important part of every aspect of life. As caregivers, we take a subservient role. By following this servant's example, we make our journey less difficult, while honoring our parents.

Additional Information

"Five Wishes" is a document that helps guide people through the preparation of their living will and advance directives. The document, once witnessed and notarized, is considered a legally binding document in most states and can be purchased through www.agingwithdignity.org.

Chapter 21

Stepping onto Shore

Making the Transition When Your Caregiving Role Ends

"Mama's care was intense for so long. We kept her at home with us, which is what she wanted. By the time Mama died, we were all relieved that she didn't have to struggle anymore, and for ourselves, too, because it had been such a hard journey. But all I kept thinking was that I killed my mama. I had a very hard time with that. I felt so guilty. I'd been responsible and felt responsible for everything for so long, why not for this? Did I do this? Did I kill Mama?

"I finally called my pastor. He reminded me of John 15:13—'There is no greater love than to lay down one's life for one's friends.'

"'You laid down your life to take care of your mother,' he said. He read Scripture to me and prayed with me. He asked God to take those difficult feelings from me. He knew I had done everything I could. Hearing him say that made it real. It was like a weight lifted from me. I realized we really did do everything possible for Mama, and I'm at peace with that now.

"The hospice nurses continued to call, checking on me and the rest of the family. After a while, I told them they could take us off their call list. We were doing fine and appreciated all they had done."—Donna

■ ■ ■

As caregiver, you have been riding tumultuous seas. Whether a few days or weeks of sudden illness, or a years-long battle with disease, death has come for your loved one.

More than likely, you feel relief mixed with guilt and self-doubt. Your boat drifts toward shore, pushed by waves of different and new things to handle, such as details for the funeral service and estate issues. But actually stepping out of the caregiving boat may require you to accept the hand of someone to help you take that leap onto shore. When you hit dry land, that place called "your life" that you've longed for from afar, expect your legs to be weak and the scenery to be less familiar than before.

You've survived the storm. Once over, many caregivers think they don't need help. They've handled everything so far, and now is no different. But it most certainly is. Allow others who have been through the storms of caregiving and death to help you recover your land-legs again. Drawing on the expertise of others, whether friends, pastors, hospice chaplains, or professional counselors, is not relinquishing control. It's smart. It's doing what you've done in your caregiving journey. You put the resources around you to the best possible use for the best possible outcome.

Grieving is a process. It doesn't begin at death and end at the funeral. It can last for months or years. Grief can't be ignored or circumvented. While it may be possible to run from grief for a period of time, it will eventually catch up with us, sometimes with more damaging results than if we'd confronted it head-on.

Years after a parent's death, you may feel a pang in your heart when you see a basket of strawberries, remembering the amazing strawberry pie Mom used to make. Or you might be standing in the choir loft, singing a familiar hymn, when you hear your father's tenor voice and tears begin to flow. These memories lead to others and to feelings of loss. Grief moments come anytime, anywhere, and without notice. As the years go by the sting will lessen, but the moments will come.

The grief process is not one you choose or control. It is simply part of your journey. You've come to a crossroad and have to turn because the road you've been on has ended. At times you may feel physically weak and distressed. But despite the tears and heavy heart, latch on to the promise that there is a place prepared for us in heaven.

Caregiver's Grief

Caregiver grief differs from the grief of someone who has had a sudden loss in that the caregiving process involves anticipatory grief. A caregiver watches her loved one lose abilities and vital life functions. When Dad can no longer walk unaided, grieving occurs for the little girl who no longer sees her big strong daddy standing beside her, ready to catch her if *she* falls. Those grief moments come weeks, months, or even years before death occurs. In some ways, it makes the actual death easier; in other ways, harder. The ease comes when the caregiver realizes the loved one was ready to leave the body that no longer supported the vital spirit within.

"In our family it is easy for us to talk about death because we don't fear it. It's a Christian legacy we pass on. At the last minute I might chicken out, but I watched my mother take her last breath calmly, and like her, I don't intend to fight death. I really believe there is a difference in the way a Christian dies and how a non-Christian dies."

—Edna

A caregiver works hard to improve quality of life, and regular bouts of grief take energy from the caregiver, making the day-to-day journey feel more of a struggle than perhaps it actually is.

"Marianne, how was your day with your mom?" Alan asked.

"Oh, fine. No major traumas, just a quick follow-up appointment with Mom, then on to buy groceries," she said.

Alan wondered why Marianne looked so exhausted on what she was describing as a light-duty day.

If asked, Marianne probably couldn't pinpoint the reason for her malaise, but that day was the first time she'd had to borrow a wheelchair from the doctor's office to get her mother back out to the car. It was also the first time her mother didn't want to go into the grocery store with her. When Marianne got back to the car, her mother was noncommunicative, staring into space. Previously a lively person, her mother seemed to be tuning out the world more and more.

When Death Comes

I'm sorry to hear your mother passed away. Was this expected?

Even "expected" death doesn't preclude sorrow. When it's apparent death is approaching, a mixture of emotions come into play—happiness that suffering will soon be over, along with guilt and questioning. But there are also special feelings of fulfillment that others do not experience in their grief. Realize that you've truly done everything possible for your parent and accept the blessings of a deep, long-lasting inner peace that came from the bond you shared combined with the care you've given. Knowing this helps a caregiver move through grief more rapidly than someone dealing with feelings of not having done enough.

Although grief is a process that has specific, recognizable phases, it is a complex issue. Each family and each person deals with grief differently. It affects adults, teenagers, and children. Unresolved grief has an impact on daily life and personalities. Some people don't even realize grief issues are behind current struggles.

"Often people come to me having dealt with one death after another," says Wayne Hyatt, counselor and associate pastor. "Perhaps their mother died two years ago and their aunt a few months later and just recently their sibling. They think they're coming to me because they're struggling with the most recent death. It's no surprise there are problems because if the steps of the grieving process haven't happened with each of those relationships, the effect is magnified."

For some, being in a support group, where others understand how they feel, offers a safe place where grieving is accepted and grieving persons don't feel judged for what they express. These are not social groups, but they're also not clinical. It's just a way for people to work through their grief through verbalization.

Usually a facilitator opens the discussion, but then lets the conversation take its natural course among the group members. Talking through grief, whether with professionals, in a group, or just with a good friend, releases the tension behind the grief in a constructive way.

The Religious Sting

Well, you're a Christian and so was your father. You'll be just fine.

When religious beliefs are used to discount or push aside the grieving person's emotional response, the grief is not honored, nor is the person experiencing it. Yes, faith helps. Knowing that your parents were secure in their beliefs that death leads to a new beginning in heaven will provide a large measure of peace. Despite the joy family and friends find in the passing of their loved one into the kingdom of heaven, there is still loss. It is the end of a relationship connected to daily life. Joy and sorrow can coexist in the grieving heart.

A Key for Caregivers

When caregivers balance their duties of love with life activities of their own, they have a basis on which to build the future. Engaging in normal activities during the caregiving process is like bringing a boat to shore on occasion to stock up on supplies. It's a reminder that land exists and you'll step onto it again at some point, even if you're currently heading back out in the choppy caregiving waters. Those who never come to shore forget what the land feels like and have much more difficulty moving forward. A caregiver who has not nurtured at least some of her own life and identity while offering care to others will suffer feelings of displacement for a much longer time and may experience a true identity crisis.

Viewpoint:

Finding support—grief counseling

Wanda's husband, John, was in charge of the family business. When he died unexpectedly, Wanda suddenly had to answer questions from bankers, lawyers, and businessmen. John's employees were counting on her to keep the business going while she was trying to help her children and mother-in-law handle John's death and grieve herself.

"It was so difficult. My life was being John's wife. I didn't have a Sunday school class but was a member of a church. I started attending a Sunday school class not long after John's death and found some support there.

"I also had a few meetings with one of our pastors and that helped, especially his suggestion to keep a journal. I recorded things in the journal that I didn't feel I could share with anyone at the time—like how I'd go sit in the closet just to smell my husband's clothes.

"As I approached the first anniversary of John's death, I saw information about the GriefShare support group, and I knew I had to be in it. It was a group of people who had lost husbands, parents, or children. We had a facilitator and pastor who were so sensitive to what we were going through. There were videos and a take-home workbook with devotionals and perspectives from different professionals on a variety of topics. They were very good, but mostly what helped was being around other people who were talking about what they were experiencing. I could share how precious it was to have friends bring me gifts on Valentine's Day, but how angry I was, too, that John wasn't there to do that.

"In group grief counseling, you may say something that helps someone else and seeing that also helps you. It's a giving and receiving process that helps with healing. There are a lot of people who could benefit from this kind of experience who haven't found it yet.

"God promises to take care of widows and fatherless children. Those promises are so true. I didn't initially feel this way when I lost my husband, but I've seen God's miracles in my life. It is so obvious that God is listening."

Living Water

> Brothers and sisters, we do not want you to be uninformed about those who sleep in death, so that you do not grieve like the rest, who have no hope (1 Thessalonians 4:13 TNIV).

Years ago, when my father-in-law was in ICU, I spent days in the waiting room with a family whose loved one had been in a motorcycle accident. Ultimately, the family had to decide whether to take this 20-something-year-old, brain-dead young man off life support. I will always remember their anguish.

I asked one family member if the boy was a Christian. She got a puzzled look on her face and said she didn't think so. That revelation left me almost speechless, because I couldn't reassure her that she'd see this loved one again.

As Christians, we have the advantage of the assurance of heaven for those who believe and trust in Jesus Christ. Death isn't a final end to life; it is the beginning of eternity. There is hope beyond the grave and the promise that we'll see our loved ones again. That knowledge keeps us from utter despair.

Additional Information

Online resources

Livestrong.com offers a wide array of articles to assist navigation through many stages of life. Coping.org, in partnership with Livestrong offers information about the stages of the loss process through www.coping.org/grief/stages.htm.

Books

When Grief Comes: Finding Strength for Today and Hope for Tomorrow, Kirk H. Neely, (Grand Rapids, MI: Baker Books, 2007).

A Grief Observed, C.S. Lewis (New York: HarperOne, 2001).

A Tearful Celebration: Finding God in the Midst of Loss, James Means (Colorado Springs: Multnomah Books, 2006).

Chapter 22

Medical Office Procedures (MOPs)

For a conscientious caregiver, traveling from one doctor's office to another is much more than miles put on the car. Keeping the office hours straight, which staffers are most helpful, the procedures used for making and changing appointments and prescriptions, as well as who handles special procedure scheduling can become a marathon event. Each office functions differently. This is where making notes about office procedures will make a caregiver's task much easier. (See chapters 5 and 23 for suggestions and forms for keeping this information easily accessible.)

When HIPAA Feels Like a Hippo

The American Health Insurance Portability and Accountability Act of 1996 (HIPAA) is a set of rules with which doctors, hospitals, and other healthcare providers must comply. It helps ensure information in medical records (and medical billing) meet certain standards to protect the privacy of patients.

For a busy caregiver, this security HIPAA provides most often feels like a headache because it requires more paperwork and hoop-jumping. Often, for every doctor or hospital visit, a patient or patient representative must sign an acknowledgement of receipt of privacy practices. Some doctors' offices provide patients with a booklet detailing their office privacy standards each year. Each service provider is required, by law, to obtain a signature verifying the HIPAA information was given and received. You may feel it is unnecessary, especially if you've been a caregiver for long time, but there are reasons for these regulations.

> Meredith had been caring for her mother for three years, taking her to every doctor's appointment and interacting with staff members regarding appointments, tests, and medication management.

> When the mail-order pharmacy sent a letter saying there was a problem with filling a prescription, Meredith called the office to request help in sorting out the situation. She was referred to a new staff member in charge of prescriptions.

> "Ms. Stone, I'd like to be able to help you, but I can't. You're not authorized."

> "Excuse me, but I am. A copy of my mother's Healthcare Power of Attorney is in her file, and I am the one listed."

> "I cannot find that, and I don't have the form signed for this year indicating that she has authorized you to act on her behalf in our office. You'll have to either let me speak to your mother directly or come in with her and have her fill out the form."

■ ■ ■

Meredith was close to losing patience with someone only trying to follow directions dictated by office policies. The office policies were designed to make sure the office was following federal laws about patient privacy.

Some offices have more stringent policies than others. Meredith could ask for intervention from a nurse in the office who knows the situation. Would that require more effort than taking the time to deliver a new copy of the Healthcare POA to the office? Was there time before the prescription ran out to handle the situation this way?

The person handling these issues can determine which course of action is best. Although a terrible strain on a caregiver, it's a necessary one, nonetheless. Here, HIPAA feels like a hippo sitting on the chest of a caregiver whose intentions are only the most honorable.

Yet look at another situation:

> Michelle is Meredith's wayward sister. She's come by for an unexpected visit and sees her mother's pain medication on the bathroom counter. She knows she could sell some of those pills, so she writes down the prescription information and calls the doctor's office when she gets home later.
>
> "Hi, I'm Michelle. I need to get my mother's pain medications refilled."
>
> "Michelle, I don't see you listed as your mother's personal representative, and I don't have authorization to refill prescriptions at your request. I'm sorry, but only your mother or her representative can request a refill."
>
> "But I'm her daughter. I'm taking care of her now, and I'm her representative. She's staying with me for a while, and I need her prescriptions called into my pharmacy since she left her medicines at home."
>
> "Well, then you'll have to bring in your mother and have her sign authorization for you to handle prescription issues for her."

Scenarios like the one above happen. HIPAA actually doesn't mandate the ways in which hospitals and medical offices identify personal representatives. States and other laws determine that. However, many office procedures designed to meet the HIPAA regulations wrap the two issues together. It is important to understand this before losing your temper with an innocent staff member.

Patients are also given the freedom to see their own medical records under the HIPAA rules.

HIPAA also covers continuance of care issues that benefit all.

> Ira flies to Virginia from his home in Oregon to visit his sister. While there, he falls, is temporarily unconscious, and taken to the emergency room of a local hospital.
>
> His sister offers information about the town he lives in, and

doctors and staff try to contact the hospital in his town to obtain medical records that will help them provide the best care. Before treating him or giving medications, they can check for allergies and other contraindications. In the process, they discover Ira is on medication for a heart condition. This information is necessary to provide the safest care possible, and it is obtained on the assumption that Ira wants care. That, however, is where the assumptions stop. No one is authorized to tell Ira's sister about his other health issues found through need-to-know efforts made on his behalf.

When Ira is released from the hospital, a report listing treatments and medications given is sent to Ira's hometown doctor. That allows the hometown doctor to follow up on Ira's care.

Paper Trails

Despite the medical community's embrace of technology and the trends toward digital medical files, many trees lose their lives in this industry. Keeping track of things involves record keeping of some kind. If you're a computer whiz who can keep notes on your laptop or smartphone, that's great. But be sure to make a backup file to protect against the unexpected computer crash. The same goes for phone numbers of doctors, appointment calendars, and so on.

Whether your notebook is digital or not, keeping the information trail clear is essential. With any given doctor you should be able to look back and see what tests were ordered, when, and why. You may need to reference this with a different doctor, so keeping up with information will make it useful and manageable. If you haven't done it yet, and you're faced with a pile of papers stuck into a "Mom" or "Dad" file, don't beat yourself up for being behind. Begin where you are. The positive feelings you receive from organizing a little will help build your motivation for the rest.

Medications

Make sure you keep an up-to-date list of medications your parent is currently taking. Remember, however, that some offices require you to bring medicine bottles with you, especially for controlled substances. Check the medical office procedure regarding medicines prior to the appointment so you aren't frustrated when you arrive.

Designate a place to save the patient information sheets that come with prescriptions. You can cut down on clutter by keeping only the latest sheet for each medicine filled or taken. It's important to read these sheets instead of just filing them. You might pick up on a side effect that a doctor or nurse reviewing the meds may not. Remember: You know your patient better than they do!

Scans and Reports

It is perfectly fine for a patient to request copies of his or her own scans and reports from scans. That is part of the HIPAA regulation. Having copies of these reports in your notebook, or in another readily accessible location, will help you navigate between doctors' offices.

Viewpoint:

The pitfalls of inaccurate paper trails—Mary's experience

"I am my sister's sole caregiver. While she was in the hospital for surgery on a broken hip, she developed a small sore on the curve of her heel that was not documented while there.

"When my sister moved to a rehabilitation facility, the size and severity of the sore increased. While the facility nurses and doctor have treated the sore, it hasn't healed in over four months. Now, suddenly, a wound expert has been called in because the sore has a foul odor and my sister's toes are turning blue.

"I have been notified by the facility that Medicare will no longer cover the treatment of the sore on my sister's heel because it is not viewed to be a result of her initial hospital stay since it wasn't documented there. Any treatment she receives for her heel from this point on will be paid out-of-pocket, and obviously, the heel must be treated to keep her from losing her foot.

"Through this experience, I have learned to request to review my sister's chart prior to discharge on any subsequent trips to the hospital."

Living Water

> Now that faith has come, we are no longer under the supervision of the law (Galatians 3:25).

The apostle Paul was an expert on Jewish law. He'd studied it, memorized it, and could quote it chapter and verse. His writings even sound like those of an attorney, don't you think?

But following his Damascus Road experience, Paul began a different sort of schooling. He started where he was and built on the knowledge he already had, but continued to learn as God instructed. While he acknowledged the wisdom and merit in having laws, he also preached salvation through faith in Jesus Christ.

In your role as caregiver, you understand the need for rules, regulations, and proper procedures, even if they often prove annoying. By accepting and complying, you save yourself frustration and stress. Remember, regulations are there for a reason.

But spiritually, through Jesus' sacrifice on the cross, we're free from myriad Old Testament rules and regulations. By grace and through faith in Christ, we don't have to jump through numerous hoops or accomplish unending works to gain salvation. It's a gift, freely given. Give thanks.

Additional Information

There are many intricacies to the HIPAA law and how it applies to individuals. For detailed breakdowns of HIPAA, visit www.hhs.gov/hipaafaq/.

Chapter 23

Forms

Forms are both helps and hindrances, but the goal is clarity and making caregiving tasks easier to manage. Here is an overview of various forms and how they are used. Some need to be obtained through an attorney, physician, state, or other agency, and require legal follow-through. Others are simple things that can be copied and used in your notebook as needed.

Legal Issues

Advance Directives

An *Advance Directive* is a legal document a person prepares to explain what kind of healthcare he should receive when he can no longer make such decisions. A *living will* is one such directive that often states a person's wishes about life-sustaining treatments such as life support, feeding tubes, and hydration. It may be helpful to have your parent talk through the realities of some of these measures before making the decision. Asking a doctor to explain what a feeding tube does may help bring clarity and peace with such decisions.

As we mentioned in chapter 20, the Aging with Dignity website (www.agingwithdignity.org) offers a tool called "Five Wishes" that covers hot-button issues in a sensitive manner. When notarized, it is a legally binding document in most states.

Power(s) of Attorney (POA)

A *Power of Attorney* (POA) is a legal document that grants someone else the right to act legally on another person's behalf. According to HIPAA regulations, however, this does not apply to healthcare issues. A "regular" POA deals with most financial and legal transactions outside the realm of health management. A POA is intended to be used if the person giving the POA is not able to handle the issues for themselves. This enables the holder to access accounts and personal information of the person authorizing it.

A word of caution: An elderly woman gave her POA to a friend she thought would always have her best interests in mind. After returning from a hospital stay, she received a call from a credit card company. The woman holding the POA had called the company and asked for a card to be issued in her name on the elderly woman's account. Although the POA holder had faxed a copy of the POA to the credit card company, they didn't act without the primary account holder's confirmation. But for some companies, the POA is enough to complete such a request. So be careful to whom this authority is given.

Healthcare Power of Attorney (HPOA)

The second type of POA is the *Healthcare Power of Attorney (HPOA)*. This document gives one person authority to manage healthcare decisions for another. It is separate from a POA, and different individuals can hold these authorizations.

For instance, if an elderly man retired to Florida and his children all live in Michigan, he could give an HPOA to one child and have a local friend or other care provider listed as an alternate. The child could also be listed as an alternate. That way, if an emergency situation arose, the local friend could help with immediate decisions until the adult child could be reached.

Different terms are used in different parts of the country for this type of authorization, so check which applies to you. In some states, a HPOA is called Healthcare Representative for Healthcare Proxy.

Do Not Resuscitate (DNR)

The DNR form is an actual order placed by a physician at the request of a patient. It states that no life-sustaining measures, such as CPR, will be attempted in the event of cardiac or respiratory arrest. A DNR is often issued by a doctor or even the medical/nursing director of a care facility when a person has a terminal disease and resuscitation is perceived as prolonging the inevitable. This is not the same as a living will. Many times when a patient is under hospice care, a case manager will have a DNR filled out and posted in the patient's room or home.

Keep copies on hand of all POAs, HPOAs, Advance Directives, and DNRs. Ideally, they will be in THE NOTEBOOK and readily available at each doctor appointment or hospital visit. A doctor will not necessarily honor your HPOA if you can't prove you have one. The same is true of Advance Directives.

Nonlegal Forms

We've included these forms at the end of this chapter, and we encourage you to photocopy them as needed or to download them from www.whenyouragingparentneedscare.com. Keep these forms also in THE NOTEBOOK.

Basic Life Checklist

Use this list to get a snapshot of the person you are caring for and how they are living their life. These conversation starters may provide a unique bonding experience. While you may think you know everything about a parent, the answers may surprise you.

Insurance Forms: Explanation of Benefits (EOB)

It's a good idea to check health insurance "Explanation of Benefits" statements for accuracy. Many individuals try to oversee this on their own, but because healthcare lingo on statements is often difficult to navigate, people sometimes opt for hiring professional watchdogs to manage healthcare benefits.

Confusion with statements often arises when a procedure performed in a doctor's office is listed as a certain name in the doctor's computer system and another in the insurance company's. This discrepancy makes it challenging to determine if services have actually been submitted for reimbursement, what has been processed, and what, if anything, the patient owes.

If your parents are receiving bills with balances that don't seem reasonable for their insurance coverage, call the doctor's office and update insurance information. Something as simple as the misspelling of a name can result in claims being rejected and the need for correction and re-filing. Other problems arise when offices change computer systems, in-house forms, or staff members, and errors crop up with those mystery numbers used to communicate with insurance companies.

Hospital Checklist

Use the hospital checklist to make a parent's hospital stay easier to manage. Vigilance with communication will help keep all comfortable and assist doctors in getting your parent home as soon as possible.

Records Request Forms

If you need to obtain records or have them sent between offices and cannot get a specific form from your new doctor, you can make and use your own. The most important part is to include all the necessary information. There may be fees associated with requesting records.

Phone Log

It's wise to keep a phone log documenting concerns you've addressed by phone, the phone numbers used, and the names of the people you've talked to. If trouble arises, which often occurs when following insurance paper trails, you have a record.

Physician Profile

Know your doctors and have their contact information accessible. Documenting knowledge you've gained from multiple doctor visits will aid someone filling in for you on subsequent visits.

Medications Log

This form is useful for long-term medication management. It's one to keep in your notebook and update regularly. It can be used to fill out the "Universal Medication Form" (available through your doctor's office) but contains additional information that doctors don't necessarily need.

When listing medications in the log include the generic name, if given. Note whether it is a (P) prescribed medication or a (N) non-prescription or over-the-counter (OTC) drug. Be sure to list all herbal supplements too.

Write in the dosage, usually in milligrams (mg), then the frequency. If it's taken only one time a day (1x), then you need to indicate (m) for morning or (e) for evening. Medications taken at noon receive a notation of (n). Use what works for you.

Some medications can cause side effects if taken at certain times of the day. Having the information when you ask about those side effects can be helpful. Make sure to note the prescribing doctor, the condition being treated, and any adverse reaction. Note the start date (SD) and the pharmacy (P) where the prescription was filled. Listing the pharmacy helps if you're using more than one pharmacy or filling prescriptions both locally and by mail order. Recording the refill date (RD) will help keep up with prescription refills and when you need new prescriptions from doctors. Note the (RD) in pencil as it will need to be updated regularly.

If a medication is changed, even if just the dosage, list it as a new medication, crossing out the old prescription entry. This will enable you to record when the change occurred and why.

Immunization Record

Vaccines need to be updated with age. Some, such as the vaccine for hepatitis, are now given in schools but were not available when our parents were in school. Forms are downloadable from the Centers for Disease Control website at www.cdc.gov/vaccines under the links for "Immunization Schedules" and "Vaccination Records." If you can't find a record of your parent's vaccinations, check with a general physician or a local health department to verify needs. Additional vaccines that aren't part of routine vaccinations in our country may be necessary if traveling to foreign countries. The "Universal Medication Form" has a place to note the most recent dates for pneumonia and flu shots.

Surgical History

Having a list of surgeries is helpful but will likely take some time to develop. Your mother may have had her gallbladder out before you were born, and remembering the year or doctor may be impossible. Do the best you can. If Dad had a hernia repaired with mesh screen placed in his abdomen twenty years ago, a doctor planning to do abdominal surgery might find it helpful to know before he heads into the operating room. Additionally, as you review surgeries, your parents may remember an adverse reaction they had to anesthesia or other medication, or they might recall an underlying medical issue they'd forgotten they'd had years before.

Medical Screening Tests

Screening tests are a tool for evaluating and maintaining long-term health and circumventing major diseases.

As women age, there is a tendency to put off annual gynecological exams, especially when they are not sexually active. Regular preventative exams are important at all ages and can often catch conditions early, thus lessening required treatment if problems are found.

Other Tests and Scans

When multiple doctors are involved in care, Dr. A might be able to use results of a test ordered by Dr. B instead of reordering the same test for a different issue. So document tests. In some medical communities, those tests (either films, CDs, or reports) can be mailed, e-mailed, or faxed to avoid additional, unnecessary tests and expense. But some tests may need to be repeated to offer comparative analysis.

Remember that patients have the right to receive copies of reports from any test as well as copies of the images, though there may be a cost for burning the images to a CD. If you do get CDs, make sure you label them.

The vast number of current medical tests makes a complete listing impossible, but following is a reference guide for the five most common:

- *X-ray*—Generally x-rays look at bone structure, but they are used for other parts of the body and may require drinking contrast liquid to highlight organs better.

- *MRI*—Magnetic Resonance Imaging uses a magnetic field, radio waves, and a computer to give detailed pictures of internal structures. Although usually not painful, some people experience claustrophobia in enclosed MRI machines. This issue should be addressed before arriving for the test.

- *CT scan*—Often called a CAT scan, this is a painless form of x-ray where images are joined together to form a three-dimensional view. The patient may be required to drink contrast liquid or have it injected through an IV. Check for allergies or concerns with the contrast liquid and for any claustrophobia issues related to the machine used.

- *Ultrasounds*—An ultrasound bounces high-frequency sound waves off organs to create images. These are painless tests that sometimes require drinking water. Doppler ultrasounds look specifically for the flow of blood in a given area of the body.

- *PET scans*–Radioactive "tracers" placed into the body reflect energy to cameras, thus creating images that help measure organ function as well as blood and oxygen flow, metabolism, and other system function. Ask about claustrophobia and potential allergy-related issues with dyes used.

Caregiver's Information Form

Keeping accurate contact information for potential caregivers is a real time-saver, so once you have the information, don't lose it! You might need it months or even years after you make the initial contact. Make sure you investigate references to verify the caregiver's suitability for your parent. Once you hire a caregiver, keep a record of the assigned duties, any duties a caregiver did not or would not accept, and how well the caregiver fulfilled the duties. Also keep a log of the caregiver's hours of availability. This information will help if you need to make a different plan for care needs in the future.

Caregiver Interview Questions

Often primary caregivers wait until they are burned out emotionally and physically before they even consider the need for hired help. By then, it's difficult to come up with questions to ask a caregiver you're looking to hire. This list will at least get you started. Your specific situation will bring others to light.

Additional Information

Downloadable forms are available at www.whenyouragingparent needscare.com.

The "Universal Medication Form" can be downloaded from www. tnpharm.org/BlankUML.pdf.

An extensive listing of various types of tests and what to expect is available at www.radiologyinfo.org.

Basic Life Checklist

Do you know...

Faith:
>   Church affiliation and local pastor
>   Favorite pastor
>   Favorite hymns
>   Sunday school class
>   Burial or cremation

Home:
>   Own or rent, comfortable or not
>   "If you could live anywhere, where would it be?"

Friends:
>   "Drop by" or by invitation only
>   Who would you want notified, and who not, if health issues arise?

Car:
>   Own, payments, insurance coverage

Social groups:
>   Memberships in clubs, prayer groups, veterans' or civic groups? How often are the meetings?

Physical activities:
>   Favorite activities

Television:
>   "Must see" shows

Movies:
>   Wanted to watch, favorite oldies, favorite actors/actresses

Books:
>   Favorite author, genre

Medications:
> Favorite pharmacy, pharmacist

Doctors:
> Primary and specialists used now, or in the past

Insurance:
> Medicare, supplements, veterans' benefits

Banking:
> Favorite bank/banker, other banks, safe deposit boxes
> Investments
> Hidden assets/liabilities

Documents:
> Location of important papers, will, power of attorney, living will
> Stocks, bonds, mutual funds

Hospital Checklist

___ **Medication Check**
- Are the meds being given the same as regular meds?
- Note the generic drug name substituted for the prescription drug name.
- Note other changes made and date; watch for reaction to changes.

  These are easier for family/close friends to notice, but always a challenge in the hospital as other conditions are being treated.

- Oxygen issues or breathing treatments? If so, what amount, how long is it given, how often?

___ **Physician Check**
- Which doctor is taking care of what diagnosis?
- How are doctors communicating with each other?

  Just knowing the doctors' notes are on the chart isn't enough. It's okay for a caregiver to ask if the gastroenterologist's medication will interfere with the new heart medicine the cardiologist has just ordered.

___ **Coordination Check**
- Is there a caseworker to manage care notes and med changes from different doctors?
- If not, how do you coordinate communication?

___ **Test Verification**
- Is the test being ordered one needed for diagnosis and treatment? If so, how? If not, why ordered?
- Keep a list of tests given in hospital.

___ Discharge Summary (DS)

- Request a "DS," which will list all tests given and evaluation of discharge condition.

___ Follow-up Needed

- Note what tests are needed as follow-up and who gets the reports.

- Get copies of initial test reports for notebook and comparison.

- Find out if the hospital has scheduled follow-up appointments with doctors or if you have to make the appointments.

___ Supply Notes

- What personal care supplies may be needed now that weren't before—special soaps, wipes, creams, etc.

- Canes, walkers, special seats.

___ Caregiving Check

- Discharge living environment: Independent? Assisted?

- Change in routine: need in-home care? If so, what kind, for how long? Who coordinates?

Records Request

To: _____

Attn: Records Department

Mailing Address: _____

_____

Patient Name: _____

Pt Date of Birth _____ Pt SS# _____

Dates of Service/ Records Requested: _____

Notes:

_____

_____

_____

_____

_____

Receiving Physician

Name: _____

Practice Name: _____

Street Address: _____

City, State, Zip: _____

Phone: (____) _____   Fax: (____) _____

Patient Authorization

_____   _____

Patient signature   Date

Phone Log

Date	Time	Office	Name of contact	Phone Numbers	Issue/Suggestion/Resolution/Follow-up needed

Physician's Profile Form

Doctor: _____ Specialty: _____

Office/Practice Name: _____

Office Street Address: _____

Office Mailing Address: _____

_____

Office Phone Numbers

General: (___)_____ Appointments: (___)_____

Nurse's Line: (___)_____ After Hours: (___)_____

Fax: (___)_____

Parking notes:

Best times for appointments: _____

Hospital Affiliation: _____

Date started as a patient: _____

Condition(s) being treated:

Tests, procedures, surgeries ordered w/dates:

Office personnel notes: (Who is most helpful, who should you avoid)

Appointment dates:

Notes:

Medications Log

Patient : _____   Date Updated: _____

Medication Name (generic)	P, N, or OTC	Dose (mg)	Frequency (1x am, etc)	Prescribing Doctor	Condition	Reaction	SD	P	RD

Drug Allergies

Medication	Reaction

Immunization Record

(record date given)

Pneumonia (pneumococcal) _____

Shingles (zoster) _____

Influenza (flu) _____

Varicella (chicken pox) _____

MMR (measles, mumps, rubella) _____

HPV (human papillomavirus—women) _____

TDAP (tetanus, diptheria, pertussis [whooping cough]) _____

Polio _____

Hep A (hepatitis A) _____

Hep B (hepatitis B) _____

Meningitis (meningococcal vaccine) _____

Other: (might have been necessary for international travel) _____

Reactions

Notes

Surgical History

Date/ Year	Type of Surgery	Surgeon	Hospital	Reason for surgery/complications

Medical Screening Tests

Test	Date	Doctor	Needs Follow-up?
CBC (complete blood count)			
Thyroid Test			
Cholesterol Check			
Blood Pressure			
Diabetes			
Depression			
Colonoscopy			
Hemoccult (checks for blood in stool)			
Prostate Exam (men)			
Bone Density (women)			
Mammogram (women)			
Pap Smear (women)			

Other Tests

(x-rays, CTs, MRIs, PET scans, ultrasounds)

Type of Test	Reason	Ordering Doctor	Date	Location of test
Example: Hip x-ray	*Fall*	*Dr. X*	*04/06/2003*	*XYZ Mem. Hospital*

Caregiver's Information Form

Name:

Address:

Organization Affiliation: (home health, etc.)

Social Security number:

Pay Rate:

Phone numbers:

References:

Days/times available:

Care duties you assigned:
Sponge bathing 1x/day
Medications
Dressing
Change bedding
Feeding assist
Change adult diapers (special directions, creams, etc.).

Household duties you assigned: (e.g., light cleaning, laundry)

Contact names you gave the caregiver:

Phone numbers you gave the caregiver:

Caregiver Interview Questions

1. What was your most difficult caregiving situation and how did you handle it?

2. If a person in your care falls, what would you do?

3. When should EMS be called?

4. How do you handle a disoriented patient?

5. Are you willing to pray and read the Bible with my parent?

6. Have you provided care for your own parent or grandparent?

7. Under what circumstances would you leave before a replacement could take over?

8. Are you a smoker? (*This can be an issue if your parent has breathing difficulties. Even if a caregiver doesn't smoke on duty, breath and clothing odor could be an issue.*)

9. What expectations do you have for your patients?

10. What expectations do you have for family members?

11. How do you manage break time during your shift?

12. How do manage the stress of your job?

13. Have you worked with hospice caregivers before?

14. How would you handle visitors?

   Other Questions:

Chapter 24

Looking Back, Looking Ahead
Kim's Vision

The caregiver's journey is not an easy one. It is fraught with physical, mental, emotional, and spiritual exhaustion. Yet it is also a journey that offers incredible opportunities for healing, bonding, and spiritual growth. This journey is yours, and God has given it to you as a gift.

There are still days that I miss my dad and mom so very much. I'm reminded of Dad's quick mind and sense of humor by things my little boy says or does or from something as seemingly silly as a cherry tomato. He loved them so much. When I hear the birds outside my office, I think of Mom and how much joy the birdfeeder brought into her life. Each bird that visited it at her backdoor became a pet. When the pang of missing them stabs at my heart, my Christian faith and knowing that they are in the company of our Lord, and together again, brings me peace. But my role as caregiver brought its own comfort I had never dreamed possible while in the midst of the challenges.

Learning catheter care, praying and worrying through surgeries, navigating emergency rooms, and realizing when the end was near were painful times, yes, but looking back on them is not. A layer of different memories has healed the hardships. It's as if time and the journey's conclusion were the ingredients needed to cure the bricks that were being molded to strengthen my own life's foundation.

The memory of the way Dad patted my hand as I drove him to yet another doctor's appointment has taken away the frustrations and fears those many appointments gave us. I remember how in a quiet moment, he said, "You know, I'm proud of you, kiddo."

The unexpected closeness of heart that Mom and I shared in her last years has dulled the pain that comes when remembering her last few days. Her death was not expected, as Dad's was, and the grieving is different. Yet I know that God's love provides us time as a tool to dull the sharp edges even more.

The gifts God gave us in the last seven years were also gifts we gave to each other. Had we not had the tough times and made the choices to face them together, the lives we were leading would not have led us to the precious moments that have lingered in my heart, eclipsing the trials that brought them to me.

Though God ended Dad's battle with cancer by bringing him home, Mom's battle was seemingly won on earth. She stood tall as a cancer survivor for more than two years. When faced with surgery for a second cancer, she moved toward it bravely. But in the end, her time had come. Her work was done, and God brought her home too.

I remember the nights curled up beside her hospital bed and how it tore my heart to pieces to have to find someone to take my place so I could go home and get some rest. Or the times I'd leave my children asking me to stay with them when I needed to be at either her side or Dad's (or both) as yet another trial was laid before us. But now, those hard times of feeling so emotionally shredded have been healed with the laughter she shared with her grandchildren or the memory of the trolley ride we made to celebrate her birthday. Had God not brought us to this place, that laughter would not have become a memory in the walls of my home or the hearts of my children. Those seats on the trolley would have been someone else's.

As I look to the future, I know there will be challenges. The journey with Mom and Dad taught me to celebrate the little joys in life. They taught me not to drown myself in worries but to remember that God's hand leads us, holds us up, and guides us through.

We, the caregivers, are commanded to honor our fathers and mothers. God will give us the strength for the tasks He sets before us.

And so I commend you heartily for being willing to brave the unknown challenges of your own caregiving situation. You don't have to look for the blessings, just keep your heart open to them. They'll tap you gently on the shoulder and give you strength when you least expect them. You don't have to look for the healing. You'll find it has come when the wound you thought was still there no longer hurts. And when your loved one is gone, you will look back with a sense of peace knowing that you've done all you could.

I believe that in accepting a caregiving role, no matter how large or small the task may seem, one day, our heavenly Father will greet us, pat our hand, and simply say, "Well done, my good and faithful servant."

Endnotes

1. "The New Alone" by Elizabeth Marquardt, 27 January 2008, www.washingtonpost. com/wp-dyn/content/article/2008/01/25/AR2008012502775.html.

2. *The Webster's New World Dictionary* (New York: Simon & Schuster, 2003).

3. Based on Florence Littauer, *Personality Plus: How to Understand Others by Understanding Yourself* (Grand Rapids, MI: Fleming H. Revell, 1992).

4. As quoted in Joshua Foer, "Memory, Why We Remember, Why We Forget," *National Geographic,* November 2007, http://ngm.nationalgeographic.com/ngm/2007-11/memory/ foer-text6.html.

5. National Strategy for Suicide Prevention—www.mentalhealth.samhsa.gov/suicideprevention/elderly.asp.

Other books to encourage you on your care-giving journey:

Billy Sprague

Letter to a Grieving Heart

In this personal letter to those facing the loss of a loved one, Billy Sprague revisits his own landscape of mourning—the tragic death of his fiancée, the loss of his beloved grandmother, the departure of a dear friend. With sensitivity and understanding, he writes about the numbing reality of grief's shadowland…and the sources of light and hope: the wise words, the acts of kindness, and the surprising revelations that eased him forward, back into the land of the living. The breathtaking, inspiring nature photography of John MacMurray enhances this thoughtful gift book.

Lloyd John Ogilvie

Quiet Moments with God

These daily, heartfelt prayers will help you nurture special intimacy with God. You will experience God's blessed assurance as you are comforted by His boundless love and His promises to provide guidance and give strength.

God's Strength for This Day

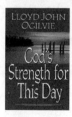

These 365 personal devotions offer you gladness, refreshment, encouragement, and renewal…the rewards of spending time alone with God and His Word. Getting to know Him and His power, you will find yourself ready to meet the challenges of the day with a strength that is beyond your own—a strength that comes from Him only.

When Someone You Love Has Cancer:
Comfort and Encouragement for Caregivers and Loved Ones

CECIL MURPHEY AND MICHAEL SPARKS

When you're caring for someone with cancer, it's difficult to know how best to respond to the twists and turns that accompany a devastating diagnosis. This comforting book will help caregivers learn how best to handle anxiety and apprehension, answer questions honestly and with love, deal with their own emotions of exhaustion and helplessness, and bring hidden feelings to the surface.

Artist Michal Sparks' soothing watercolor paintings combine with practical helps and honest "I've been there" admissions from bestselling author and longtime pastor Cecil Murphey to help readers celebrate the gift of life in the midst of troubles.

The Promise of Heaven
Randy Alcorn and John MacMurray
(AVAILABLE JANUARY 2010)

The Promise of Heaven combines solid biblical teaching from Randy Alcorn with the awe-inspiring photography of John MacMurray to give readers a tantalizing glimpse at what could be their future home.

Everyone has questions about life after death. In *The Promise of Heaven,* Alcorn provides answers based on what God tells us about Heaven in the Bible.

- Is Heaven a real place?
- What happens to us when we die?
- What will our new bodies be like?
- Will all people get the same rewards in Heaven?
- How can we know we're going to Heaven?

Heaven is a place without fear, anger, sadness, or sickness. It's also a place full of beauty, joy, activity, and rest. And it's a place where those who are in Christ will live with the wonderful and fascinating God who created them.